Everybody Does It!
Crime by the Public

This is the first book to explore in detail crime committed by the general public. Thomas Gabor challenges the prevailing stereotype of the criminal by documenting the extent to which ordinary citizens (those who are not habitually in conflict with the law) violate the law, exhibit dishonesty, or engage in actions harmful to their fellow citizens. He shows that so-called respectable citizens account for a large proportion of many kinds of crime: theft, fraud, tax evasion, assault, sex offences, business scams, political and corporate crime, environmental crime, technological crime, and mass lawlessness such as looting and vigilantism. He also discusses crime by police and other authorities in the justice system. Case-studies provide concrete examples and raise crucial questions about law enforcement.

By discussing the justifications and excuses ordinary people provide for their transgressions, Gabor draws a parallel between those justifications and the ones provided by chronic or hard-core criminals. He shows, through experimental and other evidence, that members of the public are often not firmly committed to society's laws or the legal system. Using existing theories in conjunction with an original, interdisciplinary theoretical model, he shows why criminality is so widespread, and why it varies from person to person, and from one milieu to another. He shows why some crimes are more prevalent than others, and why some people are more immune to being labelled and processed as criminals within the criminal justice system. He concludes with a discussion of approaches for dealing with widespread criminality.

THOMAS GABOR is a professor in the Department of Criminology, University of Ottawa. He is the author of two previous books, including *The Prediction of Criminal Behaviour: Statistical Approaches.*

THOMAS GABOR

'Everybody Does It!'
Crime by the Public

UNIVERSITY OF TORONTO PRESS
Toronto Buffalo London

© University of Toronto Press Incorporated 1994
Toronto Buffalo London
Printed in Canada

ISBN 0-8020-2779-2 (cloth)
ISBN 0-8020-6828-6 (paper)

Printed on acid-free paper

Canadian Cataloguing in Publication Data

Gabor, Thomas
  Everybody does it! : crime by the public

  Includes bibliographical references and index.
  ISBN 0-8020-2779-2 (bound)   ISBN 0-8020-6828-6 (pbk.)

  1. Criminal behavior.   I. Title.

HV6080.G3 1944   364.3   C93-095572-2
          1994

This book has been published with assistance from the Canada Council and
the Ontario Arts Council under their block grant programs.

To my mother, Elizabeth,
in memory of her devotion and grit.
She will forever remain an inspiration.

Contents

Case-Studies

Tables

Figures

Preface

'Everybody does it' is a justification people resort to quite frequently in explaining their transgressions, ranging from filing inaccurate income tax returns or making fraudulent insurance claims to pilfering on the job, cheating customers, violating copyrights and professional codes of conduct, or even assaulting family members. For those who use this justification, the idea that many others also engage in socially devalued behaviour somehow makes such behaviour acceptable. As long as people feel they are in good company in their conduct, the potent inhibiting effects of social disapproval will be absent. While people who view themselves as rebels may become even more defiant and extreme in their behaviour when their actions are censured, the majority of citizens tend to break rules when they feel there is a fair amount of support for doing so. There is no better indicator of such support than widespread rule breaking.

Is there any substance to the assertion, advanced by a New York City looter (chapter 10), that 'everyone's got a little thievery in them'? To some, the answer is obviously yes: of course, we all break laws and, organizational rules, and behave dishonestly from time to time; all people have a dark side that places self-interest above everything else. Others, by contrast, offended by these suggestions, consider them preposterous. How can anybody believe, they can be heard to say, that we are all criminals and therefore in the same category as the Al Capones, Ted Bundys, and Charlie Mansons?

The objective of this book is to examine the evidence on a wide array of crimes – from conventional violent and property crimes to technological crimes and those committed by society's élites and professionals, as well as those committed by justice-system personnel. The primary goal is to explore the *prevalence* of criminality – the proportion of citizens or those within a given milieu who engage in criminal or unscrupulous behaviour.

Traditionally, criminology has focused on the *incidence* or the total number or rate of infractions of a given type. The FBI even has a 'crime clock,' telling us, for example, that a rape is committed somewhere in the United States every few minutes. Official crime statistics have almost always been based on simple tallies of the number of known crimes, of each type, in a jurisdiction. Clearly, however, it is also very important to know whether the 1,000 sexual assaults in a community were committed by 20 or 300 offenders. The approaches taken to address the problem will be very different in the two cases. If assaults in the community are committed by a small number of highly active offenders, a punitive approach may be one viable solution to the problem. If the assaults are dispersed over a large number of offenders, the community may have to take a closer look at itself: at the violence in its families, the emphasis placed on violence as a means of solving problems, and the attitudes taken towards women.

I have argued throughout this book, in relation to many forms of crime, that criminal, violent, and dishonest behaviour are supported in many contexts. Although, in general terms we may frown upon theft and assaultive behaviour, in some circumstances we may condone, or at least be indifferent to, such behaviour. Thus, a formal rule (e.g., prohibiting theft by employees) may be disregarded routinely or in special circumstances, as cultures of violence and dishonesty prevail in many environments.

The reader will observe that my position represents a compromise between the two polarized views presented above. To say that we are all criminals, and hence all the same, is a gross oversimplification and distortion of the evidence. While I hope I succeed in demonstrating that virtually all of us violate various laws and social norms on occasion at least, it is clear that there is a difference between the career lawbreaker and the opportunistic offender. As I show, people differ dramatically in the frequency, seriousness, and persistence of their criminality.

I contend that criminality is most accurately viewed as a matter of degree, rather than as an attribute that we either possess or lack. The polarities of good and evil and criminal and non-criminal are subscribed to by those who take the position, mentioned earlier, that criminals constitute a marginal group of maladjusted or plain 'wicked' individuals very distinct from the rest of the population. The evidence I present refutes this notion, showing that many people take the plunge occasionally in criminal and socially disreputable behaviour. Incentives, personal stresses, provocations, peer pressure, and other situational factors may lead an individual who generally displays conformist behaviour to deviate from that pattern.

Not only does the division of humanity into criminal and non-criminal camps have self-righteous overtones, it also carries with it the tenuous assumption that human behaviour is invariant over time and across different circumstances. To claim that we are either criminals or non-criminals is to suggest that our behaviour is principally rooted in heredity and early life experience, and that later developmental and environmental influences have little effect. Much attention is devoted in this book to demonstrating how unanticipated circumstances and the milieu in which one lives and works affect behaviour and may lead to deviations from established behaviour patterns. To see a person's behaviour as alternating between conformity and deviation is to see him or her as an imperfect, not always predictable, self-determining human being. Behaviour, in my view, is adaptive and often driven by momentary self-interest.

This view of behaviour does not paint as flattering or as simple a picture of human beings as the more self-righteous view. Apart from noting the flaws in the self-righteous position, I wanted to take issue with the hypocrisy displayed by many citizens who routinely condemn what they consider to be our leniency towards convicted criminals, while they justify their own illegalities. Simplistic and Draconian policies may appeal to our tendency to project all that we find unacceptable in ourselves onto some identifiable social group, but they do nothing to help us understand or deal with criminal victimization.

There is no quick fix for crime. Policies based on blaming a small segment of society for crime overlook many social forces responsible for criminality. They ignore the serious social and economic inequities present in many countries. They ignore, especially in North American society, the triumph of individual over collective rights and of materialism over humanism, and the legitimization of violence in many contexts. Blaming a fixed segment of society for crime also ignores the strong tendency of human beings to pursue their own interests – interests that inevitably clash with those of society from time to time.

This book provides a sober rather than a Pollyannaish view of human behaviour and crime. Its aim is to debunk the polarized view of humanity that many people hold: the view that we are either criminals or law-abiding, scoundrels or trustworthy. Here, human beings are portrayed as having imperfections. Perhaps when we can accept these imperfections in ourselves we will no longer need to focus all our indignation on a given social group. Then we may see crime as it really is and take constructive steps towards dealing with it.

I owe a great debt to many people and organizations in the long journey that culminated in this book. I am grateful to Virgil Duff, Executive Editor of the University of Toronto Press, for his confidence and support. The comments of the anonymous reviewers were sometimes challenging, but always informative. The manuscript also benefited considerably from the copy-editing skills of Beverley Beetham Endersby.

Conversations and debates with my colleagues at the University of Ottawa, as well as with the students who attended my graduate seminar, helped shape my views. The projects of my graduate students proved to be a rich source of information. Researchers who worked with me included Lisa Leduc, Claude

Leger, Gurnam Singh, Jody Strean, and David Varis. It was a delight working with them. I am grateful to all those who helped in the collection of news clippings and in the transcription of interview material.

I also owe a great debt to those who consented to be interviewed and served as informants on illegalities and dishonesty in various sectors. Many thanks to Kevin Doucette and Kathy Thompson, of the Canadian Consumers Association; Gwen Levesque, of Revenue Canada; Jane Belyea, of the Better Business Bureau of Ottawa–Hull; my unnamed police informant; the Canadian Automobile Association; and the many other informants in the various trades who wished to remain anonymous.

Finally, I would like to thank my family, friends, and other 'ordinary' people with whom I had the opportunity to exchange views during the evolution of this project. This book is about all of us.

PART I
CRIME BY THE PUBLIC: THE ISSUE IN
CONTEXT

1

Introduction

An armed man enters a restaurant and begins indiscriminately to massacre its patrons. A nurse, returning to her car following an evening shift, has her worst nightmare realized: as she gets into her car and closes the door, a man who had been hiding, crouched down, in the back seat holds a knife to her throat, commandeers the vehicle to a secluded spot, and rapes her and dumps her at the side of the road. An elderly couple taking an evening stroll is taunted and then robbed and beaten by a group of young thugs seeking a few kicks; the man suffers a fatal heart attack during the incident.

Murder, rape, robbery, and assault: these are the events people tend to associate with crime. Although such incidents are horrific, they are extreme cases that tend to monopolize the media's attention. While these types of events have the capacity to arouse enormous ire among the public, they constitute a very small fraction of all criminal acts. In Canada, only 10 per cent of crimes reported to the police are violent offences.[1] Public-opinion surveys show that four out of five Canadians overestimate the extent of violent crime.[2]

The types of crimes mentioned above engender particular concern among the public not only because of the brutality involved, but because of other features that arouse consternation, fear, and anger. They are perceived as acts against complete strangers – people who have seemingly done nothing wrong other than to be at the wrong place at the wrong time.

However, many violent crimes – homicides and assaults, as well as a significant proportion of sexual assaults[3] – are committed against individuals the perpetrator knows. Furthermore, serious injuries occur in only a minority of violent crimes.[4] To say that, in many cases, violent crimes are directed at people known to the offender and that they usually do not produce serious injuries is not meant in any way to minimize the suffering of victims; rather, I merely wish to point out that the types of brutal, predatory acts against strangers referred to above are not typical even of violent crimes.

Why, then, do we focus on brutal crimes against the innocent? One obvious reason might be that unpredictable and seemingly senseless acts undermine our sense of security and our belief that the world is a 'just' place where bad things happen only to 'bad' people.[5] The idea that all of us, whether we are 'good' citizens or 'outlaws,' prudent or reckless, are vulnerable to such victimizations makes us feel both powerless and indignant.

Our obsession with extremely violent incidents may also be attributed to the mass media, which, in both news coverage and entertainment, tend to be preoccupied with the sensational and bizarre.[6] Our focus on very brutal crimes may also be prompted by the visible suffering of the victim. The consequences of mass murder, a vicious rape, or a brutal mugging are far more apparent than are the phobias of a burglary victim, the violation of trust felt by a fraud victim, the financial losses incurred by a victim of theft, or the chronic illnesses suffered by employees exposed to hazardous products as a result of illegal corporate practices.

We might also conjecture that, whereas concentrating on the most repugnant acts enables us to view criminals as the personification of evil or as psychologically maladjusted, focusing on more mundane forms of criminal behaviour entails our looking more closely at ourselves. Stereotyping criminals as murderers, rapists, and muggers distances us from the criminal and sets up a simplistic view of the world as one in which people are either decent citizens or villains.

I argue that reality is anything but simple, that dividing all of humanity into two camps – the decent and the villainous – is at odds with the facts. The view taken in this book is that almost everybody violates criminal or other laws on occasion. Thus, rather than viewing some people as conformists and others as lawbreakers, I believe it is more accurate to say that people differ in the degree to which they are committed to lawbreaking. I also make the case that the circumstances people encounter contribute to lawbreaking in a significant way.

THE EXTENT AND TYPES OF CRIMINALITY COMMITTED BY THE PUBLIC

In this book I try to show that criminal behaviour, rather than being abnormal and uncommon, is a normal and routine part of everyday life, engaged in (at least on occasion) by the majority of citizens. Consider just a few statistics:

- close to 10 per cent of all Canadians (2.5 million) have a criminal record (for males at crime-eligible ages, this figure may well be between 20 and 25 per cent);
- one in four males from a large U.S. city will be arrested for a serious violent or property crime during his lifetime;
- 44 per cent of male Britons will be convicted for a non-traffic offence at some point in their lives;
- when 1,700 New York City adults without a criminal record were surveyed, 99 per cent admitted to committing at least one of forty-nine offences listed in a questionnaire (the men averaged eighteen, and the women eleven, different *types* of offences);
- surveys undertaken in many countries show consistently that virtually all young people admit to breaking the law during their adolescent years;
- studies of honesty show that over 90 per cent of the population (including children) lie and cheat at least some of the time.[7]

In the chapters that follow, I introduce evidence documenting the widespread involvement in criminality of the public at large. Once the facts regarding this extensive involvement are established, I will try to show the link between the values we hold and the crime problem we are faced with. The major premise of this book is that crime is normal and inevitable, as it is, at times, an extension, of human nature and imperfection and, at other times, the product of deeply ingrained social values and interpersonal relationships that turn sour. Crime in general, I hope to show, is not the exclusive domain of abnormal individuals or occasioned by unusual circumstances unrelated to everyday life. Crime is not an alien phenomenon arising in a social vacuum. It is not like a localized cancerous growth that can be excised from society. Centuries of experience with capital punishment, torture, banishment, and genocide show that singling out individuals or entire groups and subjecting them to the most repressive measures have not succeeded in eradicating crime and corruption.

Crime, to continue our medical analogy, is more like the common cold – an affliction to which no one is completely immune but to which everyone is not equally susceptible. Just as they do with the common cold, people differ in their immunity to crime. Hereditary and familial factors, as well as other influences early in life, are particularly vital in shaping this immunity. But, just as with the viruses responsible for the common cold, where a strong immune system can be overwhelmed by a high level of exposure to the virus, people who are not particularly prone to antisocial behaviour may be exposed to situations that overwhelm their coping ability or convince them that criminality is justified under the circumstances – for example, in adolescence, a previously well-behaved boy or girl may suddenly 'get in with the wrong crowd' and engage in delinquent behaviour.

Crime can be contagious in many other circumstances: in a marital relationship in which our partner teaches us that physical and emotional abuse are acceptable ways of dealing with conflict; at work, where our co-workers may support and even encourage us to steal from and even sabotage our employers, or where our employers train us to deceive customers, abuse the health and safety of fellow workers, or otherwise victimize society or the environment. The virus of crime can also be spread by the mass media, which may glorify violence and substance abuse. Criminality can be spread by corrupt political and spiritual leaders, who sometimes send the message that abusing the public's trust and behaving immorally are acceptable as long as one has the power and influence to stave off the recriminations.

In short, learning about the criminality, violence, or dishonesty of others, whether directly, through word of mouth, or indirectly, through the media, tends to weaken our own inhibitions or what criminologist Maurice Cusson calls our 'resistance' to crime.[8] From others we may learn specific ways of committing disreputable acts. We may also become desensitized, observing those acts so frequently that we no longer become angry or indignant. Furthermore, if those we admire, like, or depend on break the law, we come to believe that the behaviour cannot be all that bad.[9] Very respectable and decent people can learn that breaking rules are a justifiable and even noble way to conduct their lives and reach their goals.

How many of us have taken home linens, silverware, art, and other 'souvenirs' from hotels in which we have stayed or from restaurants in which we have dined? How many of us have relieved our employers of office supplies, materials, tools, or merchandise, or redirected our travelling and telephone budgets, or other privileges, for personal use? How many people have deliberately failed to report some income when filing tax returns, made deductions that were not legitimate, or otherwise misrepresented their economic situation to lessen their tax burden? Many of us have also done one or more of the following:

– made inflated insurance claims following a fire or theft;
– driven while legally impaired by alcohol in a manner endangering others;
– used prohibited drugs or abused prescription drugs;
– failed to inform a store, customer, or bank of a financial error in our favour;
– engaged in dishonest business practices;

- failed to make truthful declarations at a border crossing;
- destroyed or damaged property maliciously;
- physically struck another person intentionally;
- exhibited disorderly conduct in public;
- illegally copied computer software or videos;
- abused the environment through dumping trash in an inappropriate place or by some other means;
- violated the human rights of others through sexual harassment or discrimination on the basis of race, disability, age, or sexual orientation;
- demonstrated cruelty to animals or hunted without a permit, out of season, or in excess of that permitted by law.

Most of these acts contravene criminal law, federal statutes, or local by-laws. At the very least, they violate moral prohibitions against dishonesty and the requirements of good citizenship.

Aside from the general transgressions listed above, people violate numerous laws, rules, and moral or ethical codes relating to their personal situations and occupations. It is not only blue-collar workers (e.g., taking home tools and materials) and clerical workers (e.g., stealing office supplies and applying office machinery for personal use) who commit illegalities and behave unscrupulously on the job. Even well-remunerated, highly educated people commit a variety of infractions on a routine basis. Fraudulent practices by physicians, for example, can include billing a medical plan for services never provided, recommending unnecessary surgery, conducting very superficial examinations to increase their number, and referring patients to a particular specialist in exchange for a kickback.

Even those responsible for law enforcement and running our prisons are not immune from dishonest or flagrantly illegal practices. There are many forms and degrees of police misconduct: accepting pay-offs, shakedowns, racial discrimination, and the excessive use of force, to name a few. Such misconduct is not always committed by 'hotheads' and 'rotten apples' within police departments; rather, it often receives support from and is even encouraged by fellow officers.

The Los Angeles Police Department's brutal billy-clubbing of Rodney King, a black man accused of speeding in March 1991, was a classic case in point. A citizen with a video camera recorded the beating administered to King – a beating that resulted in nine skull fractures, a cracked cheekbone, a smashed eye socket, a broken leg, and assorted facial cuts and injuries. Twenty-one white and Hispanic officers either watched or participated in kicking, punching, clubbing, and shooting electric darts at King. The vicious beating persisted despite protests from nearby residents. Some of the officers involved even broadcast the incident over police radio. Gloated one cop: 'I haven't beaten anyone this bad in a long time.' The police chief at the time was Daryl Gates, known for his bigoted comments and militaristic ('make my day') style of administration. The officers involved clearly believed, therefore, that they had tacit support from fellow officers, as well as their chief, and could brutalize people in their custody with impunity.[10]

The conduct of the most influential members of a society, such as politicians, business leaders, and clergy, is often less than exemplary. The scandal-ridden governments of Ronald Reagan in the United States and Brian Mulroney in Canada, major scandals on Wall Street and involving various financial institutions in the United States, business ethics in general, and the recent falls from grace of many prominent religious figures illustrate that even society's most powerful and, often, respected members are not above criminal and unethical behaviour.

One might argue that most of the activities mentioned so far are minor relative to the actions of those who endanger life and limb. Murder, rape, child molestation, armed robbery, and burglary are the types of crimes that instil fear in us and wreak havoc in the community. As a result, the hard-core criminals committing these heinous crimes merit the most attention from the police and courts.

The reader might be surprised to discover that in many instances some of the most serious offences, such as murder and assault, are committed by people who do not have a life-long history of antisocial behaviour and imprisonment. Indeed, as we shall see in chapter 5, the perpetrators of these crimes often have no criminal record at all. They tend to be, by most accounts, quite ordinary people who have responded to extreme stress, conflict, provocation, or abuse and who view their behaviour, on the basis of the situation at hand, as appropriate and justifiable. Seeing such behaviour as resulting from extraordinary circumstances does not justify it. My point is that many of those who kill and assault are reasonably well-integrated into society, with families, legitimate jobs, and no known histories of major psychiatric disorders.

Even if we look at the most serious of crimes, criminal homicide, we find that most killings in Canada (and many other countries) arise out of a dispute, often involving people very well known to each other. One of the most common scenarios falling within this category is that of a man killing his wife or girlfriend after she has decided to leave him or has taken a lover. For the majority of women who kill, the victim is a husband or lover.[11] Many killers have no previous criminal record.

A large proportion of killings, among other crimes, must, therefore, be viewed in the context of a relationship (often longstanding) between offender and victim. To fully understand such offences, one needs to examine the manner in which the interaction of the parties contributed to the killing. Probing the mind of the killer alone will not provide a complete perspective of these incidents.

This book is about crime by 'ordinary' and 'respectable' people, those who neither see themselves nor tend to be viewed, as criminals. Dishonest behaviour and some unscrupulous practices on the part of the general public are also discussed, even if technically such acts are not illegal. Many sales techniques, for example, involve deception and the misrepresentation of products. Some criminologists and sociologists would argue that such sales techniques are no different, or differ in nuance only, from outright criminal fraud. The consequence of the emphasis on free enterprise in North American society is that we tend to overlook the more routine business scams.

Indeed, if many business practices just fall within the boundaries of what is legally acceptable, it is naïve to believe that our
youth will appreciate the legal nuances and distinguish among
the various shades of dishonesty. They are likely to perceive
that their elders condone dishonest practices in the pursuit of
self-interest.

CRIMINALITY IS A MATTER OF DEGREE

To say that many respectable people violate our laws or, on
occasion, participate in unscrupulous behaviour is not to suggest that all members of our society are equally criminal or dangerous. To be sure, most of us would rather be conned by a used
car dealer or overcharged by the corner grocer than be attacked,
at knife-point, by a stranger on a dark street. Thus, most of us
would probably agree that some offences, such as violent
crimes, are more serious than other crimes, such as those committed against property. Unquestionably, therefore, *some people
commit more serious crimes than do others.*

Furthermore, people differ in terms of their commitment to
criminal or antisocial behaviour. Some are chronic offenders –
those whose lives and livelihoods revolve around criminal acts.
Such people often associate and align themselves with others
who share this lifestyle. Willie Sutton, the famous bank robber,
considered himself 'a true professional thief.' To Sutton, a professional thief 'is a man who wakes up every morning thinking
about committing a crime the same way another man gets up
and goes to his job.'[12]

Towards the opposite end of the spectrum lies much of the
public. For most people, lawbreaking is not an integral part of
their lifestyle; rather, it arises from personal stresses (such as
financial or marital problems) or unanticipated opportunities.
Most people who steal on the job, for example, do so because
they have access to items they desire, face a low risk of being
caught and reprimanded, and, quite possibly, are supported in
their activities (tacitly or otherwise) by fellow employees. They
do not seek out a job because the opportunities for theft are

there. They steal once they are on the job and recognize that opportunities are present. It is this opportunistic feature that distinguishes the casual from the chronic offender. Chronic or repeat offenders are ever alert to criminal opportunities, actively seeking them out and not merely reacting to them.

Somewhere in-between those deeply committed to an antisocial lifestyle and those only casually or episodically taking a plunge into illicit activities is a mixed bag of people, ranging from amateur thieves to unscrupulous business people.

Even career criminals tend to experience hiatuses in their criminality, for example, when they take a legitimate job or get involved in an intimate relationship. These breathers may last from a few months to several years. In a study we undertook of armed robbers in the Province of Quebec, my collaborators and I found that some individuals become very intensively involved in criminal activity for only a few months or years and then quit altogether.[13] Thus, even career criminals differ in the extent of their involvement in crime.

It is reasonable to conclude, therefore, that *people differ in the degree of their commitment to criminality, as well as in the seriousness of their transgressions.* Acknowledging such differences among us is not inconsistent with the statement that most, if not all, of us break laws, formal rules, and other social conventions at some point, and that we differ only in the *degree* to which we commit these violations and in the gravity of them.

DOCUMENTING THE PUBLIC'S INVOLVEMENT IN CRIME

Everyday crime tends to be underplayed on the six o'clock news and in daily newspapers, the principal sources of information about crime for most citizens. I invite you, the reader, to scan your local paper. You will find few reports or articles on such topics as spousal assault, employee theft, corporate crime, tax evasion – infractions in which 'respectable' citizens are heavily involved. You *will* find, however, many reports of murders and robberies, offences that represent only a fraction of all crimes. There is a saying in journalism that 'Man bites dog' is news, but the inverse is not. The media present those stories capable of arousing readers and viewers emotionally; after all, boosting television ratings and print-media circulation figures are what the networks and dailies strive to achieve. They have both the reason and the ability (as a primary information source) to convince the public that crime is synonomous with acts of extreme brutality. In the next chapter, I discuss the role political and business leaders, as well as academics, play in shaping stereotypes about crime and criminals.

In the chapters that follow, I document, through a number of information sources, including previous research and data collected specifically for this book, the public's involvement in different forms of illegal activities and dishonest practices. Research involving statistics gathered by police and other branches of the criminal justice system sheds light on such things as the proportion of the public that gets in trouble with the authorities, as well as the frequency and persistence (in months or years) of such contacts.

Another useful way of gaining information about the extent to which members of the public commit criminal acts or other indiscretions is through the field experiment. In such experiments, unsuspecting people are given opportunities to lie, cheat, and steal, and their reactions are then observed surreptitiously. My own experimental research and that of others are discussed.

Other experimental studies (discussed in chapter 10) gauge the inclination of bystanders to get involved when they witness what they think is a crime in progress. A general unwillingness of people to intervene can tell us something about their commitment to society's norms and values. Through the various experimental conditions, we can also learn about the circumstances conducive to criminal and other harmful behaviour.

Still another way of finding out about the prevalence of illicit behaviour is to query people about their involvement, through either an interview or a questionnaire. With anonymity or confidentiality guaranteed, it is hoped that respondents will provide accurate and complete information about their criminal activities. Research conducted for this book included interviews with police officers, waiters and waitresses, income tax investigators, representatives from the Better Business Bureau and consumers' groups, college students, security personnel, and automobile mechanics.

Yet one further means of assessing the extent to which an activity is widespread is to observe people in their natural settings. In order to examine employee theft in a warehouse, for example, a researcher can obtain a job on site to determine the number of employees taking goods home or bartering them for other goods and services. The advantage of such a method is that, if the observations are made discreetly, the researcher can gain a representative glimpse of everyday behaviour in that setting. Evidence drawn from such naturalistic studies is also introduced in this book.

UNDERSTANDING WHY WE ENGAGE IN LAWBREAKING

Aside from documenting and describing the transgressions of ordinary citizens, this book explores the reasons why so many people engage in criminal and other socially harmful behaviours. Traditionally, criminologists have attempted to explain why some people become criminals and others do not. Some have attributed the apparent differences between criminals and the law-abiding to innate or genetic factors, others to personality differences, and still others to social circumstances. Whatever their persuasion, these traditionalists shared the assumption that there were clear differences between criminals and the rest of society. The traditional goal of research and theory in criminology, therefore, has been to identify these differences as precisely as possible.

If it can be shown that almost all people violate the law at some point or another, the principal concern then becomes the following: Why does the potential for lawbreaking reside in all of us? What are the circumstances or conditions that lead to the realization of this potential?

In trying to understand everyday criminality, I believe it is vital that we address the ways in which people excuse or justify their transgressions. In my opinion, justifications are essential to the commission of crimes – especially when the authors of criminal acts are people who do not have a criminal identity. Such justifications can explain how those who consider themselves to be law-abiding deal with their own contradictory behaviour. Justifications are the mechanisms that allow those who view themselves as honest and respectable to take objects home from work without permission, to cheat on their tax returns, to brutalize a spouse or child, to drive while impaired, and to commit many other acts with little remorse.

Maybe the assumption that members of the public see themselves as honest and decent is oversimplified or inaccurate. It could be that people justify their own less-than-exemplary behaviour on the basis that such behaviour is necessary to survival in a highly competitive and exploitative world. Thus, if we feel that the government, businesses, landlords, and our employers are mistreating and exploiting us, we may also feel that any conduct undertaken to defend our interests in such a hostile world is justified. Such an outlook does not make it necessary to justify each and every illegal or dishonest act, as though it was a deviation from one's 'true' character. Rather, this view of the world as exploitative and of others as untrustworthy can clear the way for unscrupulous behaviour over the course of a lifetime. If this is the stance that most of the public takes, then the public adheres to a world-view often attributed to criminals. Chapter 9 deals with our rationalizations for illegal and other socially devalued acts, showing how such defence mechanisms allow us to maintain a hypocritical posture towards those conventionally referred to as 'criminals.'

ONLY A MINORITY ARE SUBJECT TO CRIMINAL PROCEEDINGS

If most of us do get involved in illegal behaviour from time to time, why is it that only a relatively small proportion of the population gets prosecuted and punished for most infractions? Some offenders are caught throughout their lives in a revolving-door situation whereby they are released by the police or from prison and, before long, are back in custody. Often, these chronic offenders have been rearrested for some minor offence.

Why is it that most of us manage to avoid the tentacles of the criminal justice system? How often do we see members of Parliament or business leaders serving time in prison? Professionals, such as doctors and lawyers, also are very unlikely to be prosecuted and face criminal sanctions. Chapter 13 discusses the systematic biases of the legal system that render some of us relatively immune from, and others highly vulnerable to, criminal proceedings. You may be surprised to find, when reading that chapter, that while political influence and economic resources are important, they are not the only factors affecting a person's proneness to arrest and prosecution.

The implications of such selective enforcement of society's laws are profound. From an ethical point of view, is it right to punish a token few if many people are involved in an activity (suppressing income on tax returns, for example)? How does a society try to enforce laws, such as those prohibiting theft, when most people violate them, and when such laws are even held in contempt in certain contexts?

Stealing from an employer, for example, may be supported and even encouraged by one's fellow employees in some work environments. Employers, at times, may be seen as complicit when they turn a blind eye to the perpetrators of these thefts in order to avoid antagonizing workers and labour unions.

THE ELASTICITY OF LAWS AND OTHER SOCIAL RULES

Ideal and Operating Norms

Should society even attempt to enforce laws that are either unpopular or simply ignored? The problem, as we shall see, is that people are frequently ambivalent in their support of a given law. Most of us agree that stealing is undesirable and that society should prohibit it. At the same time, we may excuse theft in certain circumstances, for example, when we engage in it or when the offender has been under great emotional stress. We may argue that we are underpaid and hence deserving of certain 'perks,' or that a woman has stolen because she has faced overwhelming family pressures. What we are really saying is that no laws or norms are absolute; rather, behaviour must be viewed in the context within which it occurs.

We therefore tend to distinguish between the *ideal* (or formal) and *operating* (or actual) norms of a society. There may be considerable disagreement about some of society's rules of conduct and the situations in which they apply. These disagreements are particularly evident in the case of offences against morals – gambling, pornography, prostitution, drug use, and so on.[14] There may also be different layers of rules within the same environment. A company rule (formal norm) may require that all employees report to work promptly at nine o'clock in the morning. In reality, employees over the years may arrive at work at five or ten minutes past nine (informal or operating norm) without being reprimanded. Determining the norms or rules that prevail in a given environment may be a difficult undertaking, and such ambiguity of social norms opens the door for the justification of crime and other rule-breaking.

Consequently, rule-breaking may not be seen as deviant at all. Rather, in certain contexts, it may receive support from others. Sometimes, as in the example above, the formal norms never operate; at other times, they are merely temporarily suspended.

When I was an undergraduate student in Montreal, the city one spring was paralysed by a major snow storm. Cars were abandoned throughout the city. Adjacent to the university near my home, a friend and I came upon a beer truck that had become stuck in the snow and abandoned by its driver. Somebody had pried open the panel doors of the truck, and students were pouring in from all over and looting its contents. My friend and I also grabbed a case of beer, despite the fact we rarely drank any beer. We were just caught up in the excitement of the moment, as there was much laughter and discussion of the massive party that was going to ensue. All the while, a police officer stood by passively and joked with the students. Nobody in that context viewed his or her actions as criminal. Had the truck been emptied on a normal working day by two or three ex-cons, rather than a large group of college students, the behaviour would have been viewed very differently. The blizzard had led to a temporary suspension of society's usual conduct norms.

The same phenomenon of shifting norms takes place on a much wider and more serious scale during some blackouts and riots, when looting, vandalism, arson, and assault may become commonplace activities. For a short period of time, the community as a whole may endorse and participate in a variety of illegal acts (see the discussion of blackout looting and the Los Angeles riot in chapter 10).

These unusual events may also elicit rare altruistic behaviours. During natural disasters, people often assist neighbours with whom they have had little contact over years of living alongside each other.[15] People can thus be stimulated to action, in both destructive and altruistic directions, by some cataclysmic event. The influence of people around them, whether it is more enduring or of a transient nature, may affect their social behaviour in a very profound way.

The final chapter of this book addresses the issue of how we should deal with widespread lawbreaking. As we will see, effective prevention entails the recognition that there may be more than one set of rules that apply in many milieus. Rather than merely ask, as traditional criminologists have done, why some people break laws and rules, it is important to explore the reasons for the formation of alternative conduct norms that may lead to the large-scale violation of formal rules. It is always easier to attribute deviant behaviour (e.g., scamming by waiters and waitresses; see chapter 4) to individual failings than it is to deal with the deeper and more complex roots of such actions (e.g., worker dissatisfaction or a culture of dishonesty in the service field). Some remedies for widespread lawbreaking are suggested in the final chapter.

The Shifting Boundaries of Crime

Further complicating the classification of behaviour as 'criminal' or 'deviant' is the fact that laws are forever changing as a result of evolving social attitudes, changes in the political and economic system of a society, and the emergence of new technologies. Labelling an individual as criminal not only may adversely affect his or her subsequent behaviour, but also suggests that the yardstick or standard according to which behaviour is judged never changes.

In reality, many of our laws continuously undergo change, illustrating the 'elastic' boundaries of crime.[16] For example, prior to the past ten years or so, forcing one's spouse to have sexual intercourse was not covered under rape or sexual-assault statutes in most countries. Physically beating one's spouse, too, has been legally acceptable at various times in many societies. During various periods, blasphemy, spitting, and weather forecasting were considered serious offences. Laws relating to prostitution, drug use, gambling, and pornography are constantly in a state of flux. The concept of 'juvenile delinquency' is continuously being redefined. The point is that law is not stagnant: criminalization and decriminalization are ongoing, and therefore the boundaries of what is formally criminal are ever changing.

For this reason it makes little sense to speak of criminality as a *state*. Even if a person's behaviour was seen as unchanging over time (a proposition the evidence presented in this book does not support), the evaluation of that behaviour varies over time and in different circumstances. Criminality is a *process* rather than a state, taking into account a person's readiness to act in a way that might be construed as criminal, the opportunities available to him or her, the stresses to which he or she is exposed, the risks of acting in that manner, and the way in which that behaviour is judged by others.[17] Criminality is a process in the sense that each criminal act involves a series of judgments and decisions on the part of the perpetrator – both of which are influenced by prior experience and current opportunities. Such decision making takes place even during impulsive crimes. Once the act has been committed, a further series of evaluations and decisions are made by victims, witnesses, and the authorities about how the act should be characterized; that is, whether or not it should be viewed as criminal. The example of looting during the Montreal snow storm shows how the circumstances and the characteristics of the perpetrators will affect our judgments of whether a given type of behaviour is criminal. Consequently, the term 'criminal' is used in this book with the recognition that the definition of an act as a crime is dependent on the situation and the evaluation of others, rather than merely on the nature of the act itself.

Criminality is also a process in the sense that people are influenced by the reactions of others to their behaviour. People who regularly receive negative reactions from others as a result of their actions may become more deeply involved in that behaviour. Illegal drug users, for example, if ostracized and referred to in derogatory terms (e.g., as 'junkies'), are more likely to align with those like themselves in order to have a form of support system. Their drug taking in itself may escalate once they become firmly entrenched in a milieu promoting such behaviour.[18]

The potential for crime, therefore, doesn't merely reside in the individual, but depends on the circumstances and the reactions of others. Referring to people as criminals reflects an 'all or nothing,' dichotomous view of the world in which people fit in one of two camps and according to which human behaviour is viewed as unchanging. I prefer to talk of criminal *acts* (with the qualifications just mentioned) rather than criminal *people*. I hope to show in this book that very few people, if any, are always honest and law-abiding; there are gradations of conformity. Most of us are situated somewhere on the conformity scale between the Mother Teresas, on one end, and the Al Capones, on the other.

Before embarking on our discussion of the criminality of the public, it is useful, as a point of departure, to outline the prevailing conceptions of criminality held by both scholars and laypersons. This book, I believe, provides a new way of looking at crime and the concept of the 'criminal.' The novelty of the

approach taken here can be grasped only if the traditional perspectives on criminality are examined. The following chapter,
therefore, explores the existing stereotypes of criminals as well
as the origins of these stereotypes. The rest of the book is
devoted to dispelling what this writer believes are the antiquated
views of crime held by much of the public, and even by a large
number of scholars.

A NOTE TO THE READER

I have asserted that there is rarely, if ever, total agreement in a
community on the appropriate rules of conduct with respect to
any broad category of behaviour. There is always an important
distinction to be made between formal and operating norms. I
have also shown that standards of conduct may sometimes be
transitory (e.g., during a disaster or other emergency situation).
Furthermore, I have stated that the definition of what is criminal
changes over time and may differ from one jurisdiction to
another. As such, it is inevitable that among the many examples
of violent or acquisitive behaviour introduced in this book, there
will be some that will not qualify technically as criminal. For
example, assaulting one's spouse is not universally condemned.

I have also introduced some examples of what might be
referred to as 'borderline' criminal offences. The 'theft' of time
by employees discussed in chapter 4, and 'puffery,' misleading
consumers through subjective, exaggerated claims (chapter 6),
are not ordinarily prohibited by law. Nevertheless, I have
included such examples because they represent premeditated
forms of deception designed to obtain some pecuniary advantage for the individual or corporation. I feel that prohibition of
some of these behaviours (e.g., puffery) may be enshrined in law
at some point. Difficult legal decisions sometimes need to be
made to determine whether corporate actions fall under misleading advertising legislation. There is thus some subjectivity
and arbitrariness regarding the designation of acts as criminal.

Behaviours such as the theft of time, although costing the
economy billions of dollars, may never be subject to criminaliza-

tion because laws prohibiting them are usually unenforceable without creating monumental problems in the workplace. However, I have, on occasion, included such behaviour in the discussion where it is dishonest, premeditated, persistent, and harmful to society. 'Harm,' in this case, refers not merely to economic loss, but also to the contribution of such activity to dishonesty and theft in other spheres. A major thesis of this book is that dishonesty, where pervasive, can be contagious, spilling over into more serious forms of theft and fraud. Therefore, forms of dishonesty that lie at the borderline of the criminal are pertinent to the discussion of crimes by the public.

2

'Pictures in Our Heads': Our Stereotypes of the Criminal

Can you spot the armed robbers in figure 1? I presented the photographs to the students enrolled in my graduate seminar and asked each of them to select the two men they thought were *most* likely to have been involved in an armed robbery.* Then I asked them to indicate which two were *least* likely to have participated in an armed hold-up. So as not to introduce the possibility of racial or sex-based stereotyping, all the subjects presented were white males.

In reality, these six photographs were drawn from a large pool of photos that accompanied a feature article on people killed with a handgun: some were murdered, some died accidentally, and some died of self-inflicted wounds. There are no known armed robbers in the group. Virtually without exception, the students in my class were ready to identify subjects 1, 4, and 5 as armed robbers. Thus, the consensus was that the three men who would probably be considered the least attractive and the 'toughest' looking were most likely to be the armed robbers. There was equally strong agreement regarding those least likely to have committed armed robberies – photos 2, 3, and 6.

What does this experiment tell us? It tells us, first, that people, even advanced students in criminology, are prepared to identify

*Artist's likenesses of the photographs were used in figure 1 as the original photographs could not be obtained.

Figure 1   Which of these men are armed robbers?

criminals solely on the basis of limited information, such as facial photographs. If one can generalize from this modest experiment, it means that people size up the character of others on the basis of physical appearance when only that information is available. They might then attribute character traits, including criminality, to some people on the basis of such superficial features as hair style, facial attractiveness, scars, and gestures. My students not only showed a willingness to draw inferences about character on the basis of facial appearance, but did so with a high degree of agreement. We might thus say that one aspect of a criminal stereotype relates to physical appearance: criminals are viewed by some as tough-looking and unattractive individuals.

What is a stereotype? There are many different definitions of the term. Walter Lippmann, who popularized the term while studying public opinion in the 1920s, referred to stereotypes as 'pictures in our heads' that were rigid, factually incorrect, and produced through illogical reasoning.[1] About a decade later, social psychologists D. Katz and K. Braly laid the groundwork for research on stereotypes in their classic study of ethnic and racial stereotypes held by Princeton University students. They, too, felt that stereotypes were fixed impressions that were at odds with reality. Katz and Braly saw stereotypes as arising 'from our defining first and observing second.'[2]

More recently, social psychologists Paul Secord and Carl Backman have attempted to formulate a more systematic definition of stereotypes. They view stereotypes as having three components: 1 / certain attributes assigned to some category or group; 2 / some agreement on these assignments; and 3 / discrepancies between the assigned and true characteristics of the relevant group.[3]

In this chapter, we explore the question of whether the public subscribes to a criminal stereotype. We will see whether people do tend to attribute some distinctive characteristics to criminals and whether there is some agreement on these attributions. Our classroom experiment suggests that one feature we may consider to be a criminal attribute is unattractiveness and that there may be a fair amount of agreement, on the public's part, that criminals do tend to be unattractive. If we succeed in showing that people do assign certain characteristics to criminals and that there is some agreement on these attributions, then we must still show, according to Secord and Backman's definition of stereotypes, that the traits assigned to criminals are at odds with their true characteristics. This final task is left to most of this book, which attempts to unravel traditional definitions of 'criminals' and put in their place a view of criminality as a matter of degree rather than of kind.

Why is it necessary to concern ourselves with the question of whether a criminal stereotype exists? The reason is simple: factually incorrect and rigid views of criminals, if held by many, can lead us seriously astray in our attempts both to understand crime and to control it. If the public is misled or misinformed about crime and criminality, then crime-control policies, to the extent they are influenced by public opinion, may be misdirected.

Also, members of the public are involved at each stage of the processing of a suspect or defendant. Ordinary citizens usually activate the machinery of justice in a case by notifying police of a criminal act; they serve as eyewitnesses in the investigation of a crime, and again as witnesses at trial; they serve as jurors; and their attitudes may play a role in whether ex-convicts are reintegrated successfully into society.

Those who work directly with offenders in the criminal justice system also will be affected in their work by the attitudes towards or stereotypes of criminals they hold. Police officers, prosecutors, defence lawyers, judges, prison guards, probation and parole officers, and others dealing directly with suspects or convicted persons are likely to share many of the general public's conceptions of criminals.

Stereotypic views of criminals can affect the theories we develop to understand crime. Someone who views criminals as chronically unemployed young people who menacingly hang around street corners is going to develop a different explanation for crime than one who associates the term 'criminal' with a wealthy businessman wearing a suit and a white shirt. The criminality of problem youth might be attributed to poor parenting, drugs, and a peer group regularly engaged in antisocial behaviour. The criminality of the businessman would hardly be attributed to these factors. Thus, any one image of the criminal will lead the theoretician to a unique set of explanations for criminality.

One of the most harmful consequences of stereotypes is that those to whom they are applied incorporate the views held about them. Studies of racial prejudice show that members of minority groups who face discrimination may accept the dominant group's views of them. Such acceptance of a negative stereotype is likely to perpetuate the low status of that group. In the same way, where criminality is viewed as inborn or the result of some other immutable defect, the person to whom that view is applied may see his or her own situation as hopeless. The person's acceptance of the idea that he or she possesses an intractable 'criminal' trait is likely to create a self-fulfilling prophecy as there appears to be little alternative to a deviant lifestyle. Criminologists have used the term 'secondary deviation' to describe the process whereby a person becomes progressively more deviant as a result of the way society has reacted to his or her initial deviations.[4]

Take John, a teenager whose father refuses to lend him the family car because he feels his son is not trustworthy and always gets into trouble. John might find that, no matter how he behaves or promises to be responsible, his father refuses to re-evaluate his negative view of him. John therefore finds that there is little point in behaving responsibly: his father has an opinion of him that is not changed by anything he does. As a consequence, he has little incentive for behaving in a responsible way as he receives no reward for doing so. If John is intent on using the car and unable to purchase one himself, he may feel there is little option but to defy his father and take the car without permission. This act then further reinforces his father's negative view of him.

This anecdote shows the powerful impact that fixed and rigid labels can have on human behaviour. They can produce precisely those consequences we fear the most. If we view convicted persons as distinctly different from the rest of society and treat them accordingly, and if we lead them to believe that they have a deeply ingrained criminal character, they may have few options but to act out that stereotype. For this reason we need to ascertain the extent to which society adheres to a particular criminal stereotype and whether such a stereotype, if present, has a factual basis.

RESEARCH ON STEREOTYPING

Ysabel Rennie, in a historical analysis of the way criminals have been viewed over the ages, has found that in most epochs a particular view of the criminal has predominated.[5] In Europe, during the Middle Ages, for instance, large numbers of vagrants roamed the countryside as the feudal system was disintegrating. Those threatened by these vagrants regarded them as part of an inferior or 'dangerous class' that needed to be controlled. In the latter part of the nineteenth century, with the influence of Charles Darwin, the view of the criminal as a biologically defective being took hold. Cesare Lombroso, an Italian physician, went as far as to suggest that criminals were born to be that way and had physical signs or 'stigmata' of inferiority. As a result of studies in which he compared the skulls of prisoners with those of Italian soldiers, Lombroso wrote that criminals are 'not a variation from a norm but practically a special species, a subspecies, having distinct physical and mental characteristics. In general, all criminals have long, large, projecting ears, abundant hair, thin beard, prominent frontal sinuses, protruding chin, large cheekbones.'[6] Lombroso also likened criminals to apes because of what he claimed was their tendency to have longer limbs than other people. Most of us today would find such views of criminals laughable. Criminologists, at the present time, tend to favour familial and social, as opposed to inborn factors in explaining crime.

Jessica Mitford, in her book *Kind and Usual Punishment*, put forward the following view of criminal stereotyping in the contemporary United States:

A few years ago a local newspaper reported horrendous goings-on of high school seniors in Piedmont, a wealthy enclave in Alameda County, California, populated by executives, businessmen, rich politicians. The students had gone on a general rampage that included arson, vandalism, breaking and entering, assault, car theft, rape. Following a conference among parents, their lawyers and prosecuting authorities, it was decided that no formal action should be taken against the miscreants; they were all released to the custody of their families who promised to subject them to appropriate discipline. In the very same week, a lawyer of my acquaintance told me with tight-lipped fury of the case of a nine-year-old black ghetto dweller in the same county, arrested for stealing a nickel from a white classmate, charged with 'extortion and robbery', hauled off to juvenile hall, and despite the urgent pleas of his distraught mother, there imprisoned for six weeks to wait for his court hearing.

Thus, it seems safe to assert that there is indeed a criminal type – but he is not a biological, anatomical, phrenological, or anthropological type; rather, he is a social creation, etched by the dominant class and ethnic prejudices of a given society.[7]

Do the changing views over time reflect the changing nature of crime and criminals or merely changes in the way we have viewed criminals at different points in history? While the answer to this question is very complex, as both our views of crime and the phenomenon itself are constantly undergoing change, one thing seems fairly constant: our tendency to derive oversimplified views of the criminal.

At the beginning of this chapter, a classroom experiment was presented in which the students who served as subjects demonstrated a tendency to considerable agreement when asked to select criminals from a pool of pictures. A number of more systematic studies have supported the idea that people make judgments about character and, more specifically, criminality on the basis of facial appearance alone.

In one Canadian study conducted at the University of Manitoba, the specific hypothesis that people impute criminality to those they view as less attractive was put to the test.[8] The investigators first asked one set of subjects to rate a series of photographs in order to establish agreement on the faces that were attractive and those that were unattractive. Those photographs on which little agreement was found were eliminated from the pool of pictures. The remaining photos were then shown to another group of subjects who were asked to identify those in the pictures who were most and least likely to have committed murder or armed robbery. The authors found that the pictures selected as most likely to be those of murderers or armed robbers were usually those previously rated as unattractive. The subjects, therefore, tended to associate unattractive faces with violent criminal acts.

In another study, psychologist Karen Dion asked subjects to rate the seriousness of the misconduct of both attractive and unattractive children.[9] Once again an initial rating of photographs was undertaken to determine agreement as to which children were perceived as attractive and which as unattractive. Then subjects were presented with various descriptions of children involved in acts of aggression, and a photograph was attached to each description. As an example, some of the subjects were asked to read the following vignette: 'At one corner of the playground a dog was sleeping. Peter stood a short distance from the dog, picked up some sharp stones from the ground, and threw them at the animal. Two of the stones struck the dog and cut its leg. The animal jumped up yelping and limped away. Peter continued to throw rocks at it as it tried to move away from him.' Subjects were then asked to rate the seriousness of the behaviour. A number of subjects were provided the same description, with only the photograph accompanying it varying from subject to subject. The study revealed that subjects exposed to identical vignettes would rate the child's transgressions as more serious if the child who apparently had committed them was less attractive. Furthermore, less attractive children were judged as more likely to repeat their aggressive acts than were attractive children.

In another series of experiments, researchers sought to determine whether people would match particular faces with specific types of criminals. In other words, are there distinct facial stereotypes of murderers, rapists, and so on?

In one study, subjects were asked to select from among a set of twelve photographs of middle-aged, white males the ones who looked the most likely and the ones who looked least likely to have committed each of the following four acts: homosexuality (it was a crime at the time of the study), murder, robbery, and treason. The selections revealed strong agreement in terms of those most and least likely to have committed each of these acts.[10] The authors concluded that there is a stereotype of the perpetrators of each of these acts.

In the second part of this experiment, the objective was to determine whether facial stereotypes could affect judgments of guilt or innocence in court cases where the evidence was ambiguous. A second group of subjects was asked to evaluate the extent of guilt or innocence of fictitious men in four contrived vignettes in which ambiguous evidence was presented concerning each of the aforementioned crimes. A third group of subjects also evaluated the vignettes, but this time the vignettes were accompanied by photographs of four of the twelve men. The investigators found that, for the crimes of murder, robbery, and treason, when photographs of those previously ranked as most likely to be perpetrators of these crimes were presented with the vignettes, judgments of guilt were far more likely to occur than when the vignettes were presented without the photographs. This finding indicates that if an accused has a face most people associate with a crime, this factor may tip the balance against the accused, leading to his or her conviction.

In another experiment, subjects were asked to evaluate 100 portraits of white, middle-aged men taken from a casting directory. Each subject received a response sheet that listed three 'criminal' occupations (mass murderer, armed robber, and rapist) and three highly regarded professional occupations (medical doctor, clergyman, and engineer).[11] The subjects were asked to choose one mass murderer, one engineer, one rapist, etc., from the portraits they were shown: they were assured that the array of photos they were shown contained one representative of each

of these six 'occupations.' The investigators found that the subjects agreed significantly as to who were the 'good guys' and
who were the 'bad guys'; that is, there was considerable agreement about which portraits were those of criminals and which
were portraits of noncriminals. Just as in the previous experiment, subjects showed agreement not only in distinguishing
criminals from non-criminals, but also on the particular type of
crime committed by the people in the pictures. Thus, one picture was more likely to be viewed as that of a mass murderer,
while another was picked more often to be that of a rapist. This
study supported the previous one in its finding that people may
not only have images in their heads about what criminals look
like, but also may hold offence-specific stereotypes.

Another study has gone as far as to ask subjects to construct
facial composites of different types of criminals.[12] Here, the
onus was on the subject to furnish descriptions of robbers, rapists, and other types of offenders. The investigator, once again,
found that there was significant agreement on the appearance of
offenders in each category and therefore concluded that these
stereotypic images can affect the interpretations people make
about the criminality of others.

The fact that many people link criminality with facial appearance suggests that facial attractiveness is indeed an important
aspect of criminal stereotypes. Other factors that have been
found to underlie stereotyping are race/ethnicity and social
class. Research shows that members of certain minority groups
may be associated with criminality. A study conducted in Israel,
for example, found that Israeli Arabs were more likely than other
groups to be regarded as murderers and rapists, whereas Ashkenazic (European) Jews were more likely than other groups to
be seen as fraud artists.[13] In another study, Sephardic (Oriental)
Jews, who have traditionally been of lower social status than
Ashkenazic Jews, were more likely to view portraits of other
Sephardic Jews as those of criminals than they were to attribute
criminality to Ashkenazic Jews.[14] Thus, not only members of a
dominant group can attribute criminality to the members of a
less privileged group, but members of a minority group may

have a less flattering view of their own group than they have of a dominant group. This finding not only supports the contention that people may see certain social groups as more inclined towards criminality, but also shows that stereotyping can lead to the adoption, by lower-status groups, of society's negative views of them. One might expect that, in Canada, the population as a whole may be more likely to regard aboriginal people than white people as criminal. In the United States, African Americans and Hispanics, in all likelihood, would more often be regarded as criminals than would members of the white majority.

The reader might argue at this juncture that there is a factual basis to these perceptions, that aboriginals, blacks, and Hispanics are more criminally active than their Caucasian compatriots. While this may be true for certain types of crime, it is not true for others. In any event, a stereotype is different from a statement of probability, whereby members of one group are seen as more likely to engage in designated crimes than members of another group. A stereotype is a generalization which suggests a uniformity of behaviour among the members of a group. A stereotype is also, by definition, a rigid view which impedes an individual from making a balanced observation free of prejudgment. This book, in any case, purports to show how virtually all citizens are engaged, on occasion at least, in lawbreaking, and that associating criminality with one or two groups in society is therefore erroneous.

Another aspect of stereotypes has to do with social class or status. People seem to associate the poor and lower-class membership with criminality. Consider an experiment conducted by Colleen Ryan, one of my graduate students. She presented the following vignette to her subjects:

You have just pulled up at a local gas station to get some gas and as you are getting out of your car you notice someone running from the variety store across the street. The individual has what appears to be a bag in one hand and a small handgun in the other. The individual jumps into a car not more than twenty feet away from you and quickly drives away. A few seconds later, the store owner comes running out of the store, yelling that he has just been robbed. The police arrive shortly afterward and get you to describe the suspect on the following criteria:

The researcher then listed such characteristics as sex, age, clothing, and economic status on a response sheet and asked the subjects to describe the suspect in terms of these characteristics.[15] Despite the fact that the subjects had received no information other than that contained in the vignette quoted above, all of them provided a description of the suspect. All described the suspect as male: not even one conceived of the possibility that the person committing the hold-up was a female. Three-quarters of the subjects listed the suspect's age as falling between twenty and twenty-five years. Two-thirds of the subjects described the suspect as belonging to the lower class, and 80 per cent thought that the suspect had, at most, a high-school education. The subjects went so far as to describe the attire of the suspect and even furnished descriptions not specifically solicited in the response sheet. Ninety per cent described the suspect as wearing jeans, and 25 per cent said he had been wearing a black leather jacket. Furthermore, a quarter indicated that the suspect had a scar or tattoo. This study certainly supported the idea that the image of the criminal held by many is that of a young, lower-class male wearing "tough" attire and possibly disfigured in some way.

A sceptic might argue that the descriptions furnished by the students were fairly accurate. Indeed, on some dimensions, such as the view that robbers are young males, they would be correct *most of the time*. There is little evidence, however, that robbers tend to dress in a particular way. In any event, as just mentioned in the context of race and crime, there are serious consequences to associating criminality exclusively with one age group, social class, sex, or educational group. Although robbers may *tend* to be young, lower-income males with less than a college education, there are exceptions to these cases. The students in the experiment showed that the picture of robbers in their heads was the lower-income, tough-looking young male. If the general public shares such rigid views, they will likely allow these stereotypes to influence their perceptions of behaviour when they serve as eyewitnesses and jurors in criminal cases.

There is no better example of how stereotypes influence human perception and decision making than the jury verdict that precipitated the Los Angeles riot in the spring of 1992. A predominantly white jury acquitted Los Angeles police officers following a beating administered to Rodney King, a black man who had led them on a car chase.[16] A videotape of the incident (filmed by a civilian) showed the fifty-six blows administered to King, many of them after he had been clearly injured and subdued. This tape provided clear evidence of the excessive force used. Nevertheless, the officers were acquitted on all but one charge.

The jury was drawn from Simi Valley, a community outside Los Angeles in which many police officers reside. Over half the jury had served at one time as security guards or patrol officers, were members of the National Rifle Association, or were relatives of police officers. They saw a black man being beaten by the police and must have concluded that somehow the beating must have been justified or it wouldn't have taken place. Seeing the police as 'the good guys' and a black man as a likely criminal leads to the conclusion that the latter must have deserved it. Prejudging a situation in this way makes objectivity, when observing the event, an impossibility.

A similar image of the criminal comes across as a result of research conducted in the state of Kentucky. Investigators John and Robin Reed asked a sample of schoolteachers, farmers, and maintenance men to identify the characteristics of a typical criminal.[17] The characteristics most commonly attributed to criminals were: uneducated, dirty, sloppy, dangerous, mean, evil, and lazy. Apart from being seen as motivated by evil, criminals were seen by many of the respondents as psychologically maladjusted. Differences did emerge in the way the three occupational groups viewed the criminal. The farmers and maintenance men, for example, more often held the view that criminals are evil, mean, and dangerous than did the teachers.

In a Canadian study of public opinion, subjects were asked to provide their conceptions of criminals.[18] Most frequently, the responses that emerged were strongly coloured by stereotyped thinking. In summarizing their findings, the authors noted the following:

> When we asked people to spontaneously describe what the word crime or criminal brought to mind, the images that emerged were cut and dried, without distinction, and, because of this, were like the stereotypes portrayed in mystery novels, on police programs on television, or in the criminal cases that make the headlines in the newspapers. What emerges, therefore, are serious and violent crimes (murder, rape, grievous assault, etc.) committed by hardened, dangerous, violent and incurable criminals ... The less people know about the system or the persons involved (criminals, victims, or others) and the less they are exposed to and have experienced victimization, the more the image is stereotyped and criminals seen as dangerous. The mass media, entering the home, influence and standardize people's opinion, and by a sort of social contamination, the same images are invoked over and over.[19]

In another Canadian study of public opinion, respondents were asked to estimate the recidivism or relapse rates of different categories of offenders.[20] Investigators Julian Roberts and Nicholas White found that members of the public provided similar estimates for property offenders, sex offenders, and those committing non-sexual personal crimes. Also, members of the public failed to distinguish between first-, second-, and third-time offenders. As a result, authors concluded that the public's view of the criminal is fairly unitary and that its view of criminal behaviour is based on preconceptions, rather than on the characteristics of each individual offender.

I have already mentioned in this chapter that just one of the adverse consequences of criminal stereotyping is that preconceptions about crime and criminals may affect the outcome of judicial proceedings against offenders. The identification of offenders in police line-ups, findings of guilt or innocence, and perhaps even the sentence imposed by a court may be influenced by such things as the attractiveness of the suspect or accused. A substantial body of research in social psychology supports the idea that people tend to connect attractiveness with positive traits (e.g., intelligence and honesty) and unattractiveness with negative traits (e.g., cunning and dangerousness). Thus, people tend to believe that 'beauty is good.'

One experiment, in which a jury situation was simulated, found that people tend to make a link between attractiveness and guilt.[21] Less attractive people, according to that study, are more likely to be convicted than are attractive people, where the facts of the case are the same. Where a conviction does occur, unattractive defendants tend to be punished more severely than attractive defendants.

One recent study looked at cases of wrongful conviction, that is, cases in which people had been convicted and often languished in prison, before being exonerated once new evidence had come to light.[22] In uncovering cases dating back to 1900, Professor Arye Rattner and his collaborators found that the most common factor underlying wrongful conviction was eyewitness misidentification. The investigators believed that eyewitness error often was attributable to the cultural expectations and stereotypes held by witnesses.

A classic study by social psychologists Gordon Allport and Leo Postman, conducted in the 1940s, is instructive in this context.[23] The investigators were studying the transmission of rumours. Subjects in their experiment were shown a photo of a scene in which two men were standing and talking in a subway train. One, a black man, was wearing a tie; the other, a white man, was wielding a razor blade. There were other passengers sitting in the background. Subjects viewed the picture briefly and then were asked to relate it to other subjects. These descriptions were then, in turn, passed on to other subjects until six or seven people had heard them in sequence. In more than half the experiments with this picture, the last subject in the chain indicated that the black man had held the razor. On several occasions, subjects reported that the black man was brandishing the razor wildly or threatening the white man with it. Even a number of subjects who had viewed the picture reported that the black man held the razor. The investigators used the term 'assimilation' to describe the process whereby our perceptions and recall are brought in line with our prior expectations. This study showed the ability of racial and other stereotypes to distort the perceptions of observers in relation to the facts of a case.

The research we have discussed here points in several directions. First, it can be said with some confidence that many people hold oversimplified, stereotypic views of crime and criminals. The current view of the criminal is usually one of a dangerous and violent individual who commits offences against strangers. Crimes committed against acquaintances and family members, tax evasion, employee theft, shoplifting, and corporate crimes do not tend to form a part of these predominant images. The criminal is also frequently seen as an unattractive individual, as coming from the lower class, as looking tough, and as being a member of some minority group. We have also seen some of the dangers wrought by stereotyping in this way: people can be wrongfully identified and convicted or sentenced more severely if they fit the prevailing stereotype of the criminal.

There is still a more fundamental way in which stereotypes can be harmful to a society: they can completely misinform us, leading us to adopt policies that are inappropriate in dealing with crime. What is appropriate, of course, is partly a question of social values; however, it may be desirable to tackle problems such as crime without our blinders on, free of preconceptions and prejudices. By adhering to stereotypic thinking, we are missing a large part of the reality of crime and other socially harmful behaviour. Before discussing the extent of such behaviour, let us examine where these stereotypes come from and whether they are an inevitable part of the way we view crime.

THE ORIGINS OF CRIMINAL STEREOTYPES

Where do stereotypes come from? How do so many people come to share a similar view of crime? One might answer that people share a view because they are, in large numbers, informed of the facts about crime. We will see, however, that the views of crime held by much of the public are at odds with the reality of crime. In any event, most of the public does not read criminological journals or statistical reports about crime. Then, what are the origins of the false impressions about criminality held by so many? In short, they are misinformed by the principal crime-information sources: the mass media, political and business leaders, scholars, and justice officials, many of whom have an interest in misinforming the public. Misinformation is not always cold and calculated; often it results from the pursuit of an agenda which does not include, as its highest priority, the enlightenment of the public.

Consider the mass media. The electronic and print media constitute the public's primary source of information about crime.[24] Both in entertainment and in news reporting, the images of crime and criminals presented to the public depart from what is known about the reality of crime. Police or crime dramas make up between a quarter and a third of prime-time television programs in any given year.[25] Violent crimes, such as murder and armed robbery, make up the majority of crimes depicted, although these crimes usually account for only a small proportion of conventional crimes in any jurisdiction. These programs also tend to exaggerate the frequency of 'shoot-outs' or violent confrontations between offenders and the police. Offenders are often portrayed as having the basest motives, such as insatiable greed and sadism.[26] They are even frequently made to look vicious. The preoccupation with violence in programming is a result of its appeal to both domestic and foreign markets, as well as the fact that such entertainment is usually inexpensive to produce.[27]

Crime news reporting is not much better, as coverage focuses on violent, sensational, and bizarre crimes. Take a study of an Ottawa daily I conducted in collaboration with Professor Gabriel Weimann of Israel's Haifa University. We examined all crime-related articles over a two-month period in the daily and found that more than half of them dealt with violent crimes, the majority of which were murder incidents.[28] This finding was interesting in light of the fact that only about 7 per cent of reported crimes in Ottawa are violent crimes and that there are rarely more than half a dozen killings in the city each year. Property crimes, by contrast, which account for the majority of reported crimes in Ottawa each year, received relatively little coverage. Crimes by corporations, politicians, and professionals (e.g., doctors) and those committed by employees (pilferage and embezzlement) received virtually no coverage.

Such studies show the extent to which the media can distort the facts about crime. News managers, editors, and reporters are not malevolent; they are simply aware of the effect of stimulating reports on audiences and readers. Their paramount goal is to sell their product. In their efforts to boost circulation and ratings, they also succeed in selling stereotyped images of the criminal.

Political leaders also contribute to and reinforce criminal stereotypes held by the public when they exploit and exacerbate public fears about crime. A number of U.S. administrations, such as those of Richard Nixon and Ronald Reagan, came to power on tough law-and-order platforms.[29] Nixon, in his 1968 presidential campaign, promised to restore safety to the streets of U.S. cities. Reagan, in the 1980s, supported the pre-trial detention of defendants assumed to be dangerous and presided over unprecedented increases in the U.S. prison population. In Canada, a member of the ruling Conservative party attempted to reintroduce capital punishment in 1986 through a parliamentary vote.

While all of these governments showed great indignation in relation to crime in the streets, they were racked by scandals and corruption. The Watergate and the Iran-Contra scandals, violations of conflict-of-interest guidelines, and patronage riddled their tenure in office. The sensitivity of these governments to street crime and their callousness in relation to their own misconduct convey the message that only the acts of low-status individuals qualify as crime.

Business leaders also subscribe to the view that crime is a lower-class phenomenon. The deaths, injuries, illnesses, and financial losses deriving from corporate financial illegalities and health and safety violations make the casualties and losses deriving from street crime, in many jurisdictions, seem minuscule by comparison.[30] Nevertheless, the business world tends to stand firmly by political parties with strong law-and-order platforms.

A report dealing with the fear of crime published by the A-T-O Corporation (also known as the Figgie Report) in the United States reflects the corporate view that criminals are violent predators who are degenerates rather than products of oppressive circumstances. The report promotes a simplistic 'good and evil' view of the world. Consider the following statement from the Figgie Report: 'A-T-O is pleased to sponsor *The Figgie Report on Fear of Crime* because as Americans, and as members of the international business community, we believe that there are few greater threats to our freedom than crime and the fear of crime. Approximately 1% of the population is terrorizing the other 99%. If the public and our corporate leaders do not join together to draft solutions to their common problems, the law-abiding citizen will continue to be held hostage.'[31] The imagery is powerful: 1 per cent terrorizing 99 per cent; the law-abiding public and benevolent business leaders joining together to combat the forces of evil.

The Figgie Report also discusses, on the basis of a survey of Fortune 1000 senior executives, the proposed solutions corporate officials offer to deal with crime. Overall, they take a stance that is so punitive that the hard-line views frequently attributed to the public seem benign by comparison. Almost all of these executives favour the death penalty and expanding police powers. Nearly half advocate the sterilization of habitual criminals. As the main causes of crime, the executives cite the breakdown of traditional values and the family, as well as the leniency of the courts. Not surprisingly, perhaps, they place a lesser emphasis on economic conditions in society, such as unemployment and the gap between the rich and poor – conditions to which the business world itself has contributed.

That the business sector has a vested interest in focusing on the criminality of the poor and diverting attention from its own wrongdoings may come as little surprise. What might be more surprising is the contribution that scholars in the field of criminology have made to the view that society can be divided into distinct 'criminal' and 'non-criminal' camps.

Earlier in this chapter, I alluded to some early research in criminology which purported to show that criminals have inborn defects that clearly distinguish them from the rest of society. Much of the early work focused on anatomical traits that were related to criminality; for example, the configuration of the skull, facial features, the length of limbs, and even the size of the genitals. This line of research, which was pursued seriously until well into the first half of the twentieth century, very unambiguously presented the criminal as a unique sub-species of human being. Ernest Hooton, an anthropologist at Harvard University, had the following to say about criminals in 1939: 'Criminals are organically inferior. Crime is the resultant of the impact of environment upon low grade human organisms. It follows that the elimination of crime can be effected only by the extirpation of the physically, mentally, and morally unfit; or by their complete segregation in a socially aseptic environment.'[32]

Hooton could not have been thinking, when conducting the research that led him to this conclusion, about 'insider traders' on Wall Street. Nor could he have been thinking about the accountant who embezzles thousands of dollars from his employer; the physician who performs unnecessary surgery to increase his income; the middle-class housewife who shoplifts some lingerie from a department store; and executives, such as those at Ford Motor Company who approved of the design of the Pinto, knowing that a rear-end collision could lead to the incineration of the car's occupants.

The line of research that focused on the degeneracy of the criminal pertained clearly to lower-class criminality of the traditional variety: murder, rape, robbery, burglary, and so on. Thus, that line of work promoted not only the distinctiveness of criminals but the idea that criminality was a lower-class phenomenon. These messages, however, are not confined to this earlier biological research.

Much research today, although more sophisticated and less blatantly ideological, functions on the premise that criminals and non-criminals have qualitatively distinct features.[33] A substantial body of contemporary work uses prisoners as subjects and tries to establish differences, at some level, between these prisoners and the civilian population. Scholars with a biological bent have focused on chromosomal defects, abnormally high or low testosterone levels, and abnormalities in the functioning of the autonomic and central nervous systems. Psychologists have tended to look for differences in personality traits, cognitive processes, and intelligence levels of criminals and non-criminals. Many sociologists, too, although focusing less on individuals than on their circumstances, have tried to identify those social factors (economic status, educational attainment) leading *some* people into crime.

Irrespective of the discipline from which this type of research derives, the message is unmistakable: criminals are a distinct group; they are not just different in degree from the rest of us, but fall into a distinct category. Most of the research seeking to identify differences between criminals and non-criminals also fails to see criminality as a process, whereby people, rather than being firmly entrenched in one camp or the other, can drift between conformist and deviant behaviour from one time or circumstance to another. In this sense, human behaviour is viewed as static, with people being seen as unchangeable over time or in different situations. Although most sociological criminologists might allow for behavioural change when fundamental changes occur in an individual's circumstances (e.g., his or her economic situation), they have often failed to consider more routine changes between conformist and deviant behaviour.

Furthermore, using prisoners and other convicted persons as the basis for the comparison of criminals and non-criminals seriously biases the research in favour of the view that criminality is primarily a lower-class activity of the street variety. As will be shown in chapter 13, the justice system operates in such a way as to make it more likely that those committing conventional crimes and possessing fewer legal resources are more likely to be prosecuted and incarcerated. Confining studies to convicted persons, therefore, seriously slants research, ignoring, as it does, all the illegal and exploitative activity that the criminal justice system overlooks.

A final sector contributing to simplistic views of criminals is the multibillion-dollar industry that supervises, holds, manages, and treats offenders. Officials and personnel within the criminal justice system (police, courts, and corrections) and those in the private sector (lawyers, security companies, agencies working with offenders, etc.) make a living through propagating the myth that fighting and dealing with crime is a straightforward and unambiguous task. The credibility of those dealing with offenders depends on our accepting the view that everybody agrees as to the identity of those who pose the greatest hazard to society and on how we should deal with these people. If prosecutors and police chiefs were to vacillate about whether to pursue white-collar criminals or muggers, the public would place less faith in them.

Police chiefs are often heard to sound the alarm, at budget time, that the failure to increase their funding will prevent them from keeping the streets free of violent predators and other 'troublemakers.' By having such a tangible goal as eliminating violence and by focusing on a visible and identifiable target group (street people, lower-class males, minorities), elected officials and the public will be more receptive to appeals for resources than if the police were to portray crime as it really is: very diffuse and complex, with many different types of perpetrators, acting on a wide range of motives.

Consider, also, private security companies that are called in to set up a security system for a home or business. Clients would find it confusing if such companies explained that there are many types of burglars, using a variety of tactics; that some will be deterred by an alarm system and some will not; and that some are capable of circumventing most security systems and others are not. Thus, security firms must speak with assurance about criminals, as though there were only one profile or category of offender. This confident posture earns the respect of the client and justifies, in the mind of the client, the hiring of specialists to secure a home or business.

The credibility of offices, such as that of a prosecutor and that of organizations and firms involved in crime prevention, therefore, hinges on oversimplifying the crime problem so that consumers of the services they provide can clearly see a rationale for these services. If crime is portrayed as complex and multifaceted, the efforts and resources required to combat it may not be so readily apparent. A police chief who said that the best way to prevent crime would be to redistribute the wealth of society would be regarded as a poor leader in the fight against crime. The home security company whose chief executive declared that the best way to combat burglary is to establish more community-based programs for youth would go bankrupt before very long. Both assertions are reasonable, but the police and security companies have a stake in assuring the public that there are more practical and immediate measures to prevent crime. Simplifying the crime problem is the way to make its solution seem more manageable.

IS STEREOTYPING INEVITABLE?

I have tried to show that perpetuating myths about criminals is in the interest of a number of sectors in society and how a similar stereotype of a criminal, broadly that of a lower-class violent offender, emerges fairly consistently from the reports of the media, statements of society's élites and justice personnel, as well as the publications of many academics. Still, the diffusion of simplistic views of criminals would not be successful if members of the public were not so receptive to them. Why do members of the public, in large numbers, adopt the narrow view of criminals promoted by society's opinion leaders? Do people need pariahs or are these stereotypes amenable to change?

The French sociologist Emile Durkheim was probably the first to advance the argument that crime was socially necessary and that the repression of the criminal promoted the solidarity of the rest of society.[34] He stated that punishment serves to affirm the superiority and the moral righteousness of those considered law-abiding. Durkheim further asserted that, without the punishment of non-conformists, those making sacrifices in demonstrating their commitment to society would become demoralized. According to this reasoning, an identifiable criminal group, such as the lower-class violent predator, makes it easier for us to place ourselves in the category of law-abiding, decent citizens. This 'good and evil' view of the world helps us achieve the identity we seek as all-round good citizens. Stereotypes provide texture to the images of criminals, offering a tangible object to both fear and loathe. People can gain a sense of solidarity from their common feelings of revulsion towards a mutual enemy.

The perception that criminality is confined to specific groups in society, such as the poor and minorities, also helps people cope with contradictions in society.[35] In North America, for example, there is widespread poverty, unemployment, and homelessness amid great affluence. It is hard for those who are successful to confront the suffering of others without justifying their disadvantage in some way. To acknowledge that crime may, in part, be a result of disadvantage and that its prevention requires sacrifices on the part of the affluent may be threatening to those who are doing well. It is often easier for one to justify one's own situation and to view criminals and the poor, not as victims of an unfair social order, but as shiftless people who are responsible for their own fate.

Social psychologist Melvin Lerner suggests that all people, to some degree at least, believe that a 'just world' exists.[36] According to Lerner, we all share the notion that a person's outcomes should be commensurate with his or her efforts and abilities. For example, there is the belief that one who works hard should earn a high income. Conversely, one who has a high income is believed to have worked hard. To believe otherwise (e.g., shiftlessness, as well as hard work, could produce wealth), according to Lerner, would produce considerable stress because the world would be seen to be in a state of disorder in which the consequences of our actions would be unpredictable. Lerner adds:

The 'belief in a just world' refers to those more or less articulated assumptions which underlie the way people orient themselves to their environment. These assumptions have a functional component which is tied to the image of a manageable and predictable world. These are central to the ability to engage in long-term goal-directed activity. In order to plan, work for and obtain things they want, and avoid those which are frightening or painful, people must assume that there are manageable procedures which are effective in producing the desired end states.

... there is a growing body of data which indicates that living in a chaotic environment or being rendered 'helpless', impotent to affect one's fate, produces deterioration in the physical and emotional integrity of the organism.[37]

According to Lerner, people will misperceive events and the attributes of others to preserve their belief in a 'just world.' If they observe that an individual has incurred a certain outcome, they will infer that the person's behaviour justified that outcome. In this way, prisoners and the poor may be seen as having deserved their fate. To believe that a prisoner has been incarcerated unfairly or has committed an offence because of uncontrollable events, or, conversely, to believe that a successful person has lied, stolen, and cheated, would create turmoil for a belief system predicated on an ordered and just world. Those formally charged with crimes, therefore, are thought to have traits that have quite naturally led to their fate. Since most of those against whom criminal proceedings are undertaken are lower-class criminals committing conventional crimes (murder, assault, robbery, etc.), it is this category of criminal for which the public reserves most of its scorn.

Thus, both individuals and society at large may have an interest in fostering particular stereotypes of criminals. Criminal stereotypes give people a tangible enemy and create a form of bond between 'decent' citizens. Also, by setting themselves apart from criminals, 'respectable' citizens feel they are standing on high moral ground. Stereotypes also keep intact their views of a just and orderly world. Imagine how these views would be shattered by confronting the fact that most of us, at least on occasion, are law violators. There is much at stake in letting go of simplistic, 'black and white' notions of criminality.

Another explanation for stereotyping criminals and other groups is that stereotyping is simply a learned response. We may develop prejudices and misconceptions about categories of people from the media, opinion leaders (politicians, business people, celebrities, scholars), and those we are close to. If we look at studies of racial prejudice, we can see how negative views become more concrete and articulated as a person develops. One study compared children in the fourth grade with those in the tenth or eleventh.[38] The investigators found that, in the fourth grade, children have only very general attitudes about other races, but, by the tenth or eleventh grade, their beliefs become more fixed and elaborated.

If we are fed fairly consistent images of the criminal through the media and those with whom we interact, these images will be gradually adopted. If parents and friends subscribe to the belief that the criminal is the seedy man on the street or the young hoodlum or drug addict, and this concurs with what is shown and printed in the media, these views will likely be passed on to young people. Just like most behaviours and attitudes, criminal stereotypes may be largely learned from others.

Some psychologists postulate that stereotypic thinking is not only learned but also stems from the way people reason.[39] People have the tendency, for instance, to exaggerate the association between two phenomena, say crime and violence, if they have a prior expectation that such an association exists. Such 'illusory correlations' can result from personal experience or some distinctive feature shared by the two phenomena. An example of the latter may be 'cunning' and 'criminal.' Both are negatively viewed concepts and hence may be correlated in people's minds. Such a correlation would probably conjure up images of 'street' as opposed to white-collar (suite) criminals. Also, when pondering the characteristics of criminals, people find it easier to retrieve images of street criminals because they are constantly exposed to these images and rarely to those of white-collar or political criminals. Furthermore, psychologists focusing on thinking and reasoning processes tell us that more easily imaged events, such as brutal murders and rapes, come to mind far more quickly than those that are more insidious. The embezzlement of a company's funds or the illnesses suffered by miners as a result of their employer's violation of health regulations may be very slow processes. Where the outcome of a criminal action unfolds very slowly or it is difficult to connect a specific perpetrator with a specific outcome and visible victims, people tend not to give it the importance it might otherwise receive (despite the fact that many may die as a result of, for example, corporate irresponsibility). It is simply hard for people to visualize, in their minds, a corporation killing their employees, when the process may be so complex, gradual, and diffuse.

In the same way, although sensitivity is growing, people do not tend to think of the criminal as the man physically abusing his wife. The victim is fairly invisible (the offence is infrequently reported to the police) and the participants are well known to each other. Also, the behaviour is usually ongoing, rather than unexpected, occurring within the context of many other events taking place in the shared lives of marital partners. The more dramatic nature of the stranger-to-stranger street crime more readily comes to mind when we think about crime, even though the consequences of such episodes often are less serious than those in which a spouse is battered. Predatory street crime (e.g., mugging) more easily comes to mind because it is sudden, unexpected, less usual, more visible, and instils greater fear in us.

This chapter has shown that the stereotyping of criminals is prevalent and that the predominant image of the criminal is that of an unattractive, maladjusted, lower-class male who commits conventional crimes such as murder, rape, and robbery. To say that criminal stereotyping is prevalent is not to say that it is universal or that all stereotypic views of criminals are equally rigid. I have shown where stereotypes come from and why members of the public are so receptive to them.

I have even argued that people may need to see criminals as a distinct group, very different from themselves, as a way of dealing with their own indiscretions. This ego-defensive function of stereotypes may be difficult to change, particularly as long as we have idealized views of good citizenship; that is, as long as citizens feel that they must achieve perfection in their own behaviour, they will need to cope psychologically with their own misconduct. One of the principal coping mechanisms people use is to find a group of people whose conduct is far more reprehensible than their own and to treat them as though they are a distinct group of transgressors. These mental manoeuvres are used to justify their own misconduct.

Beginning in chapter 3, we catalogue the criminal transgressions of ordinary, 'respectable' citizens. The objective is to show that a simple division of society into criminals and non-criminals is a construct created to meet our own emotional needs, rather than one that stands up under close scrutiny.

3

Is Everyone Doing It? The Extent of the Public's Criminality and Dishonesty

In his book *Criminal Violence, Criminal Justice*, Charles Silberman argues that crime and violence are 'as American as Jesse James.'[1] He shows that, from the frontier days to the present, violence, theft, and fraud have been endemic to U.S. society. In the continent that had been conquered by the musket, violence, as well as other forms of lawlessness, show few signs of abating.

Silberman offers a clue as to why criminality may be widespread and not simply a preoccupation of a relatively small number of repeat offenders or recidivists:

A society that believes winning is the only thing is likely to overlook a great deal if the victory is large enough. Certainly, the men who brought us Watergate believed that a prize as large as the presidency could justify almost any tactic. Consider this exchange between Senator Herman Talmadge and former Attorney General John Mitchell during the Ervin Committee (Watergate) hearings:

Q: Am I to understand from your response that you placed the expediency of the next election above your responsibilities as an intimate to advise the President of the peril that surrounded him? Here was the deputy campaign director involved in crime, perjury, accessory after the fact, and you deliberately refused to tell him that. Would you state that the expediency of the election was more important than that?

A: Senator, I believe you have put it exactly correct. In my mind, the re-election of Richard Nixon, compared with what was available on the other side, was so much more important that I put it in that context.[2]

The pursuit of self-interest and winning at all costs have been central themes throughout North American history. In business, as well as politics, the ends (the foremost of which has been material success) have usually justified the means. Richard W. Sears, the founder of Sears, Roebuck, began his career as a railroad telegraph operator who sold watches on the side. Sears bought them for two dollars apiece, placed twenty-dollar price tags on them, and mailed them to fictitious addresses throughout the United States. When the packages were returned as undeliverable, he would open them conspicuously in front of his fellow employees and then unload them on his co-workers at the 'bargain' price of ten dollars.[3] Such business acumen has been admired more often than it has met with condemnation.

When a large number of citizens place a higher value on success than on the fair treatment of fellow citizens, it stands to reason that criminality and other exploitative behaviour will be widespread. How widespread are these behaviours? It is assumed by most people, including many criminologists, that crime is an undertaking of a fairly small proportion of the population in any society. However, considerable evidence indicates that a significant proportion of the population of many countries engages in criminal violations.

In Canada, the files of the federal correctional service tell us that about 2.5 million Canadians have a criminal record.[4] This figure is a very conservative estimate of the number of Canadians who have violated the Criminal Code or other statutes, as the majority of crimes are not reported, many are never uncovered (e.g., numerous acts of shoplifting and employee theft), and, in other cases, perpetrators simply are not caught. Even so, about 8 per cent of all Canadians have been processed by the justice system. This official figure would be greater if males only were considered – in the neighbourhood of 12 or 13 per cent. The proportion of those with a criminal record would be higher still if those not yet old enough to get in trouble (say, persons under twelve years of age – the age at which a person can be held criminally responsible in Canada) were excluded from our calculations. Moreover, there is some evidence that people born in the last few decades have been more criminally active than previous birth cohorts.[5] Thus, if we consider only males born after about 1950 who are also old enough to have had an opportunity to get into trouble, the *prevalence* rates of criminality may well be in the vicinity of 20 to 25 per cent.[6]

These figures are not surprising in light of estimates arrived at in the United States and England. Research undertaken on behalf of the President's Crime Commission in the 1960s estimated that 50 per cent of American males and 12 per cent of females would be arrested in their lifetime for a non-traffic-related offence.[7] A recalculation using more current data found the respective probabilities of arrest over a lifespan to be 60 per cent for males and 16 per cent for females.[8] Still more recent research has found that one in every four American males from a large city can be expected to be arrested for an index offence (serious violent or property crime) during his lifetime.[9] Even more striking is the finding from the last-mentioned study that for non-whites living in large urban centres in the United States, the lifetime probability of being arrested for an index offence is over 50 per cent.

Since the U.S. crime problem is more serious than that of most countries, we might be justifiably cautious about generalizing such findings to other countries. Research in England, a country with crime rates more closely resembling those of Canada and other Western countries, indicates that there, too, a large proportion of the population contributes to crime. David Farrington, of Cambridge University, has estimated that an English male has a 44 per cent chance in his lifetime of being *convicted* for a non-traffic offence.[10]

Arrest, and especially conviction data provide conservative

estimates of criminal involvement as many wrongdoers never come in contact with the criminal justice system. One way of getting around this problem and of trying to tap criminal involvement directly is through the self-report procedure. People are asked, anonymously (i.e., through questionnaires) or with confidentiality ensured, whether they have ever participated in offences specified by an investigator. The self-report procedure is, of course, vulnerable to problems of recall, interpretation, and deliberate attempts to mislead on the part of respondents.

The evidence drawn from this body of research is astonishing. The studies, as a whole, show that most, if not all, people break the law at one time or another. One of the earliest studies was a survey conducted in New York City in which 1,700 adults were asked to provide information about their involvement in relation to 49 offences listed in a questionnaire.[11] The subjects were selected so as to include only those people who did *not* have a criminal record. Ninety-nine per cent of the respondents admitted to committing at least one of the 49 offences listed. The average number of different *types* of offences committed in adulthood was 18 for the male and 11 for the female subjects.

Table 1 provides a sample of the offences in the questionnaire and the proportion of males and females admitting to each of them. The table shows, for example, that close to 90 per cent of the men and over 80 per cent of the women in New York City, sampled in the 1947 study, committed larceny or theft at some point (at least once). Half the men had committed at least one assault. Over half the men and just under half the women admitted to tax evasion. Perhaps even more astonishing was the fact that more than a quarter of the men admitted to auto theft and almost a fifth admitted to having committed at least one burglary at some point.

The research by Wallerstein and Wyle in New York City provided some of the earliest clues to the effect that ordinary citizens have more than just a few skeletons in their closets. Since that study, much of the survey research dealing with confessions about criminality has focused on young people.

TABLE 1
Members of the Public Admitting to Lawbreaking

	Percent of Respondents Admitting to Offence	
Offence	Men (N = 1,020)	Women (N = 678)
Malicious mischief	84	81
Disorderly conduct	85	76
Assault	49	5
Auto misdemeanors	61	39
Indecency	77	74
Gambling	74	54
Larceny	89	83
Auto theft	26	8
Burglary	17	4
Robbery	11	1
Concealed weapons	35	3
Falsification and fraud	46	34
Tax evasion	57	40

Source: James S. Wallerstein and Clement J. Wyle, 'Our Law-Abiding Law Breakers,' Probation 25 (1947), 110

In a pioneering effort in the late 1950s, sociologists James Short and Ivan Nye administered a questionnaire to students in three western and three mid-western U.S. high schools.[12] They found delinquency to be both 'extensive and variable' among these students. More than half the boys in both regions admitted to committing the following acts at least once: driving a car without a permit, truancy, fighting, petty theft, and unlawful drinking. A sizeable proportion also admitted to living recklessly, destroying property, and physically bullying others.

Martin Gold, in interviews with a representative sample of teenagers in Flint, Michigan, found that 83 per cent confessed to having committed at least a few delinquent acts. His conclusion was emphatic: 'Studies of delinquent behavior itself, such as the Flint study, will, I believe, promote considerable change in our whole concept of juvenile delinquency. Most important, the idea of "the delinquent" should disappear altogether. For if social science demonstrates empirically that almost everyone sometimes breaks the law, but there are wide differences in how frequently and seriously individuals do so, delinquency should then be recognized as a matter of degree.'[13]

Gold's conclusion bears repeating: *delinquency should then be recognized as a matter of degree.* This statement captures well the theme of this book. Many people, particularly in their formative years, are engaged in a wide variety of rule-breaking and illegal behaviour.

A highly acclaimed U.S. study conducted at the University of Pennsylvania by Marvin Wolfgang and his colleagues has shown just how widespread criminality is among the general population.[14] The investigators monitored the progress of close to 10,000 boys, born in 1945, who grew up in the city of Philadelphia. By the time they reached the age of 18, approximately 3,500 (35 per cent) had been arrested at least once for an offence other than a traffic violation. The researchers continued to follow up 1,000 of the original 10,000 boys to the age of 30. By that age, 47 per cent had been arrested at least once. Furthermore, close to one-sixth of this group had been arrested five or more times by 30 years of age. Thus, at least in U.S. urban centres like Philadelphia, about half the males get in trouble with the law at some point in their lives and a sizeable proportion are involved in crime on a more regular basis. A more recent analysis of males born in 1958, by Wolfgang and his colleagues, has yielded similar findings in terms of the extent of criminal involvement up to the age of 18.[15]

The experience in other countries supports the findings of U.S. researchers. In Canada, in the 1960s, Eugene Vaz interviewed middle-class high-school boys to tap their involvement in illicit behaviours.[16] More than half of those 15 to 19 years of age admitted to driving without a licence, petty theft, fighting, gambling, and destroying or damaging property. Studies of lower-income areas have generally uncovered still more pervasive and serious criminal involvement.[17] In a more recent study of a representative sample of 1,684 male adolescents in Montreal, University of Montreal researchers Marc LeBlanc and Marcel Frechette found that 97 per cent reported having committed at least one criminal infraction during their adolescent years.[18]

In Sweden, a country known for its adherence to social-democratic ideals and for the law-abiding behaviour of its population, the numbers, although not quite as dramatic, point to the fact that criminality is not merely an undertaking of a small minority of citizens. One study examined the criminality of all persons born in Stockholm in 1953 and still living there ten years later.[19] Thirty-one per cent of the boys had been arrested at least once by the age of 26, but fewer than 10 per cent of the females had.

THE DISHONESTY OF 'LAW-ABIDING' CITIZENS

Now that we have begun to establish that criminal behaviour is widespread rather than confined to a marginal group of people called 'criminals,' let us turn to the honesty of the general public. Most crimes, after all, are those involving some form of dishonesty or deception (e.g., theft and fraud).

Dishonesty has been defined as lying, cheating, or stealing.[20] If a generalized trait of 'honesty' existed, a case could be made for placing people into 'honest' and 'dishonest' categories. In other words, if people were entirely either honest or dishonest, without being affected by the situations they encountered, a simple division of people into these two categories would be justified. However, people do not behave with complete consistency across situations. A classic study of deceit on the part of children illustrates this point.

Psychologists Hartshorne and May gave schoolchildren a variety of opportunities to participate in dishonest acts.[21] They were given chances to cheat while correcting their own tests and to falsify their performance in some athletic tests; they were asked to perform other tests with their eyes closed while being monitored for 'peeping'; they were allowed to cheat in solving puzzles; they were given opportunities to steal coins; and so on. The authors found that the performance of the children was far from totally consistent from one test to another. Their behaviour tended to be particularly sensitive to the settings in which opportunities to deceive were present (whether in the home, school, Sunday school, etc.). The results led Hartshorne and

May to conclude that honesty and dishonesty do not derive from an overriding predisposition to behave in one way or the other; instead, behaviour was felt to be specific to the situation at hand.

The debate about whether behaviour is primarily guided by personality traits or situational factors is still very much alive in the field of psychology and it will not be resolved here. Undoubtedly, both positions have merit, and their respective applicability varies from case to case. A person strongly disposed to honesty may show substantial behavioural consistency across situations and may resist temptation in the most trying circumstances. At the same time, in a very oppressive situation in which the risks of censure are profound, people may show remarkable uniformity in their behaviour. Thus the strength of personalities may override situations in some cases, and situations that allow for little behavioural flexibility may override individual differences in others.[22]

Hartshorne and May's study showed that people rarely fit into an extreme category of being either completely honest or completely dishonest. Only about 10 per cent of their subjects were either honest or dishonest every time a chance to deceive was presented to them. Most of the children cheated between 20 and 70 per cent of the time. Thus, although there were differences in the degree to which they were dishonest, most were honest some of the time and dishonest at other times. This finding suggests that certain situational factors must be eliciting deceit in some cases and suppressing it in others. These factors will be dealt with in chapters 11 and 12, when the roots and prediction of the public's misbehaviour are discussed.

Psychologists devising honesty tests for companies wishing to screen future employees tell us that people can be placed in one of three categories: totally honest, totally dishonest, and basically honest.[23] The totally honest people are incorruptible, as they will react honestly in virtually any situation, even when their need or opportunity to steal is great. This group, honesty surveys reveal, make up about 10 per cent of the population. The totally dishonest people are said to be basically untrustworthy and will steal in a variety of situations. This group is said to account for about 5 per cent of the population. The other 85 per cent of the population is considered 'basically honest' because they admit to having committed some larceny; however, this larceny manifests itself only under specific circumstances.

Apart from analysing statistics and conducting surveys, another way of gauging the extent of the public's dishonesty is to undertake experiments in which ordinary people are given opportunities to lie, cheat, and steal without realizing they are being monitored or observed. A variety of experimental techniques has been used to ascertain the public's honesty. One of the first of these studies was conducted on behalf of *Reader's Digest* in the early 1940s.[24] The objective was to test the honesty of garages, as well as radio- and watch-repair shops. Men and women, posing as couples, brought in cars, radios, and watches that were not working properly but which had merely been 'jimmied.' They found that 63 per cent of the garages, 64 per cent of the radio repair shops, and 40 per cent of the watch-repair shops made charges for repairs that were unnecessary.

Social psychologist Roy Feldman has conducted a series of cross-cultural experiments in which he tested the respective honesty of the French, Greeks, and Americans.[25] In one such experiment, investigators entered pastry shops, made a purchase, and then pretended to unwittingly overpay the cashier. The test of honesty was whether the cashier informed the investigator of the overpayment. The investigators were drawn from among both compatriots and foreigners. The study revealed that, in Paris, 54 per cent of the clerks kept the money from both compatriots and foreigners. In Athens, the overpayment was not returned to either the compatriot or the foreigner about 50 per cent of the time. In Boston, interestingly, the money was kept 38 per cent of the time from the compatriot and 27 per cent of the time from the foreigner.

The 'lost letter' technique has been used in another set of experiments to determine the return rate of letters that are left in public places and appear to be lost but, in reality, have been deliberately planted there by researchers. In one of the first studies of this kind, the investigators dropped self-addressed envelopes and postcards on the streets of a number of U.S. cities.[26] Some envelopes contained letters, and others appeared to contain a fifty-cent piece. Seventy-two per cent of the postcards and 85 per cent of the letters were mailed, whereas only 54 per cent of the envelopes containing a coin were mailed. Furthermore, some of the mailed envelopes with a coin had been tampered with. In another study of this type conducted in London, England, letters containing no cash, £1 notes, and £5 notes were dropped on the street.[27] Ninety-four per cent of the letters with no cash, 72 per cent of those containing £1, and 58 per cent of those with £5 were returned. Both of these, as well as other studies, suggest that increasing the value of an item makes a dishonest response more likely.

Many other field experiments probing the public's honesty have been conducted and, with few exceptions, they tend to show that ordinary people are only too willing to succumb to temptation when opportunities to make a quick monetary gain present themselves.

Case-Study: Dishonesty in Canada's Capital City

My collaborators and I have undertaken two studies in Ottawa to determine whether the striking findings from other countries also apply to Canada.[28] In the first of these two studies, three of my research assistants visited 125 convenience stores in the Ottawa area to test the honesty of the cashiers in these stores. The goal was not to ascertain whether cashiers in particular could be trusted, but the extent to which an occupational group that is probably largely middle class and quite representative of the general population responds dishonestly when provided with an opportunity to do so. Of the of 125 stores visited by our researchers, some were part of larger chains, others were owner-operated. Two of the students were males (one Caucasian, the other East Indian) and the other a female.

In each test situation, an investigator, posing as a customer, entered a store and purchased a local newspaper. The newspaper, costing 30 cents at the time, was paid for, in each case, with a single Canadian dollar bill. The investigator then pretended to forget the change and proceeded towards the door at a pace slow enough to give the cashier enough time to inform him or her of the apparent mistake. The test of dishonesty was whether the cashier stopped the investigator prior to his or her departure from the store in order to return the overpayment. The investigators, in each instance, recorded the sex and estimated the age of the cashier.

The change was not returned to the 'customer' in a total of 20 (16 per cent) cases. Cashiers under the age of 25 failed to return the change almost twice as often as those over 25 years of age. This difference was almost completely accounted for by the behaviour of the younger females who were two and a half times as likely to keep the change than were women over 25. As a whole, no difference was found in the behaviour of the male and female cashiers. Also, the nature of the store (whether a chain store or family business) did not appear to have a bearing on the cashiers' behaviour. As for the likelihood of victimization, the race of the investigators was not found to be important, but, interestingly, the male investigators were more than twice as likely to be victimized than the female, suggesting that some people may still be more protective of or chivalrous towards women.

In one of every six stores, therefore, cashiers appeared to act dishonestly. The argument that what appeared to be dishonesty was really an honest mistake can be ruled out, for the most part, because the transaction was very straightforward and the stores were entered only when the cashiers were not busy. Given just one opportunity, one out of six ordinary people acted dishonestly. Although this figure is not astronomical, it is significant, and other research indicates it probably would have been greater if a larger sum of money was at stake. One cashier made this point succinctly, saying, 'Seventy cents isn't worth keeping.'

The 'lost letter' technique was used in a second field experiment we conducted in Ottawa. A total of 112 stamped, self-addressed envelopes were planted securely under the wind-shield wipers of cars witnessed arriving and parking in various shopping centre parking lots throughout Ottawa. The sex and the age of the drivers were noted, and the envelopes were coded so that, if they were returned, we would be aware of the characteristics of the people returning them. The letters were accompanied by a note containing the message 'found near your car,' suggesting that the letter had been picked up from the ground by a passer-by. The envelopes were semi-sealed: half contained an old Canadian penny along with a 'formal' letter stating the coin was appraised at $150, and the other half contained only a personal 'thank you' note.

One-quarter of the letters were not returned by those discovering them on their windshield. Some of the drivers were observed tearing open the envelopes as soon as they had discovered them. Those containing coins were slightly less likely to be returned than those containing the personal note. Males were less likely to return the letters than females, and young subjects, overall, were substantially less likely than older subjects to mail the letters. As in the other Ottawa study, young females behaved the least honestly and/or responsibly, and the older females the most honestly and/or responsibly. Males of both age groups were in between these two extremes in honesty/responsibility.

A study of vandalism conducted by psychologist Philip Zimbardo, in New York City, is particularly telling about the potential for dishonesty and destructiveness of the public.[29] A car was left on the street deliberately as though it had been abandoned. Hidden cameras recorded what ensued (see figure 2). Zimbardo observed that

within ten minutes, the 1959 Oldsmobile received its first auto strippers – a father, mother, and eight-year-old son. The mother appeared to be a look-out, while the son aided the father's search of the trunk, glove compartment and motor. He handed his father the tools necessary to remove the battery and radiator ... By the end of the first 26 hours, a steady parade of vandals had removed the battery, radiator,

Figure 2   From hot rod to worthless hulk

air cleaner, radio antenna, windshield wipers, right-hand-side chrome strip, hubcaps, a set of jumper cables, a gas can, a can of car wax, and the left rear tires (the other tires were too worn to be interesting). Nine hours later, random destruction began when two laughing teenagers tore off the rear-view mirror, and began throwing it at the headlights and front windshield. Eventually, five eight-year-olds claimed the car as their private playground, crawling in and out of it and smashing the windows. One of the last visitors was a middle-aged man in a camel's hair coat and matching hat, pushing a baby in a carriage. He stopped, rummaged through the trunk, took out an unidentifiable part, put it in the baby carriage and wheeled off.

In less than three days, a battered, useless hulk of metal remained as a result of twenty-three separate incidents of destruction.

A recent poll conducted at Concordia University in Montreal

shows that fraudulent behaviour is not confined to persons with little education.[31] A total of 552 students were asked whether, in the previous six months, they had plagiarized, used the same term paper in two or more classes, or used an old exam to prepare for a test without obtaining the instructor's permission. Forty per cent admitted to one or more of these forms of academic fraud. Younger students were more likely to cheat than their older counterparts and females were less likely to cheat than males.

A U.S. study of high-school seniors also uncovered some startling results. Of the 1,093 seniors surveyed, 59 per cent answered 'definitely yes' or 'maybe' to the question of whether they would face six months of probation for an illegal deal in which they made $10 million.[32] Other findings of the survey include:

- 36 per cent stated that they would plagiarize to pass a certification test;
- 67 per cent said they would inflate their business expense reports;
- 50 per cent of the students indicated they would exaggerate on an insurance damage report;
- 66 per cent would lie to achieve a business objective.

In a book entitled *The Day America Told the Truth*, authors James Patterson and Peter Kim revealed, on the basis of a national opinion survey, that 91 per cent of Americans admit to lying regularly, 50 per cent call in sick when they are not, and only 13 per cent support all the Ten Commandments.[33] So much for the idea that a small fraction of the public has a monopoly on dishonesty.

Case-Study: Recycled Term Papers

A few years ago, in our own Department of Criminology, two professors teaching large undergraduate courses were comparing student papers when they noticed that one of the students had submitted the same term paper to both courses. The professors then checked all the papers and found that four other students had done the same thing. On just one occasion, by pure luck (but misfortune to the students), five students were caught committing one type of academic fraud – there are many other types of fraud, including plagiarism, which a number of the other students may have committed. As a consequence of these revelations, a fraud committee was established to investigate the matter.

One of the students claimed that she had accidentally submitted the same paper to the two courses and provided a very farfetched explanation in support of her position – an explanation having little credibility in the eyes of our committee. The other four students acknowledged what they had done, but all had justifications for their actions. One had family problems; the other was part of the school football team and had no time to complete his assignments; and a third, a physical-education major, claimed that criminology was irrelevant to her studies and, anyway, how should she know what the rules are in another department! This last student, incidentally, was applying for a permanent position with the Royal Canadian Mounted Police.

Several lessons can be learned from this experience. The first is that dishonest behaviour is not unusual; rather, it may be fairly widespread in many contexts. Second, dishonesty is not merely displayed by evil-doers, but is undertaken by ordinary people for a variety of reasons. The key to dishonesty and other devalued behaviour is that perpetrators manage to justify their behaviour, often in advance of it. The different justifications provided by the students indicate that there is no one cause of dishonesty. The explanation of a 'bad character' simply does not suffice.

All this is not to say that, while many normal people may act dishonestly in trying circumstances, all of us are equally prone to dishonesty and criminality. That is quite another matter. The student who had legitimate family problems was more likely to have acted dishonestly owing to his particular circumstances and is less likely to repeat his behaviour than the one who claimed she 'didn't know the rules.' Thus, in some cases, criminality and dishonesty are reactions to a very stressful situation, whereas, in other cases, they do reflect an underlying tendency towards antisocial behaviour. That is why I believe that involvement in criminality and dishonesty should be regarded as a matter of degree.

A study of academic fraud by one of my students also yielded the finding that many forms of cheating are highly prevalent.[34] The small sample of students she studied provided a large number of personal experiences with fraudulent behaviour. Here are some examples, expressed in the subjects' own words:

'My friend wrote a take-home exam, but I did not have time to do mine so he gave me his paper, I changed around the words, and we told the prof. that we worked on it together.'

'In one of my French classes, the desks are very close to one another. The test was true/false and fill in the blanks. It was very easy for me to glance sideways and see what the person next to me was writing.'

'I wrote parts of my essay (key words to a paragraph) on my hand or my desk and they triggered my memory when it came to writing the essay or the exam.'

'In my first year of psych., a friend and I established that we could cheat off each other's mid-terms. They were multiple choice questions. If we were stuck, we would write which number on the top left-hand corner and the other would either write the answer on the same corner of her paper or tap the answer; i.e., three taps for "c", four taps for "d", or we would make signs with our hands – p.s. I still did bad!'

The students also provided many justifications for their dishonesty:

'It frustrates me not to know an answer.'

'Because it was incredibly easy to cheat.'

'I wasn't the only person in the class doing it. Why should everyone else cheat and get higher marks and not me?'

'I didn't have the time to prepare.'

'I don't see what is wrong with using a paper from one course for another because it is all my own work and not plagiarized in any way.'

'Lack of enthusiasm in finding another topic.'

'I was running out of time and to copy a paragraph out of a book did not seem like such a big thing.'

'I don't think exams are a true test of knowledge.'

'Teachers should be more careful and less trusting. Face it, dishonesty is a popular quality!'

One indication of the pervasiveness of dishonesty in North American society is the growing use by businesses of honesty and psychological tests in the screening of potential employees. In the United States each year, about two million employees and job applicants are given polygraph or lie-detector tests by actual or potential employers.[35] The goal is to identify those capable of, or actually engaging in, theft on the job. Questionnaires, too, have become popular means of gauging what people have done in the past or are doing presently, as well as their attitudes towards stealing from an employer. Drug testing has also become widespread as drug abuse costs companies billions of dollars in medical expenses, absenteeism, loss of productivitiy, accidents, and theft (the means by which addicted workers can finance their habits).

The boom in the private security industry in recent years is another indication of the fears of businesses, public institutions, and private citizens. Private security personnel outnumber police officers by a ratio of two or three to one.[36] In addition to the growing number of personnel employed by the private security sector, a great deal more is being spent by companies and individuals on security systems, armoured vehicles, fences, and so on.

THE 'J-CURVE' HYPOTHESIS OF CONFORMITY

We might conclude, from the evidence presented in this chapter, that not only are criminality and dishonesty widespread but people participate in unscrupulous behaviour to different degrees – in other words, people commit disreputable acts with different frequencies. Another meaning can be attached to the idea of 'different degrees' of misconduct. Take the example of the time people report for work. Studies show that most people arrive on time or just a few minutes late. A smaller percentage arrive thirty minutes late on any given day, and still fewer report for work an hour or more late.[37]

In another example, more than 2,000 motorists were observed to determine their reactions to stop signs. The reactions were recorded only in cases where there was traffic coming at right angles to the direction of travel of the motorists concerned, so that a double incentive to stop was presented: the possibility of a collision and the presence of the stop sign. About 75 per cent of the motorists stopped completely at the sign. Another 22 per cent proceeded very slowly but failed to stop. Another 2 per cent slowed their vehicles only slightly, and 0.5 per cent went right through without changing speed at all.[38] A study conducted by a student of mine in Ottawa regarding reactions to stop signs found similar results. Observations of pedestrians, too, have revealed that most did not cross at a red light, a smaller number looked both ways and then crossed, and only a very small percentage crossed without looking.[39]

Take one further example of the degree to which people conform to rules. The behaviour of Catholics at the Syracuse cathedral was studied to determine their adherence to religious ritual. More than 1,500 people were observed on different Sundays to see whether they would stop before entering to dip their fingers in the holy water and make the sign of the cross.

Sixty-three per cent carried out this ritual in full. Fewer than 10 per cent touched the font (without dipping the fingers) and made the sign of the cross. Only about 1 per cent either made the sign of the cross without dipping the finger or touching the font, or dipped the finger but failed to make the sign of the cross.[40]

The psychologist Floyd Allport, citing these examples years ago, proposed what he called the 'J-Curve' hypothesis of conforming behaviour. What he meant was that, with respect to most rules, we will find a similar distribution of behaviour: most people will conform to the rule, a smaller number will deviate slightly from it, and still fewer people will deviate from it in a substantial way. With respect to any rule, adherence is a matter of degree rather than simply a question of conformity or deviation. The more extreme the deviation from the rule, the fewer the people who will participate in it.

People commit many types of rule violations regularly. Consider the area of traffic enforcement. A U.S. study in which drivers were filmed from a following truck revealed that the average driver committed more than nine different 'errors' in five minutes of urban driving.[41] The U.S. Department of Transportation indicates that 'the studies reviewed seem to indicate that most drivers commit errors regularly. These drivers are deviant only in that they depart from ideal or optimum behavior. Deviant drivers, in the sense of deviating from the average, do exist, but they are few in number in comparison with the average drivers who commit most of the errors and become involved in most of the crashes. A certain magnitude of driver error for any driver must be considered normal.'[42]

The sociologist Lawrence Ross used the term 'folk crime' to describe legal violations, such as traffic offences, which are violated regularly by the 'average' citizen and which carry little or no social stigma. Thus, there is little social support for these laws, or condemnation of the lawbreakers as criminals. One must distinguish, therefore, between ideal norms and those actually adhered to by most people. It is this vagueness of many social norms that makes it so difficult to draw the line between behaviour that is deviant and that which is not.

Some sociologists and criminologists go so far as to say that no rules are absolute, as their enforcement varies according to the time, place, and situation.[43] Thus, what is criminal in one context, community, or point in time is permissible in another. Smoking marijuana, for example, might have earned one a stiff prison sentence in the early 1960s, but now is usually overlooked by police despite the fact that possession laws may still be on the books. Thus, even criminal justice system personnel may tacitly approve of some illegalities. Even homicide is considered defensible under certain circumstances (e.g., in self-defence). This relativity of social norms not only blurs the picture in terms of identifying what is deviant but also makes it easier to justify illegal and dishonest behaviour.

In chapter 4, we begin our discussion of the types of crimes committed routinely by the public. It will become apparent from the discussion that many forms of theft are commonly committed by a wide cross-section of the population, partly because there is some measure of social support or, at least, no serious stigma attached to these behaviours.

PART II
THE CRIMES COMMITTED BY 'LAW-ABIDING'
CITIZENS

4

'The Root of All Evil': Property Crime

Perhaps the most common category of crime is that involving the unlawful acquisition of another's property through theft or deception. Theft by non-professionals can be committed by individuals or can take place within small networks in which individuals illegally exchange goods and services. This latter type of theft is discussed below, under the heading 'Hidden Economies.' The use of deception or fraud to acquire money or property illicitly, or to avoid paying taxes, is also dealt with below. First, let us look at common larceny or theft in general.

THEFT

The most common form of property crime is theft. Consider some of the following facts and figures:

- Canadian retailers lose over $1 million a day or about $300 million a year, to shoplifters;[1]
- employee pilferage in Canada amounts to between $2 billion and $10 billion annually and, in the United States, to between $40 billion and $200 billion per year;[2]
- losses to hotels in North America as a result of theft by guests, employees, and professional criminals is in the order of several billion dollars each year.[3] The losses are not limited to towels and ashtrays, but also include furniture, wall-bolted pictures, lamps, and heavy bedspreads;

- public libraries in the United States, on the average, lose between 300 and 500 books a year;
- even shopping carts in grocery stores are not exempt from the public's larcenous behaviour. The Kroger chain in the United States, for example, loses 10,000 of these carts yearly.

The list can go on and on, and no sphere is immune. Take the opening of the John F. Kennedy Center for the Performing Arts, in September 1971, in Washington, DC. Mostly visited by the middle class, this centre, in the words of then NBC newsman John Chancellor, was robbed blind. All ashtrays and salt and pepper cellars were taken, as were great amounts of glassware, dishes, and silverware. 'Pieces of valuable curtains were snipped off, chandeliers were stripped of glass, faucets in the washrooms detached and stolen, even brass plates around electrical fixtures pried loose.'[4] People also walked off with plants and all the menus in the restaurant, and even cut up pieces of carpet in the halls and made off with them.

The 'five-fingered discount,' or shoplifting, is one of the most common forms of theft. This offence, however, is not confined to small items. Shoplifters have walked out of stores with such things as fur coats, microwave ovens, and even canoes. In one incident in Vancouver where a canoe was taken, the perpetrator was caught when he brazenly returned for the paddles.[5]

How widespread is shoplifting? A series of studies have tried to answer this question by following a representative sample of customers from the time they entered a store to the point of their departure. When conducted in department stores in three U.S. cities (New York, Philadelphia, and Boston), these studies revealed that between one in twenty and one in twelve customers shoplift.[6] These figures are astounding when one considers that all these people were only observing customers on just one occasion. Many of the customers who did not steal on that occasion may have done so at other times. Furthermore, some of the subjects may have been deterred from stealing because they sensed they were being observed.

When we look at the characteristics of shoplifters, the only conclusion we can come to is that most are anything but hardened criminals. Security experts state consistently that amateurs make up about 90 per cent of all shoplifters, and an equally large percentage have no criminal record.[7] Moreover, no single profile can be created for the shoplifter. Research suggests that males and females are involved about equally. The behaviour, too, seems to be well distributed across different social classes; middle-class housewives, for example, figure quite prominently among shoplifters. Security experts frequently comment on the fact that apprehended shoplifters often have the cash in their possession to pay for the stolen merchandise.[8] As for the age of shoplifters, although teenagers may be overrepresented, all age groups, including the elderly, contribute measurably to this problem.[9]

Employee theft is also a problem of monumental proportions. It can range from stealing office supplies, merchandise, or taking tools to calculated, premeditated theft involving a network of employees using special jargon or signals to acquire goods and services at the company's expense. Even the piecemeal acquisition of items, can amount to a significant gain to the employee over time. In one case, an automobile worker stole car parts one by one until he had enough to assemble an entire car.[10] In another case, a bartender working in a Canadian hotel furnished his entire apartment with the property of his employer.[11] Although such large-scale thefts may be isolated incidents, the amount that individual workers can take during years of service, just from petty pilferage, can be significant. Some studies show that upwards of 90 per cent of employees pilfer in some work environments.[12] In fact, employee theft is so rampant that it has been estimated that one-third of all business failures in the United States are attributable to employee theft or dishonesty.[13]

Employee theft can be of three types: time theft, theft of cash, or theft of merchandise. Time theft has been estimated to cost businesses in the United States about $150 billion and those in Canada $15 billion. It is not defined as the occasional chat with a fellow worker; it is the deliberate, premeditated stealing of paid

TABLE 2
Types of Workplace 'Time Thieves'

Socializers – engage in non-stop chattering with other employees
Coffee/Water Drinkers – use the ploy of going for a drink to enjoy extra breaks
Short-Day Workers – habitually arrive late and leave early
Smokers – must leave the office to smoke
Entrepreneurs – run their own business on company time
Double-Barrel Thieves – steal time while committing theft against their employer
Dreamers – consistently pay little attention to the job at hand
Anticipators – close up shop 15 to 20 minutes early each day
Long-Lunchers – habitually eat on company time and then go out to enjoy their lunch hour and more
Procrastinators – deliberately work slowly, often in order to acquire overtime to complete their assigned duties
Holidayers – book off work or call in sick to have long weekends
Telephone Talkers – make and receive personal calls throughout the day
Readers – read the morning paper or best sellers while on the job

---

Source: Claude Leger, 'Employee Theft: Thievery from Within,' Master's thesis, University of Ottawa, 1990

time.[14] While time theft may not be subject to criminal proceedings, it is no different from deliberate overbilling by a legal firm or auto-repair shop. Lawyers and mechanics who regularly charge for more hours than they put in may be subject to legal action or censure by professional or trade associations. Retribution for employee time thieves is usually limited to dismissal. Table 2 lists some of the most common types of workplace loafers.

Case-Study: Working 'Overtime' at a Chemical Plant

Two good examples of time theft are provided by a maintenance supervisor who has worked for over 30 years at a chemical plant in an Ontario city.

There's a defective instrument and, let's say, the operator will report to the tradesman and the tradesman will say, 'Well don't bring it up to the foreman now. We'll wait until 3:30 and bring it up to him and then it runs into overtime.' Before I got on management I would work overtime and would see certain tradesmen who had work to do at 4:15. We would work until 4:00 and at 4:15 that guy would be going for a shower. There's no more supervision after 4:00 and that individual would wait for his supper and overtime sometimes until 5:30 and leave, and he's been paid for supper and he's earned his supper. Sometimes he would punch out at 7:00.

... I've had an individual that was my worst apple in the department and nobody wanted to work with him because if somebody can stretch a job, he can. He would step on my shovel to delay the job, so I don't work either. So I've taken a course last year in management and I learned about reverse psychology and I wanted to use it. So I walked in one morning and I gave everybody their work assignments and I walked up to him and I said, 'Your work assignment today is to do nothing.' I didn't exactly say it in those words. 'We've been paying you for years for doing nothing. So today I'm going to watch you. I want you to sit there and do nothing all day.' ... Half an hour after everybody heard about it, they started talking to him and teasing him. What is he doing today? What's he doing sitting down? Tell me how you do it? I'd like to sit and do nothing. Within an hour the guy was so ashamed of himself that he sent somebody to go and see the union president. (Interview)

Stealing cash is another form of employee theft. There are many ways to accomplish such theft, but the most vulnerable point for retailers is at the till. The most simple form of theft is merely to dip into the till and pocket the money, after failing to ring up a purchase in the amount stolen. Or the employee can ring a 'no sale' or 'line void' on the cash register and fail to give the customer a sales receipt.[15] A third method of cash-register theft involves under ringing or overcharging: the cashier either punches in a lower price but charges the customer the appropriate amount or punches in the correct price but overcharges the client. Yet a fourth method of cash theft occurs when the cashier alters the sales slip or invoice. For example, when a customer pays $12 for a $12 item, the cashier then fills out a slip indicating a $1.75 overring on the sale and pockets the difference.

Case-Study: 'Scamming' by Restaurant Employees

In Ottawa, Lisa Leduc, who has worked for a number of years in local restaurants, conducted a series of interviews of waiters/ waitresses, bartenders, and managers about 'scamming' in the restaurant business.[16] Scamming refers to actions, on the part of employees that victimize either the employer or the customer, and produce benefits to the employees and/or their family or friends. Leduc's informants, many of whom had worked for many years in the industry, indicated that virtually all employees they had known had engaged in scams of one sort or another, at least on a small scale. The different types of scams were explained by the informants:

'I remember taking a couple of shrimps now and then ... a couple of whatever's being served ... you know, you take a little something without people noticing. I think that's a scam, and I remember working one time and realizing, somebody brought it to my attention, that you could scam certain things, take the full payment for that item plus the tip and just pocket the whole thing, and I've done that because I knew there was no way that I would be found out.'

'I consider scamming as being dishonest in any way in a restaurant, for example, not punching drinks in and giving your friends free drinks, not paying for a staff drink or staff meal ... saying that you worked seven hours and you only worked six, just ripping the restaurant off in any which way you can. Scamming can be even stealing things like people's personal things, stealing cutlery for home, taking cups ... when you receive flowers at work, taking [some] home and taking home vases.'

'A manager would bring in his friends, a table of, let's say, eight, and [they would have] wings and beer, and he would go into the cooler where the beer was and grab it when the bartender wouldn't even notice, and [there would be] free dinner and beer for this person's friends ... Also, people weren't punching in drinks and [were] pocketing the money. Cooks [were] taking food home, all staff [were] taking dishes and cutlery.'

'Well, I've scammed in virtually every establishment that I've worked in, but in different ways. Certainly, when I worked at the first place I would give free food in my capacity as cook ... Friends would come, I would see them at a table and I would give them free food, or give them extra helpings ... I went through a year of being your normal average waiter who didn't scam and then I started to see people walking out with $70, $80, $90, $100, and I was walking out with $30, and of course I would shake my head and say to myself, "Now why is this happening?" And then it dawned on me that coupons were almost a fail-safe way of scamming. In this case, it was a restaurant which used to distribute thousands of coupons throughout the city for $3 off, $2 off, $1 off, and a major number of customers did not use these coupons, but because they were so readily available, the waiters would bring them in and then subtract that money from the total on the bill and pocket the difference.'

'You have a table of twelve that comes in and they're ordering some sixty or seventy items among them and you punch in some fifty of them and then you break up the bill manually and add on the twenty missing. So you're charging them for things that they get but you're not giving the money to the restaurant.'

'The challenge is fun at first, but I suppose it's a very addictive thing. Not just the challenge of scamming and getting away with it, which I suppose in the restaurant business gives you that feeling, but it's the money. The money is really good when you scam, like it really compensates for a bad night ... I think it's rampant ... Some do it through the cash, others do it with coupons, everybody has their own little way. Everybody.'

'Basically, my biggest scam [was] when the restaurant closed I stole eight knives, eight forks, eight soup spoons, and eight teaspoons. I just like a full set of silverware. I almost felt justified in that because we had all this silverware and they didn't match. I was getting embarrassed when guests came over and nothing matched on the table.'

The theft of merchandise by employees can range from the simple act of walking out the door with stolen goods to complex schemes requiring the manipulation of documents and/or involving several employees. The value of goods stolen can also range from small-time pilfering (e.g., pens, paper, cleaning supplies, tools, clothing, and scrap metal) to merchandise worth thousands of dollars. Even items of modest value, however, can cumulatively amount to considerable losses to the employer. Consider the case of a large company engaged in contract work for the U.S. government. The firm decided to take photographs of its dedicated employees leaving after a hard day's work. The gates of the plant, which were normally left open, were closed and cameramen were positioned in the watchman's tower. The workers were not informed of the picture-taking when they arrived at the gates and, as the gates were opened, the cameras clicked. As it turned out, the loyal employees left behind, on the ground by the gate, more than 4,000 items – tools, parts, soap, towels, scrap, and a fifteen-pound sledge hammer.[17]

One study of employee theft uncovered over 415 ways to steal.[18] One common way is through trash disposal. Goods are smuggled out of a building in a trash container and reclaimed after the shift by the employee or by an accomplice. Another popular method is hiding merchandise in a handbag or lunch box and sneaking items out during lunch breaks or at the end of the day. The following example illustrates the ingenuity of some employees: 'In a theft uncovered at a major electronics firm, an employee used two identical lunch boxes in a scheme to steal liquid gold. On his way to lunch each day the maintenance man slipped unnoticed into an unguarded room where liquid gold was stored in a vat. Here he dunked his lunch box into the vat until it was coated. Then he returned to his locker where he exchanged the gold-coated lunch box for the one containing his lunch.'[19] Other employees simply walk out out while wearing stolen merchandise (e.g., jewellery, scarves, coats) or simply hide it under their clothing. Workers at a Buffalo foundry stole 129,000 pounds of lead by recasting it to fit their bodies.[20] In another instance, a Ford plant assembly-line worker stole merchandise by tying it together with a piece of rope and suspending the rope around his neck while the objects (shock absorbers) hung along his deltoids and stomach. The employee then left the plant appearing to be empty-handed while the goods dangled under his jacket.[21]

In a study of employee theft at a Crown (government-owned) corporation in Ottawa, criminologist Claude Leger found that stealing was rampant.[22] Interestingly, many of the subjects he interviewed were security guards; others were cleaners and public relations personnel. The majority of the employees admitted to theft, and the average was almost five thefts per month. A typical case involved one security guard asking another to turn off a particular television monitor (used to detect and record thefts) while he or she stole electronic equipment or food from the kitchen.

Individual employees also participate in many forms of theft involving greater sophistication. These methods include:

- making false entries to pad inventories so shortages will not be noticed;
- placing 'return to manufacturer' labels on goods and sending them instead to the employee's own address;
- intentionally soiling garments or damaging merchandise so employees can buy them at reduced prices;
- sales clerks marking down goods for friends or relatives;
- cashiers adding merchandise not paid for to an accomplice's package; and
- cashiers retaining customers' sales slips and putting them on stolen goods, which the clerk keeps or turns in for a refund.[23]

HIDDEN ECONOMIES

Hidden economies involve a variety of illegal activities undertaken by ordinary working people to gain desired goods and services. Although some of these activities include stealing from an employer or the state, they differ from pilfering in general in that they are carried on by a large number of people – and are, therefore, accepted behaviour in that milieu – and/or the goods stolen are not appropriated for personal use but are used to barter for other goods, to exchange for recognition from others, or to gain currency. The extent of the activity varies greatly from one country to the next. Usually, it complements a person's lawful activities and is undertaken on a small scale, both of which distinguish it from professional criminal activity.

Sociologist Stuart Henry has described how hidden-economy activity commonly takes place in England.[24] A typical case is that of collusion between a truck driver and a warehouse worker. The warehouse employee may be required to load 100 television sets on the truck and, instead, loads 104 and subsequently 'fixes' the books or reports the merchandise as lost. The truck driver can either pay the warehouse employee a sum of money or offer him cheap goods from another warehouse in return for the 'favour.' The driver can then use these television sets as gifts or sell them for a nominal amount to friends and family. Such networks not only make desired goods more accessible to people with modest incomes, but also give workers a sense of belonging in a social network. The cost of non-participation may be ostracism. Furthermore, hidden-economy trading gives people with dull, routine jobs a greater feeling of control over their work environment.

Another example of hidden-economy activity is provided by a study of dock pilferage on the part of longshoremen in the province of Newfoundland:

The hatch checker had been alerted by details on his bills of lading concerning the contents of the crates: messages had passed from shed to vessel crew to warn them of 'good picking' to be expected. The crates were then loaded by the hold crew so that two would fall when the winch was jerked. At the appropriate moment, as the sling was poised over the quay, the signaller gave an all clear sign to the winch-man. The winchman adjusted his levers, the winch jerked and the crates fell. They were only slightly damaged but this was enough to permit entry. Following normal procedures, the crates were then moved by fork truck ... In this instance, much other cargo unloaded with the suits was bulky and packed in large cases. The fork truck driver stacked this cargo to block off the superintendent's line of vision so he could not see the sorting area from his office. At the same time the driver also built up some other of the packing cases to form a hollow square. This enclosure then served as a changing room. Thus equipped, men were able to choose their suits at leisure, trying on different ones for size and being secure from the prying eyes of the superintendent. Throughout the day, longshoremen made their way individually to the changing room ... This cargo was removed from the dock in the usual way, secreted in the clothing of men who took the goods home at the end of the day.[25]

In the case of these longshoremen, a sophisticated signalling system had been established to warn workers of the location of security personnel. Hidden economy networks frequently also use a special argot or terminology as a means of communicating their intentions to commit illicit acts. In the retail food and beverage industry, for example, the term 'brother-in-law' means underringing sales to friends or relatives.[26]

Hidden-economy activity can also result from the disenchantment of workers with a political or economic system, and the scarcity of valued goods. Where meat is scarce, for example, butchers may hoard it and only sell it to friends or those willing to pay inflated prices. Under wartime conditions or where the butcher is a state employee, the behaviour is clearly illegal. In the former Soviet Union and its client states in Eastern Europe, stealing public property or circumventing official channels to do business was routine. Crimes against 'socialist' property were among the largest categories of prosecuted offences.[27] In some cases, entire 'parallel' economies have existed. The activities of Polish peasants under the Communist system provide an example of such second economies:

In their attempts to achieve their goals, farmers use illegal means to purchase adequate quantities of fertilizers and pesticides, to construct necessary buildings and to secure needed tools and machines. As well, they must resort to illegal markets to sell their surplus produce in order to obtain funds to finance these investments. They perceive the state trade channels as uneconomical, not simply because of the low wholesale prices paid to farmers, but also because of the poor organization of transport and of state purchasing centres which mean that farmers must wait in endless lines while their products often deteriorate and thereby depreciate.[28]

'SOUVENIR' HUNTING BY TOURISTS

The hotel industry is particularly susceptible to theft by both staff and customers. Employees take such things as furniture, television sets, dishes, laundry, liquor, and meat through a variety of scams. Tourists are notorious for helping themselves to a variety of articles, often justifying their behaviour on the basis of the high cost of a room – this cost, they assert, entitles them to a few extras.

Case-Study: Hotel Linen Lifting

The *Ottawa Citizen* carried the following story a few years ago about thefts from local hotels:[29]

I was bad once, admitted Susan, standing in the lobby of the Château Laurier Hotel. 'I was staying at a hotel in Philadelphia and I don't know how many people were there, but it was a madhouse – I don't know how many hours I waited in line.' To get even, Susan took the fluffy comforter off her bed, stuffed the thing into her duffel bag on checkout day, and went home. Guilt free. 'It looked great on my bed,' she said. 'I figure they owed it to me.' No, she said she didn't think she'd take anything from the Château before heading home to Toronto.

As long as hotels and motels continue to stock their rooms with tempting items like bathrobes, towels, pillows, silverware or anything else that isn't nailed down, guests will help themselves. Hotel managers, on one hand, say the theft of hotel property is a serious issue. They insist that guests ultimately foot the bill through higher hotel rates. But on the other hand, like sports fishermen bull-shooting their buddies about the one that got away, they love to swap stories about strange thefts.

Edward Macies, manager of Macies Ottawan Motor Inn for the past 28 years, stopped by the front desk one day, then did a double-take when he noticed that a six-foot artificial tree was gone. Hume Rogers, manager of the Beacon Arms, is still puzzled when he considers the handywork required 18 months ago when someone walked off with a TV set. It was still bolted to a hefty metal stand. Westin Hotel executive assistant manager Michel Geday chuckles when describing how two efficient chaps walked off with a massive $2,000 vase and artificial flower arrangement from the lobby in the middle of the night. The new vase in the Westin lobby has an electronic trip-wire attached to the base which, if disturbed, triggers an alarm at the front desk. And Château Laurier bellman Jean-Claude Cote, who's been close to the action for 40 years, says he'll never forget the time he and another bellman went to pick up the bags from several rooms used by a tour group from Mexico. 'All the beds were stripped, so we told the assistant manager who told the tour guide what happened. They took all the luggage and opened it by the front door of the hotel,' said Cote. 'I remember it like yesterday. Sheets and bedspreads all over the place.'

Still these are the more bizarre cases. Nothing like the hum-drum but constant theft of towels and other trinkets. Hot items these days are tea-strainers and demi-tasse spoons. But it's towels that are the timeless favourite. Phil, a frequent hotel user, says without doubt the Sheraton Regina has the best towels for the taking. 'The quality of towels has dropped significantly in the last few years. Most of them are rougher than sandpaper,' said Phil, who travels the country regularly on government business. 'But these ones in Regina are the Cadillac of towels. They're super thick--you can hardly close your suitcase with two of them in there.'

Even the Westin's Geday concedes he likes to take the little packages of toothpaste that sit in that tempting $9 basket of toiletries by the bathroom sink. They might come in handy in the future. Actually, hotel managers expect guests to use some or all of these items like mini-shampoos, hand lotions or shower caps. But some guests like the look of those cute little baskets so much, they take the whole lot for their own bathroom, basket included.

Château general manager Peter Howard figures the more goodies you put in the room, the more chances people will walk off with them. 'I would assume most people who take things say to themselves, "hey, I like this, I've paid for my room so I'll just help myself".'

Susan Tomchyshyn, director of housekeeping at the Westin, deals head-on with the terrible towel trauma every day. She budgets $3,200 every three months to replace missing or soiled towels. That's 400 bath towels, 700 face cloths, 175 hand towels, and two or three terry bath robes ...

FRAUD

The forms of theft we have discussed so far in this chapter have ranged from the simple acts of shoplifting by amateurs and dipping into the till by employees to more sophisticated schemes involving the use of deception by longshoremen. Even thefts involve deception to some degree, so they differ from fraud only in terms of the degree to which deception, manipulation, and the abuse of trust are involved. There is really no clearcut difference between theft and fraud because even amateur shoplifters try to deceive an establishment into thinking they are customers willing to pay for merchandise and instead use stealth to acquire the items they desire. The 'typical' fraud, perhaps, involves somewhat more sophisticated acts of deception than the 'typical' theft, although this is not necessarily the case. What I call fraud here are actions more frequently involving a pen (e.g., creative accounting procedures), rather than purely physical acts. Frauds are also more likely, according to the way they are defined here, to involve the violation of one's position of trust in an organization or profession.

A common form of fraud is embezzlement, the fraudulent appropriation of money entrusted to the employee's care. Embezzlers often make away with large sums of money. One of the best-known embezzlers was Robert Vesco, who siphoned more than $224 million in cash from the Securities and Exchange Commission.[30] Embezzlement is facilitated by the volume of computer-related money transfers. In the United States, for example, corporations exchange more than $117 trillion annually over wire. Armed with a personal computer, modem, a telephone, and the all-important password, an employee can electronically transfer millions of dollars within seconds to a Swiss bank account.[31]

There are a number of sophisticated schemes, aside from illegal money transfers. An accountant or other person in charge of accounts receivable/payable can create a fictitious company with proper stationery and invoices. He then issues cheques to this company rather than to legitimate vendors. Another technique involves the accountant stealing the cash payment from one customer and covering it with another customer's payment. By delaying payment, he can keep this scheme going for years and embezzle large sums of money. In another scheme, an insurance broker, claims agent, or pension benefit administrator insures non-existent clients. Benefits are paid for non-existing illnesses and end up in the employee's bank acount. Or, in a slightly different variation, a payroll clerk or supervisor adds a friend or relative to the payroll. Although the recipient has never worked for the company, he or she receives a regular paycheque.[32]

Case-Study: The Fictitious Payee

The following case was described in the magazine *The Practical Accountant*:[33]

Dick's first caper was to insure the non-existent employees of non-existent corporations for accident and health coverage. He sent in a faked application and actually paid the insurance premiums. After a few months, these covered employees began to show a remarkable susceptibility to disease of all kinds, and they began sending in claims for accident and sickness benefits.

Some of these claims were quite imaginative, ranging from back pain to cardiac infarctions. The claims were accompanied by forged physicians' reports on fake letterheads. Since Dick was the person assigned to investigate these claims, they all passed scrutiny. As a result weekly checks were authorized for disbursement to claimants all addressed to one post office box number.

Dick's next step was to open fictitious personal bank accounts to handle these checks which started flowing in a steady ever-increasing stream. He visited twelve different banks and opened twelve different accounts. Lunch time found him busy making the rounds of the banks, depositing claimant's checks with forged endorsements and making withdrawals from these accounts ... In two years he was promoted to supervisor of the accident and health claims department. The wolf was now guarding the chickens. As supervisor, Dick didn't even have to submit false claims any more. He was now the final authority for passing on claims and all he had to do was give instructions to the book-keeping department to issue checks to claimants ... After a thorough review of all checks issued in the accident and health department, it was revealed that over 650 checks had been issued to or endorsed by these twelve fictitious individuals in two and a half years. These checks totalled in excess of $66,000.

The sociologist Donald Cressey, on the basis of his study of a large sample of embezzlers, concluded that they were essentially people in positions of trust with a non-shareable problem, such as a lifestyle in the 'fast lane' (alcohol abuse, gambling, woman-izing, etc.) that they knew could be resolved through their position.[34] Furthermore, the individual, according to Cressey, was able to rationalize the fraudulent act by arguing that, for example, he was only borrowing the money.

Perhaps the most common form of fraud practised by the population at large is that of income tax evasion or, at least, some suppression of income. In the British House of Commons, the chairman of the Board of Inland Revenue estimated that one in eight people fail to declare £1,000 in income and one in four do not declare £500. Furthermore, two-thirds of the respondents in a survey thought that most people would conceal a small amount of their income if they thought they could get away with it.[35] Studies in the United States suggest that between 20 and 33 per cent of taxpayers show non-compliant behaviour on at least one measure of tax evasion.[36] It has been estimated by the Internal Revenue Service that more than $100 billion in taxes go uncollected each year because people fail to report all their income. Nearly a third of that amount is from self-employed workers, such as professionals, labourers, and sales-people.[37]

In Canada, Neil Brooks and Anthony Doob conducted a survey of Toronto residents to determine compliance levels. Respondents were asked whether, in the past five years, they had failed to file a return when they thought they owed money to the government, claimed deductions they knew or thought would not be allowed if Revenue Canada had full knowledge of them, or had not reported taxable income. One of four respondents reported committing one or more of these forms of evasion over the previous five years. Furthermore, 37 per cent of the respondents indicated that they probably or definitely would commit one of these three forms of evasion in the future if the opportunity was available and they thought they would not be caught. These figures are all the more striking when it is considered that 41 per cent of the respondents reported receiving all their income as salary; therefore, for all intents and purposes, close to half the sample had no opportunity to cheat on their tax returns.[38]

Case-Study: Our Law-Abiding Tax Cheaters

The following are exerpts of an interview I conducted with a senior investigator at Revenue Canada. The interview reveals the prevalence of tax suppresion in all sectors of society.

Anytime there is a cash business operating, be it a retail store, be it an operation where you've got a salesperson going around, you're going to find a tendency to put something in the pocket ... Any business where you have cash and a lack of internal control you've probably got an 80 per cent chance that some of the money is not finding its way into the balance sheets and the financial statement that is filed with the tax department.

... You take a retailer. You go to the cash, you hand over your money, and you punch it into the cash. What's the trick some of them do? You have noticed, I am sure, if you think about it, the drawer in the cash register is slightly open. They don't punch your sale up. They put your money in. They give you your change and they may write your receipt by hand. Nothing comes up on the cash register, but they declare their sales from the cash register tape. So anything that doesn't get punched in is not on the tape.

... take someone who is a professor at a university, has a salary from the university, and may do contract work elsewhere and that contract doesn't come out on the T4A [tax form] ... There's a possibility there for that individual to not declare the full income or to overstate the expenses ... The temptation is there depending on the person's back-ground, how he feels the government deals with its tax dollars, and how much he feels he may be caught if he does it. So, what percentage of people who are in a position to, do it? ... percentage-wise it would be a sheer guess, but I think it would be fair to say 50 per cent.

[On the cash economy] We think it's major ... the jewellery associa-tions made representations to the Minister to say that there are mil-lions of dollars out there in unlicensed jewellery retailers with all cash businesses and you're losing tax from income tax point of view and customs point of view with stuff being smuggled in ... and that's just one association ... So yes, the cash economy's there, but not just in terms of legitimate operations, but also illegitimate operations: the drugs and organized crime. Millions, maybe billions.

[On small, unregistered businesses] Oh, yeah, we have lots. We have a problem with not filing tax returns. Income tax, sales tax, as well as the provincial sales tax. You've got all sorts of small and medium-sized business operations ... Basically it's a free ride.

... Waitresses, waiters, hairdressers, and other businesses, they all get tips and to a large extent they rely on their tips as part of their salary because their salaries are low. Now we found that in some medium- to high-class restaurant establishments, the waiters could make as much as $20,000 a year on tips, which is a substantial amount. So they're earning $20,000 as a base salary, they're earning another $20,000 or more as tips ... Most people in the business declare $500, if they declare that. So $500 was the token in tips. Nowhere near what they were making.

[On the reasons for tax evasion] I think it's plain and simple; it's greed. And then when people get caught, they offer excuses. They will offer explanations as to why they've done it which will be anything but greed. They will say, 'Well we are tired of the government spending our tax dollars in this fashion and the level of taxation is too high and we want to put more money in our pockets.' But the bottom line is greed ... I think we're always surprised when we find people who are committing tax evasion and they have very high levels of income. You would expect that when a person has a very high level of income that they are already declaring that the need is not there for them to avoid tax. So it always comes as a surprise when we get a higher percentage of them committing tax evasion than anyone else in the social spectrum...The perception is that either the chances of them being caught are very slim or else the opposing view is they've been too smart and even if they are audited, the tax department would never find the method that they've employed. So you get a person who thinks that the scheme that he's employed is too clever to be uncovered and then you get people who think there's too many people filing tax returns and there's very few audits being done. 'So my chances are, like the lottery, very few and if I'm caught what will they tax me for, a couple of years. Well, that's not all that bad.'

According to a feature article in *Maclean's* magazine, tax evasion in Canada now amounts to about $30 billion a year, almost the size of the annual federal budget deficit. The article, drawing from industry estimates, reports that one out of nine cigarettes smoked by Canadians is illegal; three out of every four housecleaners are paid under the table; and more than half of all home renovations are paid for exclusively by cash.[39]

Another common fraudulent activity is smuggling goods through customs. In Canada, the smuggling of cheaper U.S. goods across the border is commonplace. When the U.S. dollar gets weaker relative to the Canadian dollar and/or taxes on goods such as liquor and cigarettes rise in Canada, smuggling from the United States to Canada increases. It has been estimated that, each year, a million dollars in liquor alone is smuggled across just the Niagara Region border crossings.[40] As this is being written, the mayors of Canadian cities bordering on the United States are meeting with the federal government to stem the flow of Canadian shoppers across the border. Recent tax hikes in Canada have prompted so much cross-border shopping and smuggling that border towns on the Canadian side are being devastated economically.[41]

Amy Willard Cross, a Toronto free-lance writer, sees thrill-seeking as another motivating factor in smuggling:

It's summertime – price as marked – and open season on smuggling. In parking lots dotting the 49th parallel, everybody's doing the Border Shuffle. In this orgiastic, ritual dance, shoppers tear off their old clothes. Pull on new rags. Arms and legs jive in frenzied syncopation – grasping price tags. Kicking the steamy tarmac, dancers ask each other: 'Do my Airsoles look old yet?' Finally ready for battle, the shoppers pile into getaway cars, heading north. Only scattered price tags and full trash cans are left in their wake.

Why is this awkward dance shaking the nation? The born-to-shop know: shopping and clearing customs without declaring is more exciting than spending and telling.

Although technically a crime, amateur smuggling more resembles a game ... And everybody loves to cheat Revenue Canada out of a little duty ... You needn't exceed the yearly $300 duty-free exemption by splurging on an Armani suit in Rome. Secretly importing a two-four of Budweiser from Rochester, N.Y. delivers the same hair-raising, sweat-making thrill.

Experienced players of Beat the Customs Officer use the same ploys. They cut pocket bastings before wearing a new suit. Replace foreign labels with Eaton's tags. They decant vodka into Evian bottles ... Even canoes are caches. When capsized at the border, that familiar symbol of the Canadian consciousness reveals its contents: a microwave. One man addicted to foie gras – the uncooked, illegal stuff – puts the over-stuffed livers into sporty-smelling jogging shoes....[42]

Members of the public also often try to cash in on their own misfortune when they make exaggerated insurance claims following fires, break-ins, or accidents. In the aftermath of the severe tornado that struck Edmonton during the summer of 1987, the Alberta minister of public safety contemplated filing fraud charges against victims making outrageous damage claims.[43] One family of four, for example, claimed $198,000 in losses. Their claim, covering 46 pages and 1,300 items, included 74 bath towels, 48 hand towels, 48 face towels, a cream and sugar set valued at $620, and a cup and saucer set worth $320.

Academic fraud, too, is widespread, as indicated by the evidence presented in chapter 3. Plagiarism is a daily part of academic life and student responses to accusations are all too often less than apologetic. One instructor writing on the subject asserts that the arrogance of plagiarists knows no bounds.[44] She expects that any day now a student will approach her and complain: 'What do you mean giving me a *B* on this paper? This is an old family term paper – it got my uncle an *A* at Rutgers.'

Academic fraud, of course, is not confined to students. Books and published articles frequently do not give sufficient credit to the sources from which they have drawn material. The outright fabrication of results in research is also not uncommon; indeed, the list of eminent scholars accused of such conduct is long.[45] One of the best-known examples is Sir Cyril Burt, the British psychologist whose falsified twin data served as the basis for much of the thinking on the impact of heredity on IQ scores for almost two decades.

Another example of fraud among professionals can be found in the medical field. Misbehaviour by physicians, whether it involves fraud, malpractice, or unethical conduct, rarely receives public attention because it is handled quietly by the disciplinary arm of a medical association.[46] It has been estimated that between $300 million and $400 million worth of services are fraudulently claimed annually by medical practitioners from the various medical plans in Canada.[47] In the United States, it has been estimated that between 10 and 25 per cent of the $100 billion spent annually on federal health care is lost to fraudulent practices.[48]

Dr Peter Banks, president of the Canadian Medical Association during 1972/3, estimated that about 5 per cent of all Canadian doctors are 'outright crooks whose licenses to practise should be taken away because they will always be crooked.'[49] If this estimate is accurate, there are more than 2,000 doctors practising in Canada who are 'outright crooks.' Assuming a typical patient load, these doctors treat at least a million Canadians a year.[50] A computerized effort in the United States, undertaken in the 1970s to detect obvious abuses by doctors, identified 47,000 physicians and pharmacists who committed blatant and outrageously fraudulent acts.[51]

Physicians can defraud or abuse these Medicare schemes in a number of ways. They can examine patients superficially in order to process as many as possible and, hence, maximize their earnings. In one case, a British Columbia opthalmologist conducted and billed for more than 100 examinations of aboriginal Canadians in less than an hour. Doctors in some provinces can also claim twice the normal rate for extended consultations. This policy is abused by those who offer extended consultations when they are not needed or by others who charge extra when only a standard consultation was given. Surgeons can claim that their therapeutic intervention was more involved or major than was actually the case. Other scams include recommending needless consultations, charging for services never performed, giving kickbacks to other doctors for referring patients and, worst of all, offering unnecessary treatments and performing unnecessary surgery.

The legal profession is particularly notorious for infractions ranging from bilking clients to inducing individuals to commit perjury and 'ambulance chasing' (collecting fraudulent damage claims arising from accidents).[52] Lawyers can also overbill a Legal Aid plan. A Toronto lawyer, for example, overbilled for 2,000 hours between 1984 and 1986 and billed the plan for 25 hours of work on one day in December of 1986.[53] In the city of Ottawa, there is even a group, 'Citizens Against Bad Laws,' which serves as a forum for those who have been overcharged, poorly represented, or otherwise victimized by members of the legal profession. Countless television 'talk shows' have detailed the various horrific experiences faced by clients, many of whom were in very vulnerable positions when they retained legal counsel. The notoriety of lawyers is not a new phenomenon. Shakespeare wrote, in *Henry VI, Part II*, 'The first thing we do, let's kill all the lawyers.'

The legal profession frames the laws, and it is lawyers who interpret them. The language of legislation and legal documents is deliberately archaic and obscure so as to ensure that lawyers will have to be retained to unravel the intricacies.[54] The adversary system of justice prevailing in Anglo-American legal systems has come under serious criticism. In this system, the emphasis is on pitting two parties against each other, the ultimate goal being the victory of one over the other. This system lends itself to abuses of all kinds. As U.S. jurist William Blackstone, Jr, wrote:

As it [the adversary system] is used today in American jurisprudence, more often than not it has the effect of befogging the issues, bankrupting the participants, and sabotaging justice.

The adversary system does not look for truth: It is not interested in proof, nor does it willingly even bring out 'the facts.' It simply sets up two sides for every situation, thus providing for the employment of at least two lawyers for every case. These sides then conduct a more or less controlled debate. The judge is there to do the controlling, and the jury, if there is one, decides who won the debate. True, the jury decides on the basis of evidence presented, but not all possible evidence is presented. On the contrary, each debater will do everything possible to keep evidence from being presented that would cast doubt on his side.

The witnesses are ... urged by threats of intervention by the Almighty to tell 'the truth, the whole truth, and nothing but the truth.' Keep in mind, however, that the attorneys are *not* subjected to this threat in any way, nor is the judge.[55]

Blackstone also comments on the unsuitability of the adversary system in family law, as this sytem still prevails in this area in many jurisdictions:

When two people who were once in love decide that, for some reason known only to them, they must go their separate ways, their differences may revolve around only two or three issues, not the entire history of their relationship, nor the whole personality of each person. To employ two strangers to act as public warriors, who will then square off and vilify any and every aspect of each of the persons involved, is nothing short of barbaric. The acrimony, trauma, and devastation arising out of divorces is largely the work of the divorce court. The breaking up of the marriage is something the couple has already decided upon or things would not have gotten to this point. To put this emotion-laden problem into the hands of gladiators, who will then plunge legal tridents into raw wounds and stir them until the blood runs, can do nothing but exacerbate the problem.[56]

Blackstone goes on to say that applying the adversary system to divorce proceedings rarely benefits any of the parties involved (including children), other than the lawyers themselves.

Abraham Blumberg has written of the practice of law 'as a confidence game,' in which defence lawyers frequently have closer ties with the prosecutorial office and the court than with their own clients. Frequently, they make secret deals but try to maintain the semblance of an adversarial system in which they are acting only in the interests of their client:

The larger the fee the lawyer wishes to exact, the more impressive his performance must be, in terms of his stage managed image as a personage of great influence and power in the court organization. Court personnel are keenly aware of the extent to which a lawyer's stock in trade involves the stage management of an image ... court personnel will aid the lawyer in the creation and maintenance of that impression. ... Such augmentation of the lawyer's stage managed image ... is the partial basis for the *quid pro quo* which exists between the lawyer and the court organization. It tends to serve as the continuing basis for the higher loyalty of the lawyer to the organization; his relationship with his client, in contrast, is transient, ephemeral, and often superficial. ... The judge and other court personnel will serve as a backdrop for a scene charged with dramatic fire, in which the accused's lawyer makes a stirring appeal in his behalf. With a show of restrained passion, the lawyer will intone the virtues of the accused and recite the social privations which have reduced him to his present state ... the incongruity, superficiality, and ritualistic character of the total performance is underscored by a visibly impassive, almost bored reaction on the part of the judge and other members of the court retinue.

Afterward, there is a hearty exchange of pleasantries between the lawyer and district attorney, wholly out of context in terms of the supposed adversary nature of the preceding events. The fiery passion in defense of his client is gone, and the lawyers for both sides resume their offstage relations, chatting amiably and perhaps including the judge in their restrained banter.[56]

The legal profession, then, not only has its own share of 'rip-offs' by individual practitioners, but fosters behaviour in general that deviates considerably from the ideal. Partly because of limited resources and partly because the practice of law is, first and foremost, a business, the higher ideals of justice and human rights take a backseat to the interests of the practitioners themselves.

5

'Flesh and Blood So Cheap':[1] Violent and Sex Crimes

For many people, violent crime is associated with strangers attacking helpless victims, without warning, on dark city streets. In reality, this type of attack accounts for a very small percentage of all violent incidents. Many violent crimes take place among people who know each other, although this situation is more prevalent in some countries than others. The United States, for example, has a greater problem with stranger-to-stranger violence than do other Western countries, such as Canada and the Western European nations. However, even in the United States a large proportion of violent crimes are committed by and against family, friends, and other acquaintances.

What makes violent crimes particularly frightening in the minds of many is the myth that they are totally unpredictable; that is, that they occur without warning. Of course, when such crimes involve a victim and offender who are known to each other, the possibility of violence can sometimes be foreseen by observing their relationship. In a marriage in which there is a history of wife battering, there is certainly a possibility (even a high probability) of the behaviour recurring. People engaging in illicit drug deals, in which participants often pack lethal weapons, must recognize that the potential for violence is always present. Thus, there may be some clues at least as to the possibility of violence when it takes place in the context of an intimate relationship or illicit transaction. Even in stranger-to-stranger offences, such as hold-ups of banks and convenience stores, the victims to some degree, can be prepared psychologically as such crimes are part of the risk involved in performing in the position of a cashier or teller.

As for the idea that victims of violence are helpless, it should be noted that not only can victims prepare themselves for the possibility of an attack when they are at high risk, but that they sometimes, through certain behaviour, increase the risks of a violent attack. Killings often result from quarrels between victim and offender. Rape victims sometimes place themselves in compromising situations prior to their victimization: they may have had too much to drink, accepted a ride from a stranger, or even willingly invited a stranger into their home.[2] To say this is not to blame the victim of a homicide or rape for his or her victimization, but rather to indicate that people are not completely powerless in affecting their chances of becoming victims. Certain actions increase *statistically* one's chances of victimization. Surveys of the public repeatedly show that life-styles and victimization are linked. The more time a person spends outside the home at night and the more alcohol he or she consumes, the more likely it is that he or she will become a victim of violence.[3] The point is that much violence ought to be seen as a product of the interaction between the parties involved, rather than simply as the acting-out of 'sick' individuals.

Yet another aspect of the public's view of violence is that it occurs in a dark alley or other public place. In fact, murders, rapes, and assaults often take place in the home, and robberies often occur in a place of business.

If we combine the four elements of the public's perception of violence mentioned above, we derive a particularly ominous view of the offender. The person who engages in violent behaviour is often viewed as a predator, lurking in dark alleys and attacking victims without provocation. An examination of criminal homicide shows how erroneous this image is.

MURDER

One of the classic studies on criminal homicide was conducted by sociologist Marvin Wolfgang at the University of Pennsylvania in the late 1950s.[4] Upon examining 588 cases of homicide that occurred in the city of Philadelphia, Wolfgang found that, in a majority of the cases, the parties (offender and victim) were married, blood relatives, or friends; that many of the victims, as well as the offenders, had consumed alcohol prior to the offence; and, the most astonishing finding, that, in a quarter of the cases, the offence was 'victim-precipitated' – in other words, the victim was the first to use force in the episode leading up to the killing.

Recent research, even in the United States where stranger-to-stranger homicides are more common, supports the notion that most homicides involve people known to each other.[5] In Canada, about 40 per cent of all killings occur within the family, and another 40 per cent involve lovers or those in love triangles, close and distant acquaintances, and business associates.[6] In only a small percentage of cases are the victims and offenders total strangers. Furthermore, 40 per cent of the perpetrators in Canada have no previous criminal record.

Some criminologists have begun to focus on the interactions between the victims and perpetrators that preceded the murder. This focus represents a significant departure from the traditional view of the murderer as simply a psychologically maladjusted individual. In studying murder transactions, David Luckenbill found that many homicides take a sequential form. First, the victim makes what the offender considers an offensive move; the offender typically retaliates in a verbal or physical manner; the victim's response then shapes the decision to end things violently; the battle ensues, leaving the victim dead or dying.[7] The typical homicide, then, is not the result of wanton violence by a deranged stranger. Instead, it results from a destructive social interaction between two or more people who know each other.

The following case-study illustrates sociologist Gwynne Nettler's comment that intimacy can be hazardous to one's health.

Case-Study: Murder Is Sweet Revenge

Neil Boyd, in his book *The Last Dance: Murder in Canada,* provides a number of cases covering each category of murder. One case in which a man killed his wife is presented here because the man was, by most standards, quite ordinary. He appeared to be experiencing the type of emotional reactions that are normal when a person is 'betrayed' by a spouse, although his ruminations about the betrayal may have exceeded the norm:

The difficulties between Victor and Stella Morrison began in 1973, when Stella left her husband for another man. According to Morrison, 'Stella didn't do things the way an honest thinking person would. She was a person who liked to find somebody else first and if it worked out, then she could dump me.'

The couple began divorce proceedings, but later got back together. As Morrison recalls, he drank heavily during the separation, but otherwise handled it in good shape. His business was doing well, and their ten-year-old son was staying with him. His wife's affair did not come out of nowhere; it had been developing over a two- to three-year period. But when Stella left him again in 1982, he was in his fifties. As he put it, 'I was getting old, and I felt that I was being rejected and dumped.'

Morrison had been out of town for a few days, on a bus trip to Reno with his brother-in-law. His son met him at the bus station and the three men drove to the apartment where they found a note on the refrigerator ... the note explained that his wife was leaving him for a man ... she found very attractive, younger and more athletic than Morrison.

For a few months Morrison coped on a comfortable income; his son moved into the apartment with a girlfriend. But Morrison was still angry and still looking for his wife. He found her in an apartment not far from his own, and asked her to come back to him.

'Of course you miss your wife,' he says now. 'If you love a woman and you've lived with her for 20 years and gone through hard times and gone through good times and raised a fine son and had everything that married people in Canadian society expect you to do, naturally you miss your wife.'

One day, in May 1982, Morrison confronted his wife and her lover out in a shopping mall, where they were selling pictures. As Morrison describes the scene, 'Now this is the thing that really hurt me. All the years that I had this business, and it was a good business, my wife didn't give a shit about that business. All she'd give a shit was when there was a hundred dollar bill in the till, you know, take it and buy some new clothes or buy something for her family ... And there she was, out selling goddamned $5 reprints – art reprints for this guy on the street corner ...'

... For the next three years Victor Morrison drifted across Canada and the United States, a competent salesman and a person who could fend for himself, but also an increasingly embittered man. He remembers an evening with some friends in the southern United States as particularly significant. He and his wife had known George and Gail for years, through a shared interest in playing bridge at the duplicates bridge clubs...' she [Gail] came up and she put her arm around me ...' Vic,' she says, "I just feel terrible about you and Stella."'

As Morrison puts it, 'something snapped.' He went back to his apartment that night and cried. 'I felt terrible. It bothered me then, everything. That was almost the start of the murder ... the wheels, the wheels up here started to turn.'

A few months later, in the summer of 1985, he returned to Canada. He had purchased a number of guns ... He was prepared to kill his wife and her lover ... Morrison was becoming increasingly depressed. He went to see a doctor about his depression; he was given a drug and told to come back in a few days if he didn't feel better.

... But he was also casing the store at which his wife worked. He took his gun and went down to the mall. He saw his wife and her lover ... For several days he made the trip to the mall, 'getting deeper' into the idea of the killing. One Thursday morning he walked into his wife's place of work.

'What's this about the divorce?' he said.

'Oh, when did you get back in town?'

'I've been in town for a day or two. I guess we should get this divorce thing finished.'

'Well, I've got the thing all ready. You just have to go up to this guy and sign the papers.'

As Stella Morrison went to get the address, her husband of 24 years pulled out his gun, saying, 'I'll give you a fucking divorce you won't forget,' and shot her. She was facing him when she fell. He walked a few feet closer, leaned over the counter and pumped the remaining bullets into her ...[8]

The Morrison case provides graphic insight into the anatomy of a homicide. Killings are rarely the impulsive, acting-out of deranged individuals who select their victims randomly. Many killings occur among intimates and follow the accumulation of long-standing grievances. Although men such as Morrison may well possess certain personality characteristics predisposing them to violence, the relationship dynamics must be understood to determine why this predisposition surfaced in the way it did. I am in no way condoning such violence but merely pointing out that violence among intimates or acquaintances can be understood fully only through an understanding of the interaction of the parties. The experience of major indignities and a profound sense of hopelessness may lead otherwise quite ordinary people to engage in extreme actions.[9]

To illustrate the important linkage between relationship dynamics and homicide, observe one further case, which appeared in the *Toronto Star* in the fall of 1991. In this case, a battered woman killed her boyfriend after enduring extreme physical and emotional abuse:

A battered woman has been sentenced to 12 months in jail for killing her boyfriend when he attacked her. Yu-Ming Tran, 32, pleaded guilty in June to manslaughter in the stabbing death of her 30-year-old boyfriend, Brian Tran ...

Brian Tran became jealous after he learned his girlfriend had a previous boyfriend ... He called the woman stupid and a prostitute ... He became so physically and verbally abusive that Yu-Ming Tran sought psychiatric treatment. He twice slammed her head on the floor, dragged her by the hair and kicked her in the stomach ... The boyfriend also expected sex on demand.

Yu-Ming Tran had tried to kill herself after her tolerance began to crumble and she could see no escape ... On the morning of the slaying, the couple had stayed up all night studying. At 6 a.m. Brian Tran 'directed' her to make him a meal ... She was heating oil in a skillet when the boyfriend demanded sex. When she refused, he called her a stupid slave and stormed into the bedroom, where he then lay naked on the bed.

She went to the bedroom with the pan of oil and said: 'Brian, if you don't stop insulting me or my family, you'll get this oil on you.' Some oil splashed on the victim and he attacked her. During the struggle Yu-Ming Tran grabbed a knife that was lying nearby and stabbed him until the fighting stopped ...

When she realized what had happened, she tried suicide by hanging herself in the bathroom and ingesting pills, but neither method worked. She then drove to Niagara Falls where she intended to jump to her death, but too many people were around, court was told. Yu-Ming Tran then went to visit her brother in California, where she had planned to jump from the Golden Gate Bridge ...

She returned home, told her psychiatrist she had killed her boyfriend and police were called. Watt [the presiding judge] concluded that Yu-Ming Tran's mental and emotional state drove her to commit involuntary manslaughter. He said she is not a violent person and is no danger to the public.[10]

It is highly unlikely that Yu-Ming Tran would ever have killed had she not become embroiled in such a highly destructive relationship. The severe abuse, degradation, stress, fear, and sense of hopelessness, and the victim's provocative behaviour immediately prior to the killing, contributed to the tragic outcome. Homicides all too often fit this profile rather than that of the random slaying.

That homicide is not an act typically committed by a deranged individual is demonstrated not only by the situational context in which it occurs, but by the support for violence sometimes found in the surrounding social milieu. Marvin Wolfgang, on the basis of his extensive research on homicide, concluded: 'Our analysis implies that there may be a subculture of violence which does not define personal assaults as wrong or antisocial; in which quick resort to physical aggression is a socially approved and expected concomitant of certain stimuli; and in which violence has become a familiar but often deadly partner in life's struggles.'[11] Wolfgang argued that high homicide rates in areas such as America's urban ghettos are attributable largely to such a subculture of violence.

SEXUAL ASSAULT

Sexual assault, the legal term used in Canada for rape and other sexually violent acts, also is not confined to a small number of disturbed offenders. According to the Canadian Advisory Council on the Status of Women, one in seventeen Canadian women is sexually assaulted, through forced sexual intercourse, at some point in her life, and one in five is sexually assaulted in other ways.[12] Only one in every three cases involves total strangers and, in fact, one-sixth of the victims of forced intercourse are attacked by a friend. Some of the most common scenarios involve family members, boyfriends, and dates.[13]

The phenomenon of date rape is gaining increasing recognition. It may be so common because, rather than reflecting abnormality in the perpetrator, it is an extension of the value our society places on male aggression and sexual conquest. Several surveys of college women conducted in the United States have found that more than half of the respondents have been sexually assaulted to varying degrees (ranging from forced necking to forced sexual intercourse). A survey of women in San Francisco revealed that 44 per cent had been victims of rape or attempted rape.[14] Noteworthy is the fact that many of the women in these surveys who had been raped did not identify their experiences as rape. It would appear that their view of rape is coloured by the idea that it can occur only among strangers and is always a physically brutal act.

In reality, rape is achieved through the use of physical coercion in only a minority of cases. Usually it is accomplished through verbal threats or menacing gestures, and serious physical injuries are uncommon.[15] Furthermore, rape is not typically an explosive act committed by an oversexed or highly impulsive individual. In perhaps the most thorough study ever conducted on the subject of rape, sociologist Menachem Amir found that only a fraction of the rapes he studied qualified as explosive. Seventy-one per cent were planned; that is, the offender actively sought out a victim and had already selected a setting for the act.[16] Another 11 per cent were found to be partially planned, with the offender devising a method once presented with an opportunity.

Rape is facilitated by the offender's view of the victim as a non-person or non-victim. If the victim is drunk, uses obscene language, has a 'bad' reputation, or hitchhikes at night, she may be regarded by the offender as fair game for a sexual attack. The offender justifies his behaviour on the basis that she probably wants sex anyway, or that she has had it hundreds of times before.[17] This type of interpretation will be made not only by a serial rapist with a twisted mind, but by many other men who fail to distinguish between a daring or even promiscuous lifestyle and an invitation to have sex.

The distinction between consensual intimacy and forced sex becomes especially blurred in the case of date rape or in the context of a steady relationship (or even marriage), where the woman has already consented to sex on previous occasions or where she shows some ambivalence. Surveys repeatedly indicate that many young men consider it 'acceptable for a man to force a girl to have sexual intercourse when she initially consents but then changes her mind, or when she has sexually excited him.'[18] Almost one-third of male students at York University in Toronto agreed with the statement that 'many times a woman will pretend she doesn't want to have intercourse because she doesn't want to seem loose, but she's really hoping the man will force her.'[19]

The fact that many men possess such attitudes certainly facilitates sexually aggressive behaviour. In fact, a controversial study by two sociologists from Ottawa's Carleton University revealed that these attitudes often become translated into behaviour. Walter DeKeseredy and Katharine Kelly, surveying 3,142 students at various Canadian college and university campuses, found that 22 per cent of women questioned had been physically abused, and 29 per cent claimed to have been sexually abused by boyfriends or male acquaintances in the previous twelve months.[20] The study also revealed that 81 per cent of female respondents had experienced some form of psychological abuse, such as taunts and insults, at the hands of these male 'friends.'

Indeed, feminists argue that sexual assault is not a form of aberrant behaviour committed by inadequate or hyper-aggressive men. Rather, it is a natural extension of the social roles of men and women, of the differential power attached to these roles, and of the conception of women as objects and possessions to be used by men for their own pleasure.[21] Feminist researchers Lorenne Clark and Debra Lewis have written of female sexuality as a commodity which, like a car or appliance, depreciates with use:

the law apparently refuses to protect women who are somewhat more 'liberal' in the distribution of their sexuality. Why is it that certain types of rape victims are popularly viewed as women who 'got what they deserved', 'were asking for it', or, simply, as women who are not credible because of their 'promiscuity' or 'lewd and unchaste' behaviour? The simple explanation is that women who voluntarily give up that which makes them desirable as objects of an exclusive sexual relationship are seen as 'common property', to be appropriated without penalty for the use, however temporary, of any man who desires their services. What this public attitude seems to entail is that the voluntary granting of sexual access outside the parameters of sanctified matrimony leads to the loss of physical and sexual autonomy. Once the woman parts with her one and only treasure, she never has the right to say no again.[22]

In accordance with this 'commodity' analogy, men are seen as enhancing their self-esteem when they conquer beautiful women in large numbers. Rejections pose direct threats to masculine self-concepts and, hence, produce frustration and anger. This frustration may be accentuated in a sexually permissive society because men who experience frequent failure believe that most men are enjoying sex. What they cannot attain through persuasion and influence, they achieve with coercion. Taking sex by force, according to feminists, is facilitated by the treatment of women as property and by many cultural myths, such as the idea that all women fantasize about being raped and that some women deserve to be assaulted (e.g., sexually active women, seductive women, non-traditional women).[23]

A graphic illustration of the attitudes held by many people, in relation to sexual assault was provided by an incident occurring in New Bedford, Massachusetts, in the spring of 1983. Six men from the city's Portuguese community were charged with aggravated rape after they took turns sexually assaulting a young woman on a pool table in a neighbourhood bar. Not one bystander came to her assistance. Many members of the community (both Portuguese and non-Portuguese) contended that the woman was not a victim but a consenting participant. Some argued that she should have been tried and punished. Said a local priest: 'She led those boys into sin.'[24] Meanwhile, family and friends stated that the woman never recovered from the incident. (She died in a car accident two years after the assault.)

In a high-profile date-rape case at Queen's University in Kingston, Ontario, the Crown attorney made the following observation about life on Canada's university campuses: 'My bottom line is that universities are a world in themselves that breed and foster rapes by "normal" red-blooded college males on vulnerable co-eds ... Campuses are hunting grounds. There are no restrictions and you don't have to worry about going over your limit. It's open season ... Some young men are there on the prowl for sex, and a lot of them don't know where seduction stops and unwanted assault begins.'[25]

Much sexual abuse (including forced sexual intercourse) is perpetrated by those in positions of trust. Below, in the section of this chapter entitled 'Child Abuse,' two cases involving members of the clergy are discussed. Physicians, lawyers, psychiatrists, and other professionals have, not infrequently, also engaged in sexual acts with patients or clients that have violated the trust placed in them. In Canada, an inquiry conducted in Ontario found that 10 per cent of the province's 22,000 practising physicians have been guilty of some form of sexual impropriety.[26] Such improprieties range from taking nude pictures of patients to fondling and sexual intercourse. A report issued by a special task force appointed by the College of Physicians and Surgeons of Ontario described a fairly typical case: 'A woman reported that she and her husband had been seeing a psychiatrist for sexual difficulties. The psychiatrist indicated that the couple should have individual therapy, so that he could see the wife separately. From the beginning of the individual session, the psychiatrist had sexual intercourse with the patient. She remembered the doctor saying to her, 'This is good for you.'"'[27]

SPOUSAL ASSAULT

Much of society's violence takes place in the home. For many years, wife-battering has been swept under the rug, although it is anything but a rare phenomenon. In Canada, it has been estimated that about one household in ten is the scene of assault against a spouse or live-in lover.[28] In the United States, prevalence estimates have run as high as 60 per cent of all families.[29]

In any jurisdiction, a large proportion of calls to the police involve domestic disturbances. The injuries stemming from spousal assault tend to be more serious than those assaults occurring outside the home. Furthermore, these assaults are more likely to be repeated, so that the victim is assaulted repeatedly and hence terrorized by her assailant. Moreover, domestic disturbances are a leading cause of police killings and injuries.[30]

Is wife assault the product of psychopathology and 'sick' marriages or, as some suggest, the manifestation of a prevailing attitude towards women? Although this question is too complex to answer conclusively, it is important to realize that using physical force against one's spouse has not always been illegal and, even today, many men believe it is their sovereign right to control their wives or lovers in this way. For centuries, of course, the law permitted the male head of the house to use force against his wife and children, who by law were considered as the man's property or chattels. The expression 'rule of thumb' derives from English common law, whereby a man was authorized to beat his wife with a stick, so long as that stick was no thicker than his thumb.[31]

Del Martin, in her book *Battered Wives*, recounts an incident that illustrates how, even in the present day, people regard domestic violence as a private or 'family' matter:

Our patriarchal system allows a man the right of ownership to some degree over the property and people that comprise his household. A feminist friend learned this lesson in an incident in Oakland, California. She witnessed a street fight in which a husband was hitting his pregnant wife in the stomach (a recurring theme in stories of wife-abuse). She saw the fight as she was driving by, stopped her car, and jumped out to help the woman. When she tried to intervene, the male bystanders who stood idly by watching the spectacle shouted at her, 'You can't do that! She's his wife!' and 'You shouldn't interfere; it's none of your business.' Although the wife had begged the gathered crowd to call the police, no one did so until my friend was struck by the furious husband. (I have heard of a similar incident where a man interfered and *he* was the one who was arrested and charged with assault!)[32]

One survey found that one-quarter of adults in the United States actually approved of physical battles between the spouses.[33] Even more surprising was the finding, in that survey, that there was greater approval of marital violence among those with higher educational levels.

CHILD ABUSE

The physical and sexual abuse of children is an enormously

prevalent problem. Since children are quite powerless and dependent, we can only guess, in the most crude way, the true extent of abuse directed against them. Psychological abuse and neglect are other serious issues.

In the United States, Richard Gelles undertook a national survey of physical punishments imposed on children by their parents.[34] By parents' own admission, 71 per cent indicated that they had at one time slapped or spanked their child. Forty-one per cent admitted to pushing or shoving the child in question during the past year, and 46 per cent stated they had pushed or shoved their child sometime in the past. Twenty per cent admitted to, at some point in the past, using some object to hit the child. Ten per cent had at some point thrown an object at the child. Eight per cent mentioned that they had at least once kicked, bitten, or hit the child with a fist. Gelles and colleague Murray Straus also found that more than one million children are physically abused by their parents in any given year.[35] Even more dramatic were the results of Diana Russell's survey of women in the San Francisco area in which she found that 38 per cent had experienced sexual abuse by the age of eighteen.[36]

The problem of abuse seems no less serious in Canada. It has even been claimed tha child abuse is the leading cause of death in infants between six months and one year of age.[37] The royal commission under the direction of sociologist Robin Badgley found that one in two females and one in three males have been the victims of unwanted sexual acts – 80 per cent experienced the assaults as children.[38] In Quebec, the province's social service centres reported 27,940 cases of physical and sexual abuse in 1988.[39] In Alberta, it has been estimated that purposeful physical abuse takes place in 10 per cent of all families.[40]

Also highly significant have been revelations regarding the abuses of children in orphanages and other institutions. In recent years, Canada has seen inquiries and media coverage of a number of high-profile cases in which children and youngsters have been physically and sexually abused in large numbers. In one of the best-known cases, eight Christian brothers were convicted for the physical and sexual abuse of young boys at Newfoundland's Mount Cashel Orphanage.[41] In another case, 19 former or current Christian brothers have been charged for the assault and sexual abuse of 177 alleged victims over four decades.[42]

The secular community, too, has experienced some high-profile cases. In Prescott, Ontario, 30 people have been charged since 1990 with 150 counts of abuse against children. In Martensville, Saskatchewan, 172 charges were laid in 1992 against 9 people in relation to the sexual abuse of 30 children at a babysitting centre and nearby farm. Included among those charged in this bedroom community, which had prided itself as a haven from big-city woes, were two former police chiefs and a police corporal. The offences alleged to have been committed against children between the ages of two and twelve were unlawful confinement, assault with a hypodermic needle, sexual assault, sodomy, administering a 'stupefying drug,' and suffocating with a pillow case with intent to render a person incapable of resistance.[43]

Child abuse, of course, is frequently exclusively emotional in nature and were there any way this type of abuse could be counted with accuracy, the figures would be monumental. An extreme example of non-physical abuse is provided by the following case reported in the *New York Times*:[44]

Linda Marie Ault killed herself, policemen said today, rather than make her dog Beauty pay for her night with a married man.

The police quoted her parents, Mr. and Mrs. Joseph Ault, as giving this account:

Linda failed to return home from a dance in Tempe Friday night. On Saturday she admitted she had spent the night with an Air Force lieutenant. The Aults decided on a punishment that would 'wake Linda up.' They ordered her to shoot the dog she had owned about two years.

On Sunday, the Aults and Linda took the dog into the desert near their home. They had the girl dig a shallow grave. Then Mrs. Ault grasped the dog between her hands, and Mr. Ault gave his daughter a .22-caliber pistol and told her to shoot the dog.

Instead, the girl put the pistol to her right temple and shot herself.

The police said there were no charges that could be filed against the parents except possibly cruelty to animals.

PROSTITUTION

What has been called the 'world's oldest profession' is widespread and big business. It has been estimated that, in the United States, the profits deriving from this activity amount to ten times the annual budget of the U.S. Department of Justice. It has also been estimated that, in the United States, there are at any time half a million full-time prostitutes (there are many more part-time prostitutes) and that 315 million acts of commercial sex are committed per year.[45] In Canada, estimates several years ago put the number of full-time prostitutes in both Montreal and Toronto at between 500 and 600, with the figures increasing two to six times when occasional prostitutes were considered.[46] These kinds of statistics certainly suggest that prostitution is anything but an activity engaged in solely by a fringe group of sleazy and perverted individuals.

Although people associate prostitution with streetwalkers, much, if not most, prostitution is based in brothels, massage parlours, and 'escort' services. Depending on the sophistication of their operation, prostitutes may have a variety of people involved in a network to facilitate their activities, for example, madams, pimps, and hotel clerks. Then, of course, there are the millions of 'johns' who will often pay considerable money for sex. It is important to note that prostitution does not always involve impersonal sex, as some customers regularly visit the same prostitute.

'Johns' are not merely 'perverts' or those not capable of obtaining sex through other means. They may be people who, for one reason or another, wish to avoid serious romantic entanglements, or they may be married individuals searching for sexual variety.[47] Like prostitutes, johns come from all sectors of society and all occupational positions. Escort services, for example, routinely see professional and business people who are attending out-of-town meetings.

Men of the cloth have frequented prostitutes for centuries. In their historical account of the field of psychiatry, Franz Alexander and Sheldon Selesnick have written that, during the medieval period, 'centuries of imposed celibacy had not inhibited the erotic drives of monks and nuns, and underground passageways were known to connect some monasteries and nunneries. Townspeople often had to send prostitutes to the monasteries in order to protect the maidens of the village.'[48]

There are many contemporary examples of priests and preachers who have fallen from grace as a result of their sexual indiscretions. Perhaps, none is more dramatic than that involving Jimmy Swaggart, the popular television evangelist who has reached more than ten million people in North America and many others in 145 countries. By day, in his sermons, he heaped unrelenting scorn upon the sinners; at night, he cruised seedy motel strips, wearing disguises, and paid prostitutes to perform pornographic acts.[49]

A recent study by Roberta Perkins in Australia refutes the view of prostitutes as oversexed individuals with a deep involvement in criminality.[50] Perkins worked as a welfare worker in the Kings Cross area of Sydney and accumulated her evidence through observations and in-depth interviews with prostitutes – both streetwalkers and those operating out of bordellos or as call girls. Her bottom line was that prostitution was not so much an act of defiance against conventional morality as one of economic survival.

Contrary to general belief, Perkins found that streetwalkers did not tend to come from broken homes or to have had a history of juvenile delinquency. Also, they did not pursue promiscuous lifestyles outside of prostitution. Instead, many were mothers caring for their children. As for those working out of residences, Perkins found that most of these women, too, were single mothers who had worked or were still working as secretaries, nurses, stewardesses, or waitresses, going to college. Most of these women came from affluent backgrounds. Thus, on the whole, she found that many prostitutes were not from a working-class or severely dysfunctional home, but, as Perkins asserted, were 'basically ordinary women with only their occupation distinguishing them from others.'[51]

Although Perkins's study may not apply to all communities, there is evidence from other research that a sizeable percentage of prostitutes (especially call girls) come from middle-class backgrounds, are primarily economically motivated, and do not have extensive criminal records.[52]

6

'There Is Nothing Wrong with Greed': Corporate Crime

Speaking to graduating students at the University of California, Ivan Boesky, the Wall Street financier who earned tens of millions of dollars illegally after receiving 'insider' tips about corporate takeovers, said the following: 'Greed is all right, by the way. I want you to know that. I think greed is healthy. You can be greedy and still feel good about yourself.'[1]

Rather than being an aberration, this attitude reflects business ethics and practices throughout North American history. Many great fortunes were amassed by illicit or unscrupulous means. Corporate misbehaviour in relation to both employees and consumers, as well as the environment, is legendary. There is the case of the Ford Motor Company, which poured millions of Pintos off its assembly lines although Ford executives knew the gas tanks were defective and could rupture after a rear-end collision, burning passengers alive. There is the Johns-Manville Corporation, producer of asbestos products, which for decades failed to inform its workers that inhaling asbestos can be lethal – about 10,000 people die each year of asbestos-related cancer. There is A.H. Robins, manufacturer of the Dalkon Shield, an intra-uterine contraceptive device. Despite the fact that women using the device were dying, having still births and babies with birth defects in large numbers, as well as suffering from internal injuries on a large scale, the company for years tried to cover up the products' dangers.[2]

There have also been countless cases of illegal dumping of hazardous materials, resulting in fatalities, chromosomal damage, and chronic illnesses on the part of significant segments of the population (see chapter 8).

The greed of some of our wealthiest citizens knows no bounds. One of the most celebrated cases in recent memory has been the trial of the 'Queen of Mean,' Leona Helmsley, the New York billionairess who was convicted for income tax violations. Despite the fact she already paid $60 million a year in taxes, she and her husband tried to cut their tax bill by having their hotel empire pay for millions of dollars' worth of personal items, for example, a $130,000 indoor-outdoor stereo system, furnishings, clothing, cosmetics, and a Caribbean cruise.[3] She was known for being ruthless and for often summarily dismissing employees for the slightest infractions. On one occasion, she refused to pay a contractor for a barbeque pit. When she was informed that the man was struggling to raise six children, she snapped: 'Why didn't he keep his pants on? He wouldn't have so many problems.' On another occasion, a waiter at one of her hotels served her a cup of tea with hands trembling. She immediately summoned the maître d' for an explanation. He informed her it was the waiter's first day on the job. She responded: 'Get him out of here.' To her housekeeper she once exclaimed: 'We don't pay taxes. Only little people pay taxes.'[4]

Of all the scandals business has been involved in, the financial collapse of huge segments of the savings and loan industry in the United States may be the most dramatic. Perhaps as many as 50 per cent, or 1,700, of the s&l banks may eventually collapse. The extent of the corruption, greed, and incompetence of those who mismanaged or plundered hundreds of these institutions is almost incalculable.[5] Because the federal government instituted a program in 1980 to insure deposits in its financial institutions, s&l managers could take reckless risks knowing that the government would underwrite its losses. Ownership rules were also relaxed so that almost anyone could own or operate an s&l. Among the abuses were the following:

Erwin Hansen took over Centennial Savings and Loan of California in 1980 and threw a Christmas Party that cost $148,000 for 500 friends and guests and included a ten-course sit-down dinner, roving minstrels, court jesters, and pantomimes. Hansen and his companion, Beverly Haines, traveled extensively around the world in the bank's private airplanes, purchased antique furniture at the S&L's expense, refurbished their home at a cost of over $1 million and equipped it with a chef. Before it went bankrupt, the bank bought a fleet of luxury cars and an extensive art collection. Another case involves Don Dixon, owner of the Vernon Savings and Loan in Texas. Dixon transformed the small savings bank into one of the largest S&Ls in the state by advertising high interest rates. Dixon used company money for a $22,000 tour of Europe, to buy five airplanes, and to pay rent on a California home. The bank funded projects so shaky that when federal regulators took over, 96 per cent of its loans were overdue. It has been estimated that the collapse of Vernon will eventually cost taxpayers $1.3 billion.[6]

A combination of opportunism by business people, collusion by politicians, untimely legislation, and the inherent fragility of these institutions culminated in a government bail-out that will ultimately approach $500 billion.

Many other examples can be provided of corruption and avarice throughout North American history. How widespread is this type of corruption and greed? Colin Goff and Charles Reasons have examined the records of the fifty largest corporations in Canada between 1952 and 1972.[7] They found that all had at least one major decision against them under the Combines Act. On the average, more than three decisions were made against these companies. The greatest number of decisions have been made against combinations, misleading advertising, and mergers.

In the United States, over one two-year period, the federal government charged nearly two-thirds of the Fortune 500 corporations with law violations, half of them of a serious nature.[8] Estimates of the cost of these crimes range as high as $200 billion a year as opposed to the $3 billion or $4 billion in annual losses from street crimes.

Negligence and greed are also responsible for many deaths, illnesses, and injuries. Occupational deaths far outnumber those resulting from murder. It has been found, in Canada, that occupational deaths rank third, after heart disease and cancer, as the source of mortality, accounting for over ten times as many deaths as murders.[9] It has been estimated that over a third of all injuries on the job are attributable to illegal working conditions, and about another quarter to unsafe conditions that are technically legal. Employers often intentionally and knowingly create hazards.[10] In the United States, it has been estimated that violations of safety standards, pollution of the environment, and industrial accidents owing to negligence result in 20 million serious injuries, including 110,000 people who become permanently disabled and 30,000 deaths.[11]

Another common form of illegality is 'chiselling' or cheating customers on a routine basis. Consider the automobile-repair industry. It has been estimated that one-third of every consumer dollar spent on car repairs is wasted as a result of fraud or incompetence.[12] The following case-study illustrates the extent of unethical conduct in this industry.

Case-Study: Highway Robbery in Canada

Robert Sikorsky, in a special investigative report for *Reader's Digest*, travelled coast to coast in Canada to determine the state of the auto-repair business.[13] What he found was very similar to the startling revelations of unscrupulousness made in comparable U.S. investigations.

Before embarking on his trip, which covered 10,000 kilometres and 152 repair shops (both large and small, independent and national chain outlets), Sikorsky ensured that his car was in tip-top condition by putting it through a rigorous bumper-to-bumper inspection by the Canadian Automobile Association. Recommended repairs were done by a Pontiac dealer (his car was a 1988 Pontiac). Before each stop, Sikorsky unplugged a connector at the idle air control, an electronic motor at the top of the engine that meters the amount of air the engine receives while idling. Unplugging it caused the engine to run exceptionally fast and triggered the 'SERVICE ENGINE SOON' warning on the dash. In order to get the engine running smoothly again, a mechanic merely had to reinsert the connector, as easy as plugging in any household appliance. The dangling plug was an obvious sign to mechanics that the problem Sikorsky said he was encountering was a simple one. Sikorsky, an authority on cars in his own right, notes what happened right at the outset of his trip:

Though the car had been thoroughly prepared for the trip, I wanted to do my own inspection. I pulled a wire from a spark plug and noticed that dirt fell from the boot, the rubber cover that fits over the plug. Any dirt should have been dislodged when the spark plugs were replaced during the just-completed major tune-up. Suspicious, I unscrewed a couple of spark plugs. They weren't new. I dug out the invoice. The $295 tune-up had included new plugs, but the old ones were still on the car. Although the old plugs were in excellent shape, I bought and installed new ones. I chuckled at the irony: I hadn't even started and already I had my first rip-off.

The first service station Sikorsky visited gave him an estimate for around $570 for work that did not need to be done, and at the very next station, the manager reconnected the loose wire in less than thirty seconds, at no charge. On the whole, 57 per cent of the stations visited overcharged, performed unnecessary work, tried to sell unneeded parts, or fixed the car and lied about what work had been done. Sikorsky adds:

For the unscrupulous mechanic, my loose IAC wire was a hot line to extra profits. Many fiddled with the engine and faked work – but charged real dollars. Padding the bill with 'phantom work' was the most common deceptive practice. Real and contrived fixes ranged from complete tune-ups, 'adjusting the carburetor' (the car had none), repairing the 'multipoint ignition' (there is no such thing) and simply letting the engine cool down. Parts recommended included a new IAC motor, fuel-injector cleaner, air filter, spark plugs, a 'sealed' throttle unit and, two favourites of mine, a 'little' valve and an 'electronic doo-hickey.' In total, more than 40 different and unnecessary repairs or parts were recommended, ranging in price from $4 to $570.

One of the shops visited by Sikorsky indicated that his car needed a distributor cap and distributor rotor, even though his car did not have a distributor! At another shop, he was billed for a carburettor adjustment. His fuel-injected Pontiac, however, had no carburettor – the mechanic had simply replaced the loose plug.

The coast-to-coast trip also revealed that mechanics are not beyond the use of sleight of hand. In one station, the owner lifted the disconnected IAC plug and appeared to replace it into its socket; however, he made sure the plug did not make contact and, as a result, the car continued to idle fast. The owner then suggested that the IAC motor was the culprit and that it would cost 'big money' to replace it.

Unnecessary diagnostic tests also are commonly used as a means of padding the customer's bill. In one chain tune-up shop visited in Vancouver, a technician mentioned that scanning the engine (which in this case was unnecessary) was expensive and could take three to four hours at $46 an hour.

Sikorsky recounts two other disconcerting experiences:

Another Montreal service-station encounter was different, though no less annoying: A mechanic picked up the loose plug, then dropped it. His partner commandeered the car and raced off. A test drive, said the other man. Some 45 minutes later, the mechanic returned. After much bickering, they replaced the plug, which both knew was loose all along, and let us go for $15. The test drive? We could only speculate that the car was used to run errands. A new approach to milking a customer.

As I headed towards Toronto on Highway 401 a few days later, I stopped at one of the freeway's service stations. A young man looked at the engine and within seconds went into a long explanation of how a mass air flow sensor works and why ours was faulty. To prove it, he resorted to trickery. A connector similar to one on the IAC motor attaches to the mass air flow sensor. He unplugged it, and the engine idle dropped dramatically. When he replaced it, the engine's speed increased. That showed, he said, that the sensor was faulty. An average motorist, not knowing the engine was supposed to react that way, could have been convinced by this demonstration. His original estimate of $100 now escalated to 'over $500.' He warned us not to drive the car because it could damage the engine.

After an hour I tired of this chicanery, reconnected the wire and drove off ... I wondered how many unaware motorists, far from home, this mechanic had 'helped.'

The auto-repair business is not unique in terms of its pervasive dishonesty. Scams seem to abound in virtually every retail business. Peter Maiken, in his book *Ripoff: How to Spot It, How to Avoid It*, documented this point through detailed interviews with veterans of approximately 100 different businesses.[14] Like the movie *Tin Men*, which featured the scams of conniving aluminum-siding salesmen, Maiken's research reveals that trickery and fraud are not confined to a small group of 'rotten apples' within different lines of work: Very often, dishonesty is the norm. The following case-studies deriving from his research provide further indication of the extent to which corrupt practices characterize the nature of business in everyday North American life.

Case-Study: The 'Bait and Switch' in Advertising

A veteran of advertising for both department and furniture stores related the following about some of his practices:

When I handled advertising for a leading furrier, I would run an add in newspapers featuring a number of items on sale, including, say, one mink coat at cost or below. In other words, I'd advertise a coat that normally sells for $4,000 for $2,000. We'd say we only had one, although, in fact, we made sure we had two, a small and a large size. When a big woman came in, they brought out the small coat. Then after they'd convince her they couldn't fit her in the sale item, they would try to switch her into something they could make a normal profit on. That is one of the 'bait and switch' methods.

Of the other sale items, they would bring out furs of inferior grades: a coat made of bellies, which is not as fine a fur as the back, but it would still have a mink, or whatever, label on it. Maybe it would be a coat made from tiny pieces, or remnants, instead of full skins. Maybe the coats were made of improperly processed furs; there are reputable fur makers and schlocky ones. If a fur is not processed properly, the hair will fall out, or the dye will come off on your hands. Of course, we didn't make any of these distinctions in the advertising.

One of the greatest ripoffs in stores is the concealed stock, where the customer is strictly at the mercy of the salesperson. These stores keep only samples out, or maybe a rack of something on clearance, but everything else is behind the curtains. As a result, the customer does not necessarily get an opportunity to make a free choice. When merchandise doesn't move fast – it might be last year's, or a style that is sticky or inferior in some way – the manager may pay the salesgirl extra commission to move it. That gives her the incentive to show these things and limit the choice of the customer. Which is another thing a salesperson wants to do. When customers see too many things, they get confused, so you want to limit their choices. This tactic is used by fine stores all over the country.[15]

Disloyalty and deception are the tools of the trade commonly used by salespeople in many retail businesses: they are not merely employed by a small disreputable group. Whether the customer is buying a fur coat, a car or video-cassette recorder, the salesperson attempts to develop some form of bond with him or her. Salespeople develop this bond through presenting themselves as allies of the customers and depicting management as the enemy. The salesperson will often inform the customer about some defect in a product, while pretending that such a disclosure would terminate his or her employment, should the employer learn of it. This feigned loyalty to the customer (and apparent disloyalty to the employer) is designed to elicit trust and loyalty from the customer. Once the customer feels indebted to and trusts the salesperson, and has become wary of management, he or she becomes highly vulnerable to being switched to the product the salesperson really wants to sell.[16]

Case-Study: The Horrors of Driving

A driving school instructor relates the way instructors under-mine the confidence of students and thereby justify more driv-ing lessons than might be otherwise necessary:

Remember, the students getting into our cars are terrified to begin with. Many are women whose husbands have told them, 'You'll never learn. I'm disgusted with you. You're ruining my car.' So they want to hear someone who says nice things to them, and that's what the instructors are paid to do ... Now there are many different ways that you can talk to people. You can undermine their confidence and put the fear of God in them, and that was one of the things we did. Instruc-tors will precipitate crises for the express purpose of saying, 'See, I told you you couldn't do it.' You could rile up people – get them very ner-vous – and throw them out into a traffic situation they're not ready for, like driving on expressways or in snow. They'll say, 'Oh I can't possibly do that,' and you tell them they can't avoid driving on expressways or in the snow, and they'll keep pleading that they're not ready. So you tell them, 'Well, you see now, we need more lessons.'
  Or you give them maneuvers that are so precise, they can't do them and lose control. Say they're parking, and you tell them, 'Line your car up with the lead car, cut your wheel, and go back, back slowly,' and they might hit the curb. So you tell them that if they do that they'll fail their road test, and if they fail it three times in one year, they've had it. And they've got to get their license, because they're taking a new job and have no transportation. So we tell them they need at least two, and possibly more, hours on parking. What's the person going to say?
  You can always work a few hours in without very much problem,

because you're the expert; you can get them to the point where they look upon you as God. You can say, 'It's up to you if you don't want any more lessons, but if you have an accident, your insurance rates will go up, so in the long run isn't it better to pay $40 more in lessons than $100 more in insurance premiums?' Or tell them that if they make a mistake typing a letter, they can always start over, but if they make a mistake driving, they could lose their life. If you call any driving school and ask how long it will take you to drive, they'll say it depends – which is true, but they stretch the truth. When you see a lot of money coming in, you get greedy. You take advantage of people. So if you can keep a student out an additional three or four hours, you get more money, and you justify it in your own mind by saying that the person really needed the extra lessons.[17]

Case-Study: The Door-to-Door Hustle

Door-to-door salespeople sell a variety of wares, but, without exception, whether they are selling encyclopaedias, cosmetics, cleaning or repair services, they have one thing in common: they must try to convince the homeowner that there is a need for the goods or services they provide. This need can be 'created' through persuasion or through a variety of fraudulent tactics that prey on the ignorance of those lacking expertise in the domain in which the salesperson is operating. A career sewer repairman illustrates how these hustles can work:

I know almost every sewer repair company in the area, and I never found an honest one in my life. I used to have a crew, and we'd drive down alleys. We might have eight guys on the truck; six would be hustlers and two laborers. Every sewer company sends out trucks like these. Then you'd start going door-to-door with cards, saying, 'Hi, I'm a sewer man in the area, and I've been doing a lot of the people's work around here for years.' Maybe you have, and maybe you haven't, but what you say the average public believes.

Just to win their confidence on a job, you'd suggest they get three good estimates. You'd know you had them in the palm of your hand, when they would say, 'Yeah, I agree, but I trust you.' So you tell them you are there to check their sewer trap and see about cleaning it. Some of the guys would open the lid and say, 'Damn, it sure is filthy,' and there would hardly be anything in it ... So we would offer to go down and clean it out for a very low price, and the customers would go for it.

Then we'd say, 'Oh, well, as long as we're down here, turn on your water so we can see if it is coming out of the pipe all right. We'll check it out for you free of charge.' So when the customers went into the house, one of the guys would take a crowbar and break the clay that leads from the house into the sewer, or loosen some of the bricks on the side of the sewer. Now, instead of a cut-rate cleaning job, they've got a repair job. Or, we could say, 'The water's coming out of your line real slow. It needs to be rodded.'

... All we wanted to do was get the rod [a cleaning device] inside the line, so when we started pushing it to the street, we could say: 'Oh, oh. I hear something!' We would start feeling the rod and holding it like we were banging on something and say, 'You have a broken tile.' All of a sudden, a $10 job comes out to be a $2,000 job. So we'd get hired to dig up the street to replace the one broken tile, and half the time we would not replace anything. We'd just cover it right back up as if some work had been done.[18]

The scams in different industries are endless. I asked the Consumers Association of Canada and the Better Business Bureau in Ottawa what major problems they encounter. The Better Business Bureau, serving a population of under one million people, receives about 15,000 complaints a year from consumers. Both organizations mentioned mail-order companies as being the leading cause of consumer concerns. In a typical scenario, a person will order a product by mail and fail to receive it, or receive inferior or damaged merchandise. An official of the Consumers Association of Canada explained what commonly transpires in these mail-order transactions:

The complaints that we get from people about mail-order firms usually are of this type, 'I had ordered this pen and it didn't come so I contacted the company with all the documentation that I had on this

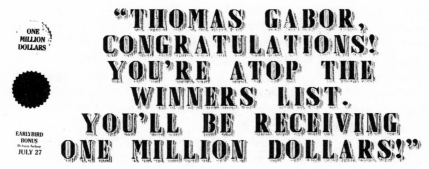

Figure 3   A millionaire once again!

order, sent it in and they sent back something saying, "Well, we need a photocopy of the other side of your form."' So that's one thing they try to use, the delay, to delay it as long as possible. 'We need both copies of this or we need this and that, you sent us this but you didn't send us that.' They'll use all kinds of excuses [to wear the customer down]. We don't know at the end what ultimately it was that caused the delay because they don't really explain it.

... We get a lot of [complaints about] direct mail where they tell you you've won a prize. It's free, you only have to send $10 to get your prize and of course there's some sort of catch in the fine print. There was a big one [scam] a few years ago. A diamond ring mail order company was promoting their catalogue and by promoting it they were saying you could win a diamond ring or $5,000 or $2,500 ... and I think in every case they won this diamond ring and what it was, it was a brute diamond which is considered commercial grain, what they use in sand paper, that sort of thing ... and the band was one of those expandable types. It wasn't a proper band for a ring. I don't even think Cracker Jack would [use it], that's how bad it was ... Some people had the ring appraised and $5 was tops for what this ring was worth.[19]

While writing this book, I received notification by mail that I had won a million dollars (see figure 3). This is the umpteenth time I have 'won' such a sum of money. Farther along in the brochure is the catch: I must return the attached stub which commits me to subscribing to a popular news magazine. The stub no longer speaks of the 'Gabor' million dollars. It merely indicates that I am *eligible* to win that amount. Such marketing ploys may technically conform to the legal guidelines governing advertising, but they are none the less fraudulent, preying as they do on the naïvety of the consumer. Needless to say, I did not return the stub. (Who knows, perhaps the offer was genuine!) Is it not significant that so many people reflexively toss such material into the nearest wastepaper basket?

Consumers' groups also receive many complaints about travel scams. In some cases, consumers receive a letter or phone call painting an enchanting picture of free or discount travel.[20] The travel firm, upon being contacted by the 'contest' winner, then sets the hook: the customer is asked to pay a deposit or membership fee in a travel club of up to $150. Some scams end here, where the money is taken and the firm disappears.

A more commonly used scheme resorts to issuing travel certificates that bear the name of a major airline or cruise operator. The consumer usually makes a deposit and then discovers that the travel is so restricted that the certificate is virtually useless. Plans routinely have fifteen or more hurdles to navigate, so most people find it impossible to make it through all the hoops. Deposits are rarely returned.

Another area of concern for consumers' groups is misleading advertising. Fraudulent claims and misrepresentation appear to be the norm. Terms such as 'pure,' 'light,' 'natural,' and 'fresh,' when referring to various food products, are frequently manipulated and misused, even with the advertising guidelines that exist. A label on a jar claiming that the contents are '100% pure strawberry jam' suggests that the jar contains nothing but jam. In reality, the jam may be pure but makes up only 50 per cent of the contents of the jar – sugar and preservatives, for example, may be added.

Puffery, praising an item with subjective opinions, superlatives, or exaggerations, is another common feature in advertising. An advertisement may represent a product as the 'best,' 'greatest,' 'finest,' or use some other superlative.[21] Examples include, 'Blatz is Milwaukee's finest beer,' 'Ford gives you better ideas,' or 'Wheaties is the breakfast of champions.' Puffery is usually allowed by law because there is no factual claim made about the product (e.g., it prevents disease) that could be verified. In puffery, no claims are made about specific facts; only opinions are advanced. While advancing these opinions may not be illegal, technically speaking, such opinions are misleading because they are not based on systematic surveys of consumer preferences. They are merely instances of self-aggrandizement that are given the appearance of credibility.

Another feature of advertisements is the mock-up.[22] Mockups alter the appearance of a product to project a more favourable image of it. Mashed potatoes may be used in ice cream commercials because ice cream melts quickly under studio lights. Soap and shampoo suds may be used in beer commercials to enhance the appearance of the beer head.

Packaging is another area where deception is often practised. Consumer products are frequently packaged in such a way that the contents appear to be greater in volume or weight than they actually are. Cereals, potato chips, laundry detergent, deodorants, and countless other products often only half-fill their packages. Consumers frequently have no way of knowing, short of muddling through confusing labels, how much of the product they are really getting. Also, consumers are not informed when packages contain less of the product than previously. For example, a box of detergent may now contain five rather than the six litres of detergent it formerly contained, yet the price may remain the same.

My informant from the Better Business Bureau indicated not only that 'rip-offs' of customers are prevalent in countless businesses, but that the victimization of businesses by customers is becoming more commonplace. She related the following story as an example:

Over the years ... we have seen more and more consumers try to rip-off business ... One of the examples I like to use is that of a renovator working on a contract. The contract was all laid out, what everyone was supposed to do. While in the home, the wife asked him if he would put up a shelf in the living room which she had purchased. She could never get her husband to do it. So he put it up with the material she supplied as a goodwill gesture. Within a short time, somebody maybe slammed the door and the shelf fell. The clock on the shelf fell with the shelf and broke. She was now trying to charge the contractor for the cost of the clock, the holes in the wall, and for the bad job she claimed he did ... She thought she could get something from him. We find that more and more people want $1,000 worth of work for $400 and $500. There's just more and more examples of people complaining about companies, maybe not completing all of what's in the contract and when we request a copy of the contract, the company has done exactly as the contract stated. There just seems to be more, 'Let's get the company.'[23]

The adversarial relationship between business and consumers is fostered by corporate irresponsibility that sometimes knows no bounds. Unsafe cars, tires, appliances, children's toys, cosmetics, and drugs are often produced and marketed with the knowledge they are dangerous. Companies often adopt the rationalization that their competitors are engaging in similar activities or that they are meeting legal standards. These standards, however, are set at a minimum level, and products can be dangerous well beyond these standards.[24] The Consumer Product Safety Commission in the United States estimates that more than 170,000 children suffer toy-related injuries each year. As many as half of all car accidents have been attributed to poor design or failed equipment.[25]

Another example of negligence about the welfare of consumers can be found in the food industry. Restaurants, for example, routinely fail to pass health inspections. In the fashionable Byward Market area in Ottawa, 40 per cent of the restaurant inspections during 1990 yielded an unsatisfactory rating.[26] Only a fifth of the eateries passed all of their inspections for the year (there are usually about four inspections a year). Some of the problems uncovered included kitchen filth, insects, clogged toilets, and cooks smoking while they prepared food. In Montreal, for the same year, the city's 6,300 restaurants incurred a total of 6,927 warnings for health code violations.[27]

Another form of unethical practice is the marketing of worthless products or those designed to be obsolete within a short period of time. Cereals, for example, are often advertised as having high nutritional value. One study of sixty well-known cereals showed that forty of them had a nutrient content so low that they did nothing to prevent malnutrition.[28] As for planned obsolescence, the automobile industry and those producing electrical appliances have been famous for providing short-term warranties, knowing their products were designed to require servicing or replacement in a relatively short period of time.

Other unethical practices include kickbacks to purchasing agents and government officials, as well as the abuse of corporate resources by management at the expense of stockholders (e.g., inflated salaries, the abuses of expense accounts, and other 'perks').

One could provide many more examples of unscrupulous and illegal behaviour on the part of businesses, both large and small, as well as of customers victimizing businesses. Are these instances of misbehaviour attributable to character flaws on the part of perpetrators or do they reflect the prevailing state of business ethics?

One of the more persuasive theories of corporate crime, that of corporate culture, accommodates both considerations. According to corporate culture theory, many organizations adopt values and objectives that are conducive to criminal violations. The values of managers at the highest levels, particularly the chief executive oficer, will set the tone of the corporate culture, including its tolerance for violations of the law.[29] Market forces, too, will have an impact on this culture.

Corporations may pressure employees to engage in unethical and illegal behaviour in direct and subtle ways. 'Whistle blowers' may be fired, while those demonstrating 'loyalty' to the company through illegal behaviour may be rewarded through promotions and other means. Upper-level management may pressure middle-level managers for results, without indicating whether these results should be achieved ethically or legally.

Employees throughout the organization come to understand that results are more important than methods.[30]

At the same time, since no specific directives are given to violate the law and since upper-level managers often distance themselves from wrongdoings, it is hard to hold them legally accountable. Several U.S. executives have even indicated that they held the position of 'vice-president responsible for going to jail.'[31] Their companies' activities were so centred around law-breaking that they had even designated certain individuals to take the fall should legal action be taken against the company.

Although corporations differ in terms of the degree to which they adopt a culture promoting unethical behaviour, it is safe to say that many North American companies condone illegalities to some extent. The prevailing attitude is that the goal of business is profit maximization, not social responsibility. Nobel Prize–winning economist Milton Friedman is a leading advocate of the position that corporate executives who talk about social responsibility are undermining the free-enterprise system. Actions that aim to meet society's needs (e.g., pollution control or extra safety features in cars) and result in reduced returns to stockholders constitute a misappropriation of their investments. Expenditures made for other than profit maximization, according to Friedman, are also at the expense of the consumer, who pays a higher price for the product, and the employee, who may receive lower wages than would otherwise be the case.[32]

The argument has also been made that business cannot assume social responsibility because business people are not properly trained for this type of work. This argument is feeble in that large corporations have experts in many fields (such as consumer preferences) and, in any case, all businesses can contribute to the welfare of the community simply by refraining from those practices and producing those products that have a high probability of causing harm to employees and consumers. Expertise is not required for this to occur, only common sense and compassion.

Crime, fraud, and corruption in the business world are not the exclusive purview of corporate officials or management. Many labour unions have displayed less than exemplary behaviour. Probably the most notorious case has been that of the Teamsters, which has represented workers primarily in the transportation sector (truck drivers, railway workers, etc.). Until major reforms were achieved in 1991, the union was riddled with corruption.[33] The Teamsters had been infiltrated by U.S. organized-crime families since the 1920s. A number of Teamster bosses were charged and convicted for such offences as racketeering, embezzlement, mail fraud, bribery, and jury tampering. Union executives typically enjoyed lavish lifestyles. Jackie Presser, for example, drew an annual salary of $280,000 and enjoyed such extras as a private jet, chauffeured limousines, and a condominium in Puerto Rico. Other top Teamsters held several titles at once and thereby drew multiple salaries, along with pensions valued in the millions. The union pension fund not only financed some of the perks enjoyed by the executives, but was used to advance money to organized-crime officials in such undertakings as the building of Las Vegas casinos. It was not until 1991 that the executive truly became accountable to the union's membership. The election held in that year involved, for the first time, a secret-ballot vote in which the entire membership participated. Previously, union leaders were elected once every five years through a show of hands of delegates at the convention. Under that system, considerable intimidation and influence were used to keep the old guard in power.

7

'What's Good for the Goose ...': Crime by Society's Leaders and Law Enforcers

Among the most harmful crimes to society are those committed by people held in high esteem by the public, whether these are political, corporate, or religious leaders, or television personalities. The misbehaviour of such individuals is highly visible, and because they are often adopted as role models, their fall from grace leads to a general disillusionment with the values of honesty and good citizenship. When the rich and powerful lie, cheat, and steal, those with lower social status can hardly be expected to maintain high ethical standards.

Although the media today are perhaps more vigilant in bringing to light political scandals, recent governments, such as those of Brian Mulroney in Canada and Ronald Reagan in the United States, seemed to be plagued with an unprecedented number of scandals. Patronage had been a hallmark of the Mulroney government (particularly, perhaps, in its first term), as many major federal appointments went to political supporters and relatives of Cabinet members. When John Crosbie was Justice minister, the law firms employing two of his sons were appointed legal agents of the federal government.[1] An advertising company headed by then Finance minister Michael Wilson's brother-in-law was awarded a contract with the Finance Department.

Several other Cabinet members tried to amass large personal fortunes through their influential positions. These included the ministers of Public Works, Transport, and Industry. In the last case, Sinclair Stevens, who resigned after allegations of conflict of interest, not only tried to enrich his family through his position as Industry minister, but cost the Canadian taxpayers $3 million in the inquiry that followed. Also, Progressive Conservative campaign money apparently had been used to help finance Brian and Mila Mulroney's extravagant lifestyle.[2] As one example, a $300,000 loan was secured by the Mulroneys from the PC Fund to finance custom renovations in their home. Moreover, a number of ministers in Mulroney's government abused personal expense accounts to a profound degree. Robert Coates, who served as Defence minister in 1985, spent $70,000 for travel and hospitality during his five months in that position. During the same year, Secretary of State Walter McLean spent between $100,000 and $150,000 on a trip to Africa with his wife and one aide.[3]

Likewise, in the 1980s, the Reagan administration was embroiled in a number of major scandals, not the least of which was the Iran-Contra Affair in which virtually every conceivable type of government misconduct took place. Foreign policies were carried out without the legally mandated approval of Congress; the officially espoused Reagan government policy not to deal arms for hostages was breached; and, finally, taxpayers' money was siphoned off in the various transactions by key players who charged outrageously for their services. Furthermore, while Reagan was in office, more than a hundred of his government's officials faced allegations of impropriety, including a number who were very prominent.

Political corruption is certainly not confined to North America. Martin Woollacott, a political commentator writes:

Scandals are chronicles of governmental death foretold. The scandals of the Leonid Brezhnev era were pointers to the revolution that eventually came in the shape of Mikhail Gorbachev and which ended by demolishing the entire country. The corruption of the Royal Court in Iran fuelled the fires which destroyed the Shah. The excesses of the Marcoses in the Philippines paved the way for Corazon Aquino's victory.

Now from Europe to the Far East, we can look out onto a positive panorama of corruption, with the money politics of Japan and Italy, the help yourself corruption of deregulated northern Europe, and looting of public assets in the former Soviet states all contributing sickly hues to a dismal scene.

Italy's case is extreme: It is entirely possible that virtually every senior politician in the established parties and most business executives of importance in that country are corrupt. One estimate is that 60,000 people would have to go through the courts if everybody suspected were to be charged. The anti-corruption campaign threatens to uproot the state itself.

The Japanese situation is similar in the awful degree of corruption revealed ... Japanese-style politics have even leaked into the United Nations, where the Japanese head of the World Health Organization has been accused of buying his re-election.

In Spain, there are fresh revelations of corruption in the building of the world fair facilities in Barcelona. In France, scandals sprout like acne in every political quarter.

In the former Soviet Union, in spite of widespread evidence of corruption, not a single case has come to court. Government ministers and officials have private business interests; sharp operators are exporting Soviet assets, falsifying the documents, and popping the money into bank accounts in Switzerland and Austria. This capital loss is crippling investment.

What the Japanese call their 'money politics' belongs in the same category with the Italian system. Money passes from business to parties and from parties to their supporters, clients, and the general public.

There is a more modest version of this in Spain. In the rest of the continent, the individual politician who looks for bribes, sweeteners, and illicit political funds seems to be becoming more common, together with his counterpart, the unprincipled business executive ...

In the Anglo-Saxon world, we have a less obvious form of corruption (alongside our fair share of the kickback and bribe). It is the growing phenomenon of personal enrichment that may not often clearly break the rules or the laws; the free building work; the concealed perk; the tax evasion or, in the business world, the salary increase unjustified by performance.[4]

We have already discussed, in chapter six, the extent of unethical behaviour in the business world. A poll of Chicago business executives revealed that 73 per cent felt that practices in their own industry were unethical.[5] Furthermore, 21 per cent admitted that if they owned a construction company, they would bribe a city inspector if it would speed up procedures. That public officials would be amenable to such bribes also may not be surprising. A national survey of Canadians conducted in 1990 found that the population had little faith in its political leaders.[6] Three-quarters of the population, according to the poll, believe that politicians cannot be trusted, and about 70 per cent feel that all political parties are basically the same.

Case-Study: Sleazy Politics in Nova Scotia

Political activities in the Province of Nova Scotia may help explain the erosion of trust people have in their leaders. In the spring of 1989, five workers for the provincial Liberal party were convicted for buying votes for their local candidate. Party workers would drive workers to an advance poll and offer them cash or bottles of liquor in exchange for a vote for their candidate. Subsequent investigations revealed that vote buying is a common practice, on the part of both major parties, throughout the province.[7] Another series of scandals in the past few years includes the conviction of several members of the provincial legislature for abusing or cheating on their government expense accounts. In another case of impropriety, a Social Services minister in the province was convicted of releasing confidential information to reporters from the file of a single welfare mother who criticized him in public. A former Tourism minister resigned in 1988 following reports that he had made a deal with four banks to write off $100,000 in debts. In another incident, a

New Democratic Party candidate in the 1988 elections stopped campaigning after she and her husband were accused of growing marijuana on their farm. Finally, in the early 1980s, Liberal party fund-raisers were convicted of conspiracy to peddle influence. When the Liberal party was in power in the 1970s, they forced liquor companies wanting to sell their products in Nova Scotia to contribute to the party.

Case-Study: Speaking like a Politician

Nothing exemplifies political life as well as the rhetoric used by politicians. The manipulative use of language permits the user to deflect potentially embarrassing questions. Politicians are coached on how to field questions. J.R. Duffy, a communications consultant, has written about the tactics used by master politicians:

What makes a politician sound like a politician? *They're all lying*, screams the average Canadian, with the charming naïveté that makes this such a fine country in which to be a practising shyster. If only this were true, the whole business of divining what evil schemes the pols have in store would be simple: just expect them to do the opposite of what they say.

The fact is, they are trying their damnest *not* to lie. For the professional politician, getting caught uttering falsehood is a first-order disaster to be avoided at all cost. The cost of such avoidance is opacity and vagueness, which are the only means at the pol's disposal of keeping open every possible avenue of interpretation of what he or she says. The job of the talking politician is not so much to get a message across as to blither through the allotted time without saying anything that could wind up belied by future action.

Consider the prime minister's experience with the phrase 'sacred trust.' An inexperienced Brian Mulroney once referred to universality of social programs in this way and turned into a liar when he was forced to reconsider. Had he refrained from hyperbole and merely termed universality 'one of those commitments without which very serious questions about who we are must be asked,' he would have been home free and could have told the screeching grandmother at the protest rally to check her notes before getting all worked up. Mulroney wasn't lying when he placed universality in the empyrean; he probably just meant to say that he thought this universality thing was kind of neat. But by pinning it down with a word like 'sacred' he closed the door on the chance to abolish it, and hasn't reopened the matter since.

The highest praise that can be paid to a politician is to say, as a minister's aid of my acquaintance was once told, 'Your boss says nothing very well.' The name of the game is to keep your options and your mouth open at the same time.

What are the special tricks of the trade, the slings and arrows of slipperiness and evasion at the pol's disposal? To find out, take a common question: 'Is today Tuesday?' Let's start with the obvious answer, 'Yes, it's Tuesday,' and see how far we can skate away from the irresponsible level of certitude implied by that answer. We can begin by saying, 'I think it's Tuesday.' We can further distance ourselves by characterizing the question as a mere opinion: 'I think there are those who feel that way.'

This answer is almost garishly evasive, so add a note of conviction: 'There's no doubt that some people feel that way.' Folks expect their politicians to be decisive, so what harm in adding the clause, 'and I agree with them.' What harm? Plenty! Never say you agree with anything unless you're damn sure that everyone agrees with you too ... You review what you've said and see an escape. So: 'There's no doubt that some people feel that way, and I agree with them ... that it's a question we have to take a very serious look at.'

Good. Phew! Out of the woods for now. But the guy who asked the question is looking at you funny. He seems troubled, lost, looking for answers on the issues that concern him. O.K., time to show leadership: 'And I can assure you that I will take your views fully into account as I make my decision.' Wrong!

Never use the active mood if you can avoid it; it implies that someone, maybe even you, might actually have the ability to do something. The passive is much better, since it implies that things just happen, and if someone doesn't like the outcome it wasn't your fault. The correct answer, then, to the highly charged question: 'Is today Tuesday?' is this: 'There's no doubt that some people feel that way, and I agree with them that it's a question we have to take a very serious look at. I can assure you that your views will be taken fully into account as the decision is, in point of fact, made.'[8]

One final word on political leaders, lest the reader remain unconvinced about the harms occasioned by society's élites. Amnesty International, the London-based human rights organization, marked its thirtieth anniversary by declaring that two out of three people in the world are ruled by governments that torture and kill their citizens.[9]

THE SINS OF THE PIOUS

Religious leaders, in recent years, also have taken a considerable fall from the pedestals upon which they formerly stood. Large religious and business empires, such as Praise the Lord in the United States, have been jeopardized by scandals that have alienated the flock. Aside from the notorious sexual escapades of televangelist Jimmy Swaggart, the best-known religious scandal in recent years has involved television personalities and preachers Jim and Tammy Bakker. The Bakkers had amassed a large personal fortune: they had a combined salary of over $1.6 million, four homes, a Mercedes-Benz, a Rolls-Royce, a houseboat, and an air-conditioned dog house, and Tammy Bakker had a wardrobe exceeded perhaps only by those of Imelda Marcos and Liberace.[10] Although their lavish lifestyle, stormy marriage, and her drug habit brought them notoriety, what finally did them in was the revelation that he had had an affair with a church secretary and had paid for her silence out of church funds. Jim Bakker had also defrauded followers of $3.7 million when he sold hotel rooms to 153,000 people at his Heritage USA religious retreat. In reality, only 258 rooms had been built to accommodate these people.[11]

Accusations against religious leaders have not been confined to church celebrities. In Canada, over the past few years, a rash of abuses by religious figures has come to light. The most noteworthy has been that of the Mt Cashel Orphanage in Newfoundland, in which Christian brothers and church officials have been convicted of sexually abusing children under their care. These types of scandals have been so numerous that the Roman Catholic Church in Canada has undertaken to review its hiring and training practices for priests. Currently, all new recruits to the priesthood undergo psychological testing and background checks when they apply. Now, as part of their training they participate in discussions on sexuality, as well as undergoing continued assessment by their teachers and the parish priests they are working with.[12]

U.S. churches, too, are now confronting the fact that sexual abuse by clerics is more than an isolated problem. Both the Presbyterian Church and the United Church of Christ are developing national policies on sexual-harassment issues.[13] In Minnesota, churches have set up a statewide interfaith committee to deal with sexual exploitation by clergy. Because most Americans turn first to the clergy with their personal problems, the seduction of members of the congregation strikes at the essence of pastoral work. Congregants approaching their local pastor may be highly vulnerable to victimization because of both the problems they are experiencing and their regard for the pastor as a God-like figure.

Very little research has been conducted into the actual prevalence of sexual impropriety among the clergy. For obvious reasons, the publication of statistics on this issue would prove highly embarrassing to church officials. Nevertheless, one U.S. study has shown just how commonplace such activity is. A three-year survey of religious and secular counsellors undertaken by the Wisconsin Coalition on Sexual Misconduct found that 11 per cent of the perpetrators were clerics.[14]

CRIME BY SOCIETY'S LAW ENFORCERS

Those who are empowered to ensure that society's rules are enforced are themselves not immune from illegal and unscrupulous practices. Police officers, judges, and other personnel connected with police departments, the courts, and correctional services are not infrequently found to have engaged in questionable, if not blatantly illegal, activities. People in these positions can commit traditional crimes; be involved in extortion and corruption; commit acts of brutality; and otherwise violate the rights of suspected offenders, as well as the public's trust.

U.S. cities, such as New York and Chicago, have been particularly notorious for having corrupt police departments. The Knapp Commission, appointed in 1970 to investigate allegations of corruption in New York City, was a particular eye-opener. The commission found that police corruption was widespread, ranging from small gratuities accepted by constables from local businesses to payoffs in the thousands of dollars received by senior officers from gamblers and narcotics dealers.[15] The commission also found that construction companies made payoffs to have police ignore city ordinances, such as double parking, obstruction of sidewalks, and noise pollution. Bar owners made payoffs so they could operate after hours and to offer immunity to prostitutes, drug pushers, and gamblers operating on their premises. Drug dealers allowed police to keep money and narcotics confiscated during raids in return for their freedom. Police also gave confiscated narcotics to informers for their own use or sale to others. Gamblers made regular payoffs (often monthly) to keep their operations going.

Corruption in U.S. police departments has not ended with the Knapp Commission's report. For example, in the early 1980s, twenty Philadelphia police officers were indicted for extorting money from bar owners and video-game vendors. The second-in-command in the Philadelphia police department was sentenced to eighteen years in prison in the case.[16] Also, during the past twenty years, police burglary rings have been uncovered in a number of U.S. cities.[17]

Some recent scandals illustrate that corruption and criminality are certainly not unknown in the Canadian criminal justice system. The Edmonton police department was rocked by scandals in 1987–88.[18] Ten officers had been charged with criminal offences over an eighteen-month period. The offences included attempted murder, assault, theft, fraud, and drug trafficking. In one highly publicized case culminating in the resignation of an officer, an Edmonton prostitute alleged the officer had hand-cuffed and raped her, as well as bought cocaine for her. In 1989, a constable charged with sexually assaulting a female officer, shot and killed his wife before fatally shooting himself.[19] In 1991, another constable was charged with kidnapping and sexually assaulting two eight-year-old boys and a ten-year-old girl. In the same year, two officers were charged with offences relating to impaired driving, and a third officer was sentenced to six years in prison after being convicted for sexually assaulting a suspected shoplifter.

In January 1988, a major scandal surfaced in Winnipeg, Manitoba, as eleven persons, including a provincial court judge, two magistrates, a Crown attorney, and two other lawyers, were charged.[20] The chief provincial court judge was also removed from his position. The charges were laid after an accusation was made that the defendants had been involved in a conspiracy to fix traffic tickets in return for pay-offs.

More recently, in Winnipeg, an inquiry has been conducted into the 'Pollock affair.'[21] Harvey Pollock, a veteran Winnipeg defence lawyer critical of the city's police department, was apparently set up by members of the department. One day, on the way to his office, he was arrested on a charge of sexually assaulting a female client and, as he was led into custody, a *Winnipeg Free Press* reporter and photographer were waiting to cover the story. Two months later, the Crown prosecutors dropped the charge after the alleged victim recanted her testimony. She had been encouraged by police officers to make a complaint against Pollock. The newspaper also had been tipped off by a member of the police department.

The Winnipeg inquiry also uncovered deep mistrust between Winnipeg police officers and top justice officials in Manitoba. Several senior police officers accused the provincial Justice Department of favouritism in deciding to pursue or avoid prosecutions. At the same time, prosecutors accused police of letting personal conflicts affect their professional judgment, even to the extent of withholding information crucial to criminal investigations.

TABLE 3
Varieties of Police Misconduct

Mooching	–	Receiving free coffee, cigarettes, meals, liquor, etc. as compensation for being underpaid or for future acts of favouritism
Chiselling	–	Demanding free admission to entertainment, price discounts, etc.
Favouritism	–	Using licence tabs, window stickers, or courtesy cards to gain immunity from traffic arrest for self, family, or friends
Prejudice	–	Giving differential treatment to minorities and others who have little political influence and, hence, cannot cause trouble for the officer
Shopping	–	Picking up small items such as candy bars and cigarettes when a store is accidentally unlocked after business hours
Extortion	–	Demanding payments for traffic violations in lieu of issuing tickets
Bribery	–	Accepting cash or gifts (of greater value than in mooching) and, in return, not providing evidence against an accused person(s)
Shakedown	–	Taking items (of greater value than those involved in shopping) while investigating a burglary
Perjury	–	Lying to provide an alibi for a fellow officer who has been caught engaging in unlawful activity

The number of people involved in both the Edmonton and Manitoba scandals suggests that the criminality and unscrupulousness of police, lawyers, and judges often are not simply a matter of character flaws among a few 'rotten apples' but rather indicate the existence of conduct norms that are favourable to misbehaviour. Ellwyn Stoddard has written about the informal code that fosters police deviance or 'blue-coat' crime.[22] He found that criminal activity on the part of the police was widespread in most major departments. Some of the activities police officers engage in are listed in table 3.

Stoddart's informant, an ex–police officer, emphasized the pressure placed on new recruits to go along with illegal practices. Officers who are overly honest are regarded with suspicion as they may disclose illicit activities. The informant states: 'take a man that has just joined the department, has good intentions and is basically honest, ... these aren't degrees. It's all either black or white. And the illegal activity I know shocks a lot of these young men ... because it was the thing to do. It's a way to be accepted by the other people. It's a terrible thing the way one policeman will talk about another. Say an old timer will have a new man working with him and he'll tell you, 'You've got to watch him, because he's honest!'[23]

One police officer told Mark Baker, author of *Cops: Their Lives in Their Own Words*, the following about honesty in police departments: 'In any department, anywhere, you can take 5 per cent of the cops and they will be honest under any circumstances and they'll never do anything wrong. They are the priests of the department. Five per cent on the other end of the spectrum would have become criminals had they not become policemen. They are, in fact, criminals who happen to be cops. The remaining 90 per cent will go whichever way the peer pressure goes.'[24]

This formula sounds very similar to that provided by authorities on employee theft and other types of crime. If it is correct, it tells us that most people are capable of dishonesty, that behaviour is largely governed by the situation at hand, and that the attitudes prevailing in a given milieu will have a lot to do with the type and extent of misbehaviour we can expect to find there. I will have more to say about the factors contributing to widespread lawbreaking in chapters 9–12.

Baker goes on to explain how the morals of a police department can slowly erode:

Racism, corruption, brutality can slowly become institutionalized throughout a police department simply because so many officers are willing to be indifferent, to let the standards erode from inattention, to go along and follow the crowd. Slowly the pendulum swings toward criminality. A locality gets a reputation for its dangerous or larcenous police officers. Those cops who are unwilling to participate are overruled or driven out and replaced with individuals who are attracted by the prospect of living above the law. The community, the people the police are sworn to protect, must live in fear.[25]

Another of Baker's informants explains how pressures are exerted on new recruits to accept established practices:

I was assigned to a precinct where there wasn't a guy that had less than fifteen years on the force, which is to say they were all hairbags and I was a rookie. I had the first case of corruption almost immediately. They assigned me to a Golden Gloves match at an Irish parish ... It's three old hairbags and myself. They're already drunk when we come on duty. We have this wonderful job of watching the lads beat the shit out of each other in the ring and it's going to be a fun night. No dealing with violent crime out there, we are going to drink beer and eat all night. They're going to do this. I didn't.

... What am I doing in a church watching guys fight? I want to get out there and lock up bad guys. They thought they were doing me a favor ... When we got there one of the guys says, 'Lad, do you want a beer?'

'No,' I said, 'I don't drink while I'm working.'

'That's very good, lad. You're going to go far in this job. Now, I'll tell you what you're going to do. You're going to go out there and just walk around the ring. You see, there's more fights that happen outside the ring than in. They're not bad boys; they really just get a bit carried away because there's a wee bit of drinking that goes on.'

The end of the evening, these guys come out and they can't even walk now. The monsignor is a very outspoken and drunken monsignor. He is shaking all the cops' hands, 'Goodnight. Thanks, lads, you did a fine job this year.' These guys must get this post every year. He gets up to me and shakes my hand. I feel there ain't something right in my hand. It's a twenty-dollar bill. A priest has just laid twenty bucks on me. He had paid me off to do my duty. So I turned around and I say,

'What's this?'

The old-timer looks at me and says, 'It's a twenty-dollar bill, lad.'

'I know that. What's it for?'

'Ah, the monsignor is a good guy. Every year he does this. It's just his way of thanking us for keeping the peace.'

'I don't want it.'

'You don't want it?' Whup, it was out of my hand so quick and he's splitting it with the other guys.

What that whole experience did for me was get me catching dead bodies almost every night of the week, because they didn't trust me. When somebody dies in an apartment or something, you got to guard the body until the medical examiner comes and says that it wasn't a homicide, it was just a normal death. This can go on sometimes for eight hours straight. He's a young cop and he didn't take the money. Better not have him exposed to too much shit.[26]

Many police officers and departments condone the use of physical force, at least off the record, for reasons other than the restraint of a suspect. One officer put it this way:

Some guys need a beating. In the street or the back of a precinct, there's a guy who needs a beating. And you got to do it. If you don't do it, the next situation that a cop runs into this character, it's going to be bad.

It's hard for people to understand or believe that. But the fact of the matter is, if this guy runs into a cop, gets into a fistfight and really beats the shit out of him, he believes he can beat up all cops, if you arrest him without working him out. He's got to know that the next time he does this, he's going to get his ass kicked in.

So I have no problem with that. Neither did any cop I've ever known have any problem with that. As long as you don't do it in public, as long as the guy really needs it, and as long as you don't carry it too far. Give him a beating and that's it. Don't break his ribs, you don't knock his teeth out, you don't crack his skull and give him a concussion.

It's simple. Have a guy hold him. You rap him in the shins a couple of good times. Let him know that he's going to get his ass kicked and it's going to hurt.[27]

Favouritism and discrimination are also a part of everyday policing. Discrimination does not merely refer to the differential treatment of racial or ethnic minorities; it also applies to the differential enforcement of laws as a result of one's demeanour and attitude towards authority. Favouritism, too, is a major factor in the city policed by my police informant, as a large number of prominent public officials reside there. The veteran officer I interviewed discussed some of these practices and described them as very prevalent. Differential treatment, he told me, is facilitated by the amount of discretion police officers have in enforcing the law:

I got dumped on at one particular traffic offence that shows how young or naïve I was too. They were supposed to be close friends of the deputy chief and the driver says, 'If the deputy chief finds out that you're giving me a ticket for this you're going to be in deep shit.' So I sort of skated around it and backed out of it ... I'm not going to get into that. I don't need that.

I've pulled over cars in the past or typed in their licence plate or called out the licence number and not even thought of it and then realized, when I got up to the car, the licence plate is SEN, meaning a senator ... So you end up letting them go because of who they are ... I guess I justify it in my own mind whether it's right or not ... If I only give one out of five anyways [i.e. one ticket for every five people stopped], I'm giving this guy a break whether he's one of the four breaks today. If it just happens that he is the senator ... But I mean, that's not right. Like I know that I'm not giving tickets to him ... I'm backing down because I'm afraid of what influence this guy's going to have on my job ... I've heard of an officer, a colleague, who arrested a guy for shoplifting and then found out that he's a member of CSIS [Canada's Security and Intelligence Service]. It's a petty shoplift, a garbage incident and I said, 'Like, what are you doing throwing away your job for ...?'

It's not worth the ticket [when influential people are involved]. They receive gratis because of who they are ... It's identifying who the individual is or what he represents ... I guess you would stop more muscle [sport] cars and guys in leather jackets than a businessman in a three-piece suit. I tend to think that I'm stopping the muscle car for a traffic violation in the hope that I'm about to find a criminal violation as well.[28]

As for those instances in which laws are most likely to be enforced, my informant takes the following approach:

Personally, I might hand out a written ticket one in five traffic stops. So I'd give them four warnings, four verbal tongue-lashings, so to speak, as opposed to a written ticket ... Whether it's right or wrong, I stop the car for a violation and guess in some respects I let the driver decide what his penalty is going to be. If I'm there to point out the fact that he made an improper left-hand turn ... and he wants to be an idiot and

fight it and tell me that I'm wrong, and that I don't know what I'm telling him about the law, okay, then let's argue about this in court. I'll
give you the ticket and you can pay the fine or you can come to court
and discuss it with the judge to see if there's a left-hand prohibited
turn or not ... It's just sort of a personal preference on how you apply
the law ... Within a certain traffic section there are police officers that
strive to hand out the most tickets in a month and would hand out anywhere from 25 to 30 a day, so they're handing out anywhere from 500
to 700 tickets a month and I hand out 15 a month.

This black guy thinks police hate him, so automatically when he's
stopped by policemen he's aggressive with them. My humane
approach to traffic enforcement would be thrown out the window with
him because he's so ignorant and aggressive with me that he ends up
getting the ticket and he's arguing that he's getting it because he's
black. But I say no, 'It's because you argued with me or that you won't
admit that what you've done is wrong.'

Thus, law enforcement is often highly selective and even
capricious, based on the personal inclinations of each police
officer. My informant's testimony shows that the attitude of a
suspect may be as important (if not more so) than his or her
actual behaviour in determining whether a matter is pursued
legally, at least where less serious offences are concerned.

There are also certain 'perks' associated with being a police
officer. As the officer states:

I think 'mooching' [occurs] more along the lines of 7-Eleven and other
convenience stores giving coffee to the policeman for free. There used
to be a McDonald's and a Burger King in one area of town that policemen could arrive at five minutes after closing and receive all the left-
over food from the day ... [There are] particular restaurants, whether it
be fast-food or a Chinese food restaurant, that the policemen would
refer to as the policeman's special. You go in there and eat all you want
and you don't pay a cent for it. One of the reasons why it was cut out
because policemen were showing up off duty and there a particular
incident [occurred] involving one of the policemen who went to a Chi-

nese food restaurant off duty, in uniform, to pick up for a party he was having at his house.

Another type of perk afforded by police work involves free admission to sporting events, concerts, and the like: 'The policeman just uses his badge to get into a rock concert or hockey game or something like that. In uniform, you just wander in. I can't take the time to watch the entire hockey game, but if I'm in uniform and if I take my lunch, I may go down and watch the playoffs or a quarter of the football game or a baseball game ... You just walk through [the gate]. The off-duty police officer uses his badge [to obtain these types of benefits]. I've done it.'

Prison life is replete with examples of illegalities. In Canada, there are several high-profile, ongoing cases involving allegations (and some convictions already attained) of sexual and physical abuse of residents of reformatories in Ontario. Not only do prison officials and personnel sometimes violate the rights of inmates, but they may also introduce contraband into their institutions. Drug use among correctional personnel, for example, is quite commonplace. Virtually every American state undertakes drug testing of its prison employees; in some states employees are tested randomly and in others testing is performed when there are suspicions of drug use.[29] When random testing was introduced at the Georgia State prison in 1984, 40 per cent of all tests were positive.

A good example of the pervasive corruption that can be found behind the walls of a prison is that of the Philadelphia city jails. In 1988, more than 200 correctional officers were arrested or disciplined for a variety of infractions of prison rules.[30] Some guards were charged with smuggling drugs, money, and weapons into prison, while others were caught helping inmates escape. Also uncovered was a major drug ring in which guards on the payroll of an inmate kingpin supplied narcotics to large numbers of prisoners on a daily basis. Still other guards were indicted for taking bribes to turn one unit of a prison into a social club for reputed mobsters.

Corruption by society's leaders and those responsible for bringing perpetrators to justice is therefore an all-too-common phenomenon. The credibility of society's rules is seriously compromised when those in positions of trust, those responsible for the public purse, and those maintaining public order and discipline demonstrate a disregard for the public interest and the rules they are supposed to enforce. While it may be unrealistic to expect that society's élites and law enforcers adopt a superhuman morality, the continuous exposure of people to scandals can convince them that deception, power, and political influence, rather than morality, are the key ingredients to achieving status and material success.

8

Other Crimes

The general public is actively involved in a number of other forms of criminal activity, ranging from illicit-drug use to technological crimes. This chapter provides only a sample of these offences.

SUBSTANCE ABUSE

The use of illicit drugs, underage drinking, and alcohol abuse are all widespread in our society. Speaker after speaker at crime conferences I have attended have underscored the rampant abuse of illicit drugs and alcohol. Not only is the use of certain substances a crime in itself, but it has an undeniable connection with various forms of crimes. Alcohol is involved in many violent crimes (including domestic violence) as well as accidents, accounting for many injuries and fatalities on the road. Illegal drugs may lead to crime and violence through their mood-altering, disinhibiting, and habituating effects, through the transactions in which they are obtained, or through the territorial disputes over control of the drug traffic.

In the United States, public officials and the media have characterized the extent of the drug problem as 'epidemic' and as warranting a full-scale war on the part of the coast guard and law enforcement agencies. A survey of a representative sample of high school students in the United States found that 59 per cent had used marijuana, 16 per cent had used cocaine, 70 per cent had consumed alcohol in the previous month, and 14 per cent had used stimulants in the preceding month.[1] Thirty per cent of all college students will have tried cocaine by their senior year.[2] Americans spend between $15 billion and $20 billion a year on cocaine alone.[3] Drug abuse is so pervasive that about a third of all major businesses and government operations have established drug-testing programs for their employees.[4]

The demand for drugs crosses all sectors of society; however, their cultivation, production, and distribution are often undertaken by ordinary working people. Whether the crops are marijuana and opium in Thailand or coca leaves in Bolivia, farmers find that growing them can be far more profitable than cultivating more traditional crops; in fact, the drug traffic can be essential to these farmers' survival. Further confounding the problem is the use of these plants for medicines, religious ceremonies, or social rituals.[5] Also, a number of governments have cooperated with those in the drug trade or have actually engaged in trafficking (Panama's former dictator Manuel Noriega was a case in point), and law enforcement personnel, as we saw in chapter 7, are not frequently corrupt. Furthermore, at the street level, the burgeoning traffic in 'crack' and allied substances has provided lucrative employment, in the capacity of look-outs and couriers, for many inner city-teens and pre-teens.

Although the problem is not as widespread as it is in the United States, substance abuse is prevalent in Canada, too. As a national survey has shown, about 40 per cent of Canadians between the ages of eighteen and twenty-nine have used marijuana at some point. The same survey indicates that 58 per cent of young Canadians consider themselves to be regular drinkers. Also, a substantial proportion engage in multiple drug use (e.g., alcohol and marijuana).[6] Over 6 per cent of Canadians have used cocaine.[7] About one in ten adults living in Ontario are considered to have a drinking problem.[8]

TABLE 4
Facts about Impaired Driving

. In 1986, 28,036 licence suspensions were registered for charges relating to drinking and driving in the Province of Ontario. More than 30 per cent of these suspensions were for second or subsequent offences.
. More than 50 per cent of drivers admit to driving after drinking at least once a month.
. More than 14 per cent admit to driving while impaired at least once a month.
. Alcohol is estimated to be involved in approximately 50 per cent of all traffic fatality crashes and 30 percent of all personal injury crashes.

Source: Addiction Research Foundation, 'Ontario Report,' in *The Journal* 2/4 (1988), 2

The annual number of users of some legal and illegal drugs in Canada are:

Alcohol   16,000,000
Amphetamines   <100,000
Cocaine   300,000–500,000
Heroin   <100,000
LSD   <100,000
Marijuana   1,500,000–2,500,000
Tobacco   6,000,000–8,000,000
Tranquillizers   1,500,000–2,500,000[9]

A good barometer of alcohol abuse is the extent of impaired driving, conduct which today is in considerable disrepute. According to the Addiction Research Foundation, males under twenty-seven years of age are most likely to be killed or injured in an alcohol-related car crash.[10] Some of the foundation's other findings are contained in table 4.

The non-medical use of drugs to enhance performance in sports has received considerably more coverage since Canadian sprinter Ben Johnson was disqualified from the summer Olympic Games in 1988. At that time, some athletes estimated that anabolic steroids were used by as many as 90 per cent of the athletes in many countries.[11]

ENVIRONMENTAL AND ANIMAL ABUSE

The sociologist Don Gibbons has used the term 'environmental abuse' to refer to actions ranging from the malicious destruction of property (vandalism) to the dumping of refuse on back roads by suburbanites. Vandalism can range from graffiti and petty property damage committed by minors to industrial sabotage on the part of politically motivated individuals.[12] Graffiti itself can vary from the inoffensive to the racist. The graffiti-ridden urban projects and transit systems in U.S. cities provide a good example of the environmental damage inflicted by amateur 'artists.'

The damage posed by vandalism extends well beyond the obvious economic costs of defacing or destroying property. Vandalism exacerbates the public's fear of crime.[13] Signs of urban decay, to which vandalism may contribute significantly, send the message to the community that the authorities have lost control of the neighbourhood to local gangs and hoodlums. Just as a clean, orderly, and well-maintained neighbourhood offers its residents a sense of security, one characterized by incivility, decay, and disorder can engender a paralysing fear of crime.[14] Acts of vandalism, of course, are not committed only by hoodlums and thugs. There is no shortage of vandalism in universities, churches, public libraries, pricey restaurants, and in parks located in affluent neighbourhoods. A study of university library books in Ottawa, for example, found that 74 per cent were mutilated in some way; that is, pages were missing, earmarked, or contained some type of comment, note, or highlighting of material.[15]

Environmental abuse also can take the form of littering, involving anything from a candy wrapper to truckloads of personal or industrial waste. The latter is particularly serious where hazardous materials (such as toxic chemicals) have been dumped illegally in order to save the costs of proper disposal. One of the most notorious cases of corporate dumping was that of the Hooker Chemical Company, which buried thousands of tons of toxic chemicals near Niagara Falls, eventually forcing the entire community of Love Canal to be evacuated. The rates of cancer, other illnesses, and chromosomal damage in the community were well above national rates.[16]

Another aspect of environmental abuse is poaching. By hunting more animals than a permit allows, the poacher threatens the delicate balance of wildlife. Poachers may use a variety of illegal tactics to catch their prey:

They spear pickerel and jig sturgeon when they are swollen with eggs and ready to spawn. They set snares to strangle moose and ruffled grouse. In speeding motorboats with guns blazing, they charge flocks of resting ducks – and if a great blue heron flies by, they kill it too. It doesn't matter that the big bird is a protected species ... They can sell it for $200. It will end up on a mantlepiece ... They entice deer with ripe, juicy apples that are imbedded with fish hooks and anchored to trees with steel wire. Sometimes the deer is already dead when they make the rounds of their trapline. Often it is still struggling on the hook ... [The poacher] kills any animal he can, any time he can, any way he can.[17]

Such sordid scenes are not the work of only a handful of individuals. In Quebec alone, 10,000 poachers are convicted each year.[18]

One of the areas in which the abuse of animals is most pronounced is in research (both biomedical and psychological), where millions of cats, dogs, monkeys, and rodents are tortured and put to death every year. In the United States, it has been estimated that between 17 million and 100 million animals are used every year in laboratory experiments.[19] Much of this research is unnecessary, having nothing to do with fighting disease, for example, lab experiments conducted by the cosmetics industry.

The Mobilization for Animals Coalition, an international network of animal-protectionist organizations, wrote the following about some of the abuses in psychological research with animals:

Animals are given intense, repeated electric shocks until they lose the ability even to scream in pain; animals are deprived of food and water and allowed to suffer and die from hunger and thirst; animals are put in isolation until they are driven insane or die from despair and terror; animals are subjected to crushing forces that smash their bones and rupture their internal organs; the limbs of animals are mutilated or amputated to produce behavioral changes; animals are victims of extreme pain and stress, inflicted out of idle curiosity, in nightmarish experiments designed to make healthy animals psychotic.[20]

Consider the following experiments:

In a 1972 paper in the *Journal of Comparative and Physiological Psychology,* for example, researchers at the Primate Research Center in Madison, Wis., described placing baby monkeys alone in a stainless-steel tank for periods of up to 45 days. They wanted to see whether confinement in this 'well of despair' would cause lasting psychological damage. It did. The animals exhibited what the researchers termed 'severe and persistent pathological behavior of a depressive nature.' But the paper stressed the preliminary nature of this finding, saying further studies were needed to determine whether the symptoms could be 'traced specifically to variables such as chamber shape, chamber size, duration of confinement [or] age at time of confinement.'

... In other papers, the same scientists described efforts to gauge the effects of child abuse on young monkeys. In one experiment they designed mechanical surrogate mothers who would eject sharp brass spikes as the youngsters hugged them. The experience seemed to have no serious effect; the infants 'simply waited until the spikes receded and then returned and clung to the mother.' So, in a refinement of the experiment, the researchers forcibly impregnated females who had been driven mad through social isolation, and turned them loose on their offspring. 'One of [the mothers'] favorite tricks,' they wrote, 'was to crush the infant's skull with their teeth.'[21]

Although such experiments may not yet be illegal, they reveal a degree of insensitivity and brutality that may be less tolerated with the growth of the animal rights and environmental movements.

TECHNOLOGICAL CRIMES

A whole series of crimes have developed as a result of technological advances, especially in relation to the burgeoning microcomputer market and the growth of computerized information systems. Law enforcement agencies must deal with a new breed of criminal, the computer hacker, who illegally penetrates the computers of private corporations and public institutions by gaining access to their security codes. The term 'hacker' tends to conjure up images of young computer whizzes, obsessed with their personal computers, who playfully try to penetrate various computer systems and are a mere nuisance when they succeed. In reality, there are many forms of computer crime and criminals, as well as different motives for this type of activity. The volume of these crimes is greatly in excess of that known by law enforcement agencies as companies and other organizations that have been penetrated tend to hush up incidents in order to conceal their own vulnerability.

Indeed, some computer hackers, many of whom are males in their late teens and early twenties, try to gain access to systems for the sheer thrill of it. Others have infiltrated military computers and have compromised the national security of a country.[22] The fear is that tampering with critical hospital computer information on drug dosages and financial systems will become more prevalent.

Computer viruses afford another destructive weapon in the arsenal of the electronic saboteur.[23] These viruses are programs that are designed to erase data or cause damage to disks. They are also designed to make copies of themselves any time an 'infected' computer comes in contact with an uninfected piece of software. These viruses can spread like epidemics as computer users swap disks or send programs to each other through telephone lines. Some viruses can have a world-wide impact, such as the 'Michelangelo' virus activated in March 1992. Viruses have been spread by businessmen angry at consumers for using pirated programs, by students seeking attention, and by individuals taking revenge against their former employers.

Employees with access to company computers constitute a major source of computer-related sabotage.[24] Disgruntled employees have used 'logic bombs' to knock out entire computer systems. Employees can alter computer access codes and blackmail their employers into paying them a large sum of money before revealing the new code. A bank employee can transfer small amounts of money (even pennies) from thousands of bank accounts to his or her own account – this form of theft is referred to as the 'salami slice.' Other forms of illegality include the unlawful use of another's computer account and stealing information from a rival company. Most computer criminals have no criminal record, have good social standing, are well educated and, hence, tend to be treated leniently by the courts.[25]

Probably the most prevalent form of computer crime is software piracy. The illegal copying of computer software or programs costs the software industry about $2 billion a year in the United States and $100 million to $400 million in Canada.[26] It has been estimated that for every program sold, three to seven copies are made and distributed illegally.[27] A study of university students in Ottawa has found that 50 per cent of those who owned a personal computer had pirated computer programs or games. All students interviewed who did not own a computer, when informed of the cost of software, stated they would pirate programs if given the opportunity.[28] Many perpetrators downplay the seriousness of their behaviour; however, its consequences are no less serious than those pertaining to other, more conventional, property crimes. As David Silburt reported: 'The young man at the computer terminal does not look like he is committing a burglary. He is not wearing a black cat burglar's suit, he has not smeared shoe polish on his face, and he does not have a crowbar. He just sits there, tapping keys in short, staccato bursts and peering intently at green figures marching across the screen. He may look rather innocent, but what he's doing is tantamount to breaking into a computer software dealer and stealing a program worth several hundred dollars.'[29]

The copying of software is commonplace, and is not solely the act of the type of individual described above. Such pirating takes place in business, government offices, and universities. As an example, the Canadian Broadcasting Corporation, following rumours of a police raid, conducted an inventory of illegally obtained software in its offices and found a large quantity, which was subsequently destroyed.[30]

Another area in which pirating is prevalent is in the entertainment industry. Video pirating is said to cost Hollywood more than $1 billion a year.[31] The pirates range from small-time operators to well-organized syndicates that copy movies and sell or rent the tapes, often at discount prices. Sometimes films are copied by movie-industry personnel even before they are shown in theatres. It has been estimated that 15 per cent of all movie videos in U.S. stores have been pirated.

In Canada, as of the summer of 1991, more than a million tapes had been seized since video-security offices had opened six years earlier. Typically, the retailer purchases one original video cassette (about $90 wholesale) and then, with the aid of two VCRs and a blank tape, can produce additional copies for about $10. In some stores, as many as 40 per cent of the videos have been pirated.[32]

ORGANIZED CRIME

'Everybody calls me a racketeer,' Al Capone said during the 1920s. 'I call myself a businessman ... I make my money by supplying a public demand. If I break the law, my customers, who number hundreds of the best people in Chicago, are as guilty as I am. The only difference between us is that I sell and they buy.' That was not the only difference; Capone's customers did not generally eliminate business rivals by murder. But Capone thought his customers were hypocritical in calling him a racketeer. 'When I sell liquor, it's bootlegging,' he complained; 'when my patrons serve it on a silver tray on Lake Shore Drive, it's hospitality.'[33]

Capone's justifications for his activities, whether fully accepted or not, point out the symbiotic or highly interdependent relationship between organized crime and the community. Most of the activities of organized criminal networks provide services, albeit illicit ones, to those pursuing prohibited pleasures or to those in dire financial need. Drug distribution, gambling, prostitution, and loan-sharking are some of the mainstays of groups associated with organized crime.

Some scholars prefer the term 'service crime' to 'organized crime' because of the many myths surrounding the latter term. Organized crime has been viewed traditionally as comprising highly centralized and cohesive networks modelled on some Sicilian mafia organizations. Criminologist Larry Siegel writes:

The term 'organized crime' conjures up images of strong men in dark suits, machine-gun-toting bodyguards, rituals of allegiance to secret organizations, professional 'gangland' killings, and meetings of 'family' leaders who chart the course of crime much like the board members at General Motors decide on the country's transportation needs. These images have become part of what criminologists refer to as the *alien conspiracy theory* concept of organized crime. This is the belief, adhered to by the federal government and many respected criminologists, that organized crime is a direct offshoot of a criminal society – the *Mafia* – that first originated in Italy and Sicily and now controls racketeering in major U.S. cities. A major premise of the alien conspiracy theory is that the Mafia is centrally coordinated by a national committee that settles disputes, dictates policy, and assigns territory.

Not all criminologists believe in this narrow concept of organized crime, and many view the alien conspiracy theory as a figment of the media's imagination. Their view depicts organized crime as a group of ethnically diverse gangs or groups who compete for profit in the sale of illegal goods and services or who use force and violence to extort money from legitimate enterprises. These groups are not bound by a central organization but act independently on their own turf.[34]

There are literally thousands of groups in North America engaging in organized criminal behaviour. These groups range from the highly to the very loosely structured and transient. Some are based on an ethnic or racial bond; others are not.

The general stereotype of organized crime is that of a group of thugs who are at war with society. They are seen as corrupting public officials, preying upon innocent citizens, and infiltrating legitimate businesses.[35] Organized crime is viewed as parasitical and alien to society, rather than as a natural outgrowth of society's laws and institutions.

Gangsterism, according to sociologist Don Gibbons, has, in fact, normally involved collusion among criminals, police and city officials, citizens, or businesses. Cooperation rather than conflict has marked the relationship between these groups.[36] Furthermore, Francis Ianni, a leading authority on organized crime, has pointed out that those involved in organized crime are no different from other entrepreneurs, other than in the services they render and the techniques they use.[37]

North American, and even more specifically U.S. society has been particularly conducive to the formation of criminal groups that provide illegitimate services. One reason is that there has been a greater tendency to legislate morality in the United States and Canada than, for instance, in most European countries. There has been an inclination on this continent to draft unpopular laws in areas in which there is a high demand for goods and services. Such legislation merely drives underground the market for these goods and services – the legal prohibition of alcohol in the United States in the 1920s was a case in point. As the enterprises that meet these demands are illegal, there can be no regulation by law. The stabilization or expansion of markets is therefore achieved either through informal deals (these are quite rare) or through violence.

The preoccupation with upward mobility and success in North America is another cultural element that fosters the development of illicit crime networks. In the United States, in particular, much of the legend and history deals with the entrepreneur who, despite humble beginnings, ultimately achieves success. It is from these stories that folk heroes emerge: the means used to achieve success are less relevant than the success itself, as innovation and daring are highly regarded characteristics. The admiration for racketeers not only exists in the community but extends to public officials as well. Consequently, they are not regarded as outsiders but people with whom business can be done. American 'mobsters', as a result, have been able to influence political campaigns and law-making to a greater degree than could similar figures in other countries.[38]

PART III
EXPLAINING THE TRANSGRESSIONS OF THE PUBLIC

9

'Everybody Does It': Rationalizations, Justifications, and Excuses for Criminal Behaviour

Those working with convicted criminals have noted the all-too-common propensity of offenders to blame everybody but themselves for their actions. Clinical workers often complain that their clients not only fool others to obtain various advantages (e.g., a reduced sentence or an early parole) but also are remarkably adept at convincing themselves they have done nothing wrong. Thus, they frequently present themselves as the victims of circumstances or of an unjust legal system. This way of thinking, of course, offers a profound challenge to those hoping to assist habitual lawbreakers mend their ways, as presumably the first step in dealing with any problem is to accept some personal responsibility for it.

The mental gymnastics involved in justifying or excusing one's behaviour, I will argue, are an integral part of law violation and other antisocial behaviour. In this chapter, I present what I believe are some novel views of rationalizations of behaviour. It is my view that understanding these rationalizations is crucial to understanding all antisocial behaviour, since the point of view of the offender, as distorted as it may appear to be, is as vital to the comprehension of his or her behaviour as are more obvious criminogenic factors such as economic want or dysfunctional families.

I also hope to show that ordinary people invoke justifications that closely resemble those used by more hardened or career criminals. It stands to reason that if career criminals (who usually do view themselves as different or, at least, as out of the mainstream of society) have a need to justify their behaviour in their own eyes, those who view themselves as decent citizens have a particularly overpowering need to justify any illicit behaviour on their part. Somehow, their behaviour must be reconciled with their self-images as law-abiding people. By justifying or excusing their transgressions, 'respectable' lawbreakers can leave intact their view of themselves as decent citizens.

Yet, in the past, sociological and psychiatric theorists have sometimes treated the tendency to rationalize antisocial behaviour as a distinct quality of the criminal. In the 1950s, two sociologists, Gresham Sykes and David Matza, advanced the idea that delinquency, rather than arising from a different value system adhered to by delinquents, arose because the young offender was able to neutralize the impact of society's norms. The 'neutralization techniques' used by delinquents were said to help them cope with the guilt produced by their illicit behaviour, as well as the recriminations resulting from such behaviour.[1]

Sykes and Matza identified five principal neutralization or coping techniques through which delinquents could deal with their own behaviour. The first technique is the *denial of responsibility*. In denying responsibility for his or her actions, the perpetrator is excusing behaviour by saying 'I didn't mean it' or 'It wasn't my fault.' Delinquents using this defence can claim either that their actions were accidental or were committed when they were out of control (e.g., prompted by anger or intoxication). Another twist to the denial of responsibility is the excuse that the actor is a perennial victim owing to unloving parents or a disadvantaged background, and thus had little choice but to become a delinquent. The delinquent, in this case, views himself or herself as a helpless victim or pawn who merely reacts to circumstances around him or her. This type of denial includes the feeling that the delinquent's actions can make no difference in improving his or her situation or can have little impact on his or her environment. Such a view can afford a lifelong excuse to avoid acting responsibly.

A second neutralization technique identified by Sykes and Matza is the *denial of injury.* Here the delinquent is saying, 'I didn't really hurt anybody.' Shoplifting and burglary can be excused by the fact that the victim is affluent and can therefore afford the loss, or by the fact the victim is insured. In auto theft, the delinquent claims only to have borrowed the vehicle. Gang fights are justified as private quarrels. In denying injury, the delinquent draws a distinction between crimes that really cause harm and those that do not. His or her crimes, not coincidentally, tend to fall in the latter category.

A third type of justification for delinquent behaviour is the *denial of the victim.* The delinquent, in using this defence, is saying, 'They had it coming.' Lawbreaking is excused by assigning some negative characteristics to the victim. By virtue of the fact the victim is a homosexual, a member of a minority group, an alcoholic, or a stool pigeon, or is seen as sleazy in some respect, he or she is viewed as less than a full person and, therefore, as undeserving of the rights accorded other human beings. It is thus considered acceptable to assault, rape, or rob such individuals. The perpetrator using such logic sees his or her role as simply that of an avenger or even as contributing positively to society, rather than as delinquent or criminal. His or her justifications may be reinforced by the attitudes of others in the milieu in which he or she lives. Denial of the victim is also invoked when the victim is an organization rather than a person (as in the case of a large department store chain) or is intangible (as in the 'victimless crimes,' e.g., drug use or gambling where the parties to the offence are consenting participants).

A fourth neutralization technique identified by Sykes and Matza is referred to as *condemning the condemners.* In using this argument, the delinquent shifts the focus from his or her own actions to the behaviour of others and excuses those actions by saying, 'Everybody does it' and 'Everyone's picking on me.' The delinquent suggests that all of society is corrupt and he or she is being singled out for punishment because of misfortune or lack of economic resources or political connections. The delinquent will argue that the police are brutal and prejudiced, politicians are corrupt, teachers show favouritism, and parents are hypo-critical; thus, if it is acceptable for authority figures to misbe-have, it should also be acceptable for him or her to do likewise. Certainly, such a defence will gain credence if there is more than a grain of truth in the accusations.

A fifth neutralization technique uncovered by Sykes and Matza is the *appeal to higher loyalties*. Here the delinquent accepts responsibility for his or her conduct but claims that 'I didn't do it for myself.' The perpetrator claims to have engaged in illicit behaviour for a higher cause. Violence may be excused on the grounds that it was intended to defend the family honour. Illegal activities perpetrated with fellow gang members are said to have been undertaken out of loyalty to the group. The delin-quent thus transforms his or her behaviour from dishonourable to honourable.

These five neutralization techniques are not merely hypothet-ical: they are encountered in everyday life by those working with defendants and convicted persons, and used in everyday life by 'respectable' citizens confronted with their failures or transgres-sions. As an illustration, table 5 compares the justifications and excuses of those involved with the legal system with those pro-vided by ordinary citizens following a car accident or traffic vio-lation. The top of the table lists some of the different types of rationalizations heard by probation officers, while the bottom of the table lists the excuses given by accident victims or 'speeders' to the police.

Even the most prominent members of society use neutraliza-tion tactics routinely to deal with questionable behaviour. There is, for example, the 'ritual of wiggle' performed by governmental officials who are trying to elude responsibility for their deviant activities.[2] When confronted with wrongdoing, political leaders tend to deny the activity in question has taken place, or at least that they have knowledge of the activity. In both the Watergate and Iran-Contra scandals, U.S. presidents denied knowledge of illegal activities on the part of their subordinates. Where illegali-ties involve individual officials, the neutralization tactic used is often one of evasion, or ignoring the activities in question. These

TABLE 5
Comparing the Rationalizations of Convicted Criminals with Those of
Non-convicted Citizens

CONVICTED CRIMINALS

Denial of Responsibility
'I didn't do it.'
'I didn't mean to do it.'
'It was his idea; I just went along.'
'They made me do it.'

Denial of Injury
'But it wasn't anything all that big.'
'But it's not like I really hurt anybody.'
'The insurance will pay for it.'
'They're a big outfit; they'll never miss it.'

Denial of the Victim
'He was asking for it.'
'That dope left his door unlocked; I was simply going to teach him to be more careful in the future.'

Condemning the Condemners
'But everybody does it.'
'The cops were laying for me.'
'That D.A. [District Attorney] is trying to get me.'

Appeal to Higher Loyalties
'I wanted to give my family a good Christmas.'

ACCIDENT VICTIM OR TRAFFIC VIOLATOR

Denial of Responsibility
'The other car collided with mine without giving warning of its intentions.'
'A pedestrian hit me and went under my car.'
'You mean it's only 30 (km/h) here?'
'My speedometer's not working – I don't know how fast I was going.'

Denial of Injury
'Do cops not have anything better to do, like go out and catch real criminals.'
'Well, I was only going five miles over the speed limit.'

Denial of the Victim
'The guy was all over the road. I had to swerve a number of times before I hit him.'
'When I saw I could not avoid a collision, I stepped on the gas and crashed into the other car.'

TABLE 5 (continued)

Condemning the Condemners
'You're just picking on me because I've got a powerful machine.'

Appeal to Higher Loyalities
'To avoid hitting the bumper of the car in front, I struck the pedestrian.'
'I received an emergency call from my wife and I'm rushing home.'
'I'm breastfeeding and I'm late for the next feeding.'
'I'm late for work.'

Sources: Charles L. Erickson, *The Perils of Probation* (Springfield, IL: Charles C. Thomas 1980), 167–8; Sherri Armstrong, *The Ottawa Sunday Herald*, 21 September 1986, 29; Tilden Car Rentals, internal document

officials often go into hiding, disconnect their phones, or simply refuse to comment when questioned by the media. The government may refuse to take action against such officials by insisting that the facts of the case do not justify governmental intervention. Still another tactic is to accuse the accuser. People such as Richard Nixon and Gary Hart accused the media of 'having it in for them.' The government can also claim that illegal actions on their part were in the interests of the nation (e.g., national security). Yet another classic evasion tactic is to promise a thorough investigation of a controversial matter. President Nixon surprised even his own aide John Dean when he announced on national television that he had conducted a complete investigation of the Watergate incident. In reality, he tried to squash its investigation.

If the examples provided in table 5 and those relating to governmental 'wiggling' are any indication, then it might be reasonable to assert that people not involved habitually with the legal system (those whom we have called 'ordinary' people), as well as some of society's most respectable members, are as likely to excuse or justify their behaviour as are habitual offenders. Yet, some psychologists and psychiatrists contend that the most basic distinction between criminals and the rest of us can be found in the way criminals think and justify their conduct.

Some psychologists view criminals as highly impulsive individuals who rarely think before they act and who tend to ignore the consequences of their actions for themselves, as well as for their victims.[3] To be sure, many habitual offenders fall into this category; however, many individuals functioning reasonably well in society also fit this description. Furthermore, many violent crimes – not merely more sophisticated white-collar offences – involve at least an element of planning or occur after long-standing differences between offenders and victims. Furthermore, many other categories of crime could hardly be labelled impulsive; for example, tax evasion, embezzlement, computer crimes, political corruption, organized criminal behaviour, and even the behaviour of those in disciplined street gangs. Albert Bandura, a leading exponent of the 'social learning' approach in psychology, contends that much socially harmful behaviour, including violence, does not result from a lack of self-control, but from the ability of perpetrators to justify their behaviour: 'cognitive skills and self-control are enlisted all too well through moral justifications and self-exonerative devices in the service of destructive causes. The massive threats to human welfare are generally brought about by deliberate acts of principle rather than by unrestrained acts of impulse. It is the principled resort to aggression that is of greatest social concern but is most ignored in psychological theorizing and research.'[4]

Still, there are those who consider the tendency to justify behaviour as a hallmark of criminality. Psychiatrist Samuel Yochelson and clinical psychologist Stanton Samenow, in their well-publicized, but highly controversial book *The Criminal Personality*, argued that criminals exhibit deficits in thinking (cognitive deficits) that set them apart from the rest of society.[5] They drew this conclusion on the basis of having studied 240 hardcore offenders, many of whom had been judged criminally insane. They stated that criminals are all habitual liars who fail to put themselves in the place of others, see others as pawns or objects to be exploited, are impulsive and irresponsible, and view themselves as victims. This view of themselves as victims, Yochelson and Samenow claimed, leads to the ready rationalization of their actions. These errors in thinking and patterns of justification were said to set criminals apart as a separate breed of human beings. Although the authors acknowledged that non-offenders, too, exhibited thinking errors, the magnitude of these errors exhibited by criminals was seen as so different that they were 'almost as a different breed of person.' To Yochelson and Samenow, the propensity to blame others for their fate, on a routine basis, was generally confined to the criminal population. Furthermore, the authors viewed this propensity, and other cognitive deficits, as almost an inborn trait of criminals, rather than as attributable to social, educational, and family experiences.

Perhaps the most troubling aspect of the work of Yochelson and Samenow is the fact that they drew their highly influential conclusions from a very specific, highly active, and disturbed criminal group, who, in fact, were hospitalized in St Elizabeth's Hospital in Washington, D.C., a psychiatric prison. We have seen by now that most members of society violate the law at one point or another. Even among incarcerated offenders, Yochelson and Samenow's subjects constitute an extreme group; hence, the authors' findings cannot be generalized even to other prisoners, let alone to all violators of society's laws.

JUSTIFICATIONS IN EVERYDAY LIFE

All categories of offenders, whether hard-core or more casual, use some fairly standard justifications for their actions. Justifications can protect one from one's own conscience or from the accusations of others. Before exploring the specific nature of these justifications, it may worthwhile exploring the work of scholars in the behavioural sciences who have considered rationalizations and excuses as normal and commonplace ways of coping with personal transgressions, failures, guilt, and pain.

Sigmund Freud developed the concept of the ego defence mechanisms. This concept has been adopted not only by followers of Freud (psychoanalysts), but by many clinical psychologists and psychiatrists. Essentially, we develop defence mechanisms from infancy to cope with the demands of the real world and with anxiety. External threats, such as devaluating failures, and internal threats, such as guilt, may overwhelm us unless we negate them in some way. The different defence mechanisms afford a variety of means of coping with these threats. Generally, the defence mechanisms serve to deny or distort reality, reduce emotional involvement in the threatening situation, or counteract the threat.[6]

All people resort to the use of some of these mechanisms; however, some may use them more consistently as their primary means of dealing with stress. Lawrence Kolb, the author of one of the most widely used textbooks in clinical psychiatry, has written the following about the defence mechanisms:

Through the long period of development the personality acquires various psychological techniques by which it attempts to defend itself, establish compromises between conflicting impulses, and allay inner tensions. These mediating and integrating activities, functions of the ego as described before, are internal mechanisms of control, unconsciously selected and operating automatically. The personality develops defenses designed to manage anxiety, aggressive impulses, hostilities, resentments, and frustrations. All of us make continual use of defense mechanisms. In themselves they are not necessarily pathological. Life would be unbearable without resort to rationalization and similar psychic protections. Neither is it always the goal of therapy to eliminate them. Since at times they may promote the individual's ability to live in peace with himself, it may, in fact, be a therapeutic objective to strengthen them. The type of motivating device unconsciously selected to meet emotional needs and stresses and to provide a defense against anxiety, the extent of its employment, and the degree to which it distorts the personality, dominates the behavior, and disturbs the adjustment with others determine the measure of mental health. Processes similar in kind take place, therefore, in both the 'normal' and the 'abnormal.'[7]

The *denial of reality*, perhaps the most primitive of all defence mechanisms, involves the refusal to acknowledge disagreeable realities. Much as in Sykes and Matza's *denial of injury* and *denial of the victim*, the transgressor can claim that his or her actions caused no harm or hurt no one of consequence.

Rationalization, another defence mechanism, involves the justification of inappropriate behaviour through the use of faulty logic or the attribution of it to noble motives that did not in fact, inspire it. A person essentially thinks up logical and socially approved reasons for past, present, or prospective behaviours. Here again, a link can be drawn between a common defence mechanism and Sykes and Matza's neutralization techniques that were said to be employed by delinquents. In the *denial of responsibility*, the perpetrator rationalizes his or her transgressions by claiming that others are to blame, or that he or she is in a socially disadvantaged situation and therefore has little choice but to engage in harmful behaviour. Also, just as in the defence of rationalization, the delinquent *appealing to higher loyalties* ascribes his or her behaviour to socially approved or honourable motives, such as loyalty to a group or a set of values held in high esteem.

The fifth neutralization technique identified by Sykes and Matza, *condemning the condemners*, also has its counterpart among the ego defence mechanisms. In condemning his or her accusers, or society in general, the delinquent is attempting to exonerate himself or herself through the defence mechanism of *projection*. Projection involves the attribution of one's unacceptable desires, failures, and actions to others. Just as students failing exams frequently blame their professors for inadequate teaching or unfairness, law violators may claim the police are unfair or that all of society is corrupt.

The negation of reality or the use of some form of distorted logic to defend behaviour is a universal process, akin to those defensive processes that traditionally have been attributed, in the field of criminology, primarily to offenders and other antisocial individuals. Social psychologist Leon Festinger's theory of *cognitive dissonance* helps explain the need to develop distorted explanations for our actions.[8] According to the theory, when a person's behaviour is inconsistent with his or her attitudes or values, an uncomfortable state of tension results. The more profound this inconsistency, the more uncomfortable the tension and, therefore, the more urgent the need to reduce the tension.

If the harmful behaviour has already occurred, it cannot be erased; however, the individual's perception of it can be altered to realign his or her behaviour and values. Thus, if a person takes objects home from work without permission but values honesty, dissonance exists between the value he or she has placed on honesty and his or her actual behaviour. To reduce the state of tension caused by dissonance, a person can either change his or her behaviour or values, or merely re-evaluate his or her behaviour. Changing either behaviour or values is less likely than redefining actions. A person can excuse victimizing her employer by telling herself that she has been treated unfairly or is underpaid and, thus, in this very special circumstance, her behaviour is not dishonest but merely compensation that was due her. This way of viewing her circumstance allows her to continue her behaviour, while maintaining the value she places on honesty with a minimum of tension.

Psychologist C.R. Snyder has written about the way excuse-making helps people maintain a positive image of themselves for both an internal audience (themselves) and an external audience (everyone else).[9] Excuses, he argues, are triggered by any action that fails to meet an individual's own or society's standards. The more closely the person is linked to the misconduct and the more negatively it is viewed, the greater the likelihood of excuse making.

Snyder argues that there are three forms of excuses: 'I didn't do it,' 'It wasn't so bad,' and 'Yes, but ...' A form of hierarchy takes place in terms of the sequence in which these excuses are used. According to Snyder, when confronted with some misdeed, people often start by disavowing personal responsibility for the behaviour in question; thus, it was not they but someone else who committed the act. An assembly-line worker accused of taking tools home from work, for example, may simply deny that he was responsible for such a theft.

When people cannot sever the link between themselves and the act, they resort to the next level of excuses: they downplay the gravity of the act. Thus, if physical evidence or witnesses link the factory worker to the theft of the tools, he can no longer claim he did not commit the act. What he can do is claim it 'wasn't so bad,' thereby softening or minimizing the act. In this way, the act is cast in a more positive light. 'After all,' he might say, 'what are a few tools to a multibillion-dollar corporation?'

If excuse makers accept responsibility ('I did it') and further admit 'It was bad,' they can resort to yet another line of excuses – the 'Yes, but ...' variety. People can point to extenuating circumstances that weaken their accountability for their actions. The assembly-line worker can claim that, while he did take home the tools, he was in dire financial straits and could not afford to purchase them. Or he could claim that he had every intention of returning them, that he was merely borrowing the tools. Another excuse of the 'Yes, but ...' variety would be that other workers are doing the same, thereby demonstrating that others with similar economic circumstances also succumb to the pressures of everyday life.

To Snyder, therefore, excuses are not used merely by select individuals. They are used by everyone on occasion and have an adaptive function, although he acknowledges that some people do resort to excuse making more regularly than others, at which point it becomes maladaptive. For most people, most of the time, excuses provide a way of negotiating life's uncertain terrain while keeping their self-esteem intact. The tendency to make excuses and rationalize behaviour is not monopolized by any one segment of the population.

From the interviews conducted by myself and others, I believe that justifications for illegal and other socially harmful behaviour fall into two basic categories: justifications pointing to the inequities and injustices of society in general (what I call 'global justifications'), and those relating to one's specific circumstances at a given time ('situation-specific justifications'). I believe that the style of justification one tends to rely on (whether the first or second) will have a significant bearing on one's social behaviour, as it is my contention that these justifications are a powerful driving force behind criminality.

Theories of criminal behaviour have tended to focus on the objective conditions of the perpetrator (i.e., family life, marital life, economic situation, substance abuse, education, etc.) and have largely ignored the perspective of the offender, his or her indignation about perceived injustices, and his or her sense of hopelessness. While it is true that very aversive events, such as severe physical abuse during childhood, will be experienced similarly by most individuals, not every person will react the same way even to such extreme events. Some victims will repeat the aggression against a sibling, spouse, or child; others will turn the aggression against themselves in the form of substance abuse, self-mutilation, or an eating disorder. Still others may alternate between other- and self-directed aggression. Others may develop symptoms of severe psychopathology, such as dissociative reactions (i.e., multiple personalities), that actually shield them from the pain of early-life trauma. Yet others may manage to overcome such adversity and cope fairly well as they grow up.

Many factors influence the different behavioural reactions to life's aversive events. Among others, there are the coping skills one has learned and the compensating positive influences; for example, where one is abused by one's father, are the other relationships in the family similarly dysfunctional, or do they to some degree compensate for this negative element? Equally vital in shaping one's behavioural response to such traumatic events is one's overall evaluation of it. Does a person who was physically abused by his father come to distrust and hate all authority figures (teachers, bosses, police officers, etc.), will he merely hate his father, or will he develop empathy for his father? A multitude of factors will affect the way in which such events are experienced, including an individual's susceptibilities and unique experiences.

From our unique experiences, we each develop a view of the world, or what social psychologists refer to as an 'implicit personality theory.'[10] The idea of an implicit personality theory refers to the notion that people tend to have a fixed set of biases in judging others. Without realizing it, people are said to have a 'theory' about what other people are like, and this 'theory' influences their judgments and behaviour towards others.

GLOBAL JUSTIFICATIONS

People who are habitually in trouble with the law are often found to possess a very negative view of others. Samuel Yochelson and Stanton Samenow, in their work with hard-core offenders discussed earlier in this chapter, found their subjects considered the world as a predatory one, full of injustices, in which no one could be trusted and they were frequently victimized.

Whether the negative world-view of chronically antisocial individuals merely justifies their behaviour or is a force behind it is open to debate. The tendency has been to regard rationalizations as after-the-fact explanations concocted by people to purify or cleanse their behaviour. I would argue that such a view is very limited, and that justifications, even if they are not stated openly or are even out of the individual's awareness, often precede behaviour. I would contend that our implicit theories about the world enable us to engage in certain behaviours and inhibit us from indulging in others. At the same time, when confronted by others for specific misdeeds or by stirrings of conscience, people will need to develop *ad hoc* explanations following the behaviour in question.

A good example of a general or global justification for illegal practices was provided by a worker engaging in hidden economy 'trading':

People today feel that they are being got at from all sides, particularly by commerce. From morning to night they are being bombarded with advertizing slogans and high-pressure salesmanship. They get forced into buying things they don't want at prices they can't afford. Then when they get home, they find the goods are faulty anyway. They take their cars to garages and find the work charged for hasn't been done. They find the milkman starts delivering a kind of milk they haven't asked for just because he gets a bigger profit for it. Those things are happening to them all the time and it seems like they have no redress. So they get resentful and try to get their own back by stealing a little here and cheating a little there. Everyone does it so why shouldn't they?[11]

Black rapist and later activist Eldridge Cleaver, in his collection of essays *Soul on Ice*, asserted that 'it delighted me that I was defying and trampling upon the white man's law, upon his system of values, and I was defiling his women.'[12] Another black writer of the 1960s, Imamu Baraka, formerly Leroi Jones, glorified the criminality of black Americans in some of his writings:

You know how to get it black people! You can't steal nothin from a white man, he's already stole it. He owes you anything you want, even his life. All the stores will open if you say the magic words. The magic words are: Up against the wall motherfucker this is a stick up! ... Run up and down Broad Street niggers, take the shit you want. Take their lives if need be, but get what you want what you need ... We must make our own World, man, our own world, and we can not do this unless the white man is dead. Let's get together and kill him, my man, let's get to gather the fruit of the sun, let's make a world we want black children to grow and learn in.[13]

The type of views espoused by these black writers, as well as by the hidden-economy trader, reflect graphically a desperation and a profound sense of alienation from society. The authors of these statements see the world as highly exploitative and competitive. They either explicitly or implicitly question society's legal institutions, as the law is considered a tool of those in control – the law merely legitimizes the exploitative activities of the powerful. Thus, it need not be respected; in fact, the black writers quoted above consider defiance of the law as a positive way of striking back at their oppressors. The world, according to these perspectives, is seen in very adversarial terms, as one in which one is either victor or vanquished. Such a perspective clearly paves the way for criminality of all kinds before specific opportunities for crime arise. This type of 'survivalist' perspective opens the door for the individual to actively seek out rather than merely respond to criminal opportunities. People who possess this type of world-view can be expected to violate rules in a wide variety of situations.

SITUATION-SPECIFIC JUSTIFICATIONS

Most justifications for illegal or other socially harmful behaviour are of the type that excuse the behaviour in question in light of the particular circumstances of the perpetrator. Justifications pertaining to social injustices provide those resorting to them with a virtual *carte blanche* to engage in antisocial behaviour of all kinds. Justifications of the global type remove the need to invoke separate justifications for each kind of misbehaviour.

Most people who are not habitually violating the law presumably do not view the world in the adversarial terms described above. Because their violations are less frequent than are those of habitual criminals or anarchists, they may experience a stronger need to justify each transgression, or at least each different type of transgression. The individual with the 'decent citizen' self-image, in some respects, has a stronger need to justify his or her criminality.

Situation-specific justifications pertain to one form of dishonesty or illegality, in a specific context, but not to other forms in other contexts. Guests pilfering goods from hotels, for example, often regard them as souvenirs to which they are entitled after paying for their rooms. Employees can justify stealing on the job as revenge for mistreatment or for being underpaid. A wife-batterer can claim that his wife works him up to a rage, after which he loses control. Drug peddlers and their customers can maintain that the use of illicit substances hurts only the user and, furthermore, that alcohol and other dangerous substances are not illegal. Business people can claim that false advertising and dishonest sales techniques are all accepted business practices. Computer hackers can say they were just playing around and meant no harm. Tax evaders often contend that the government already takes too much of *their* money and then wastes it anyway. Each of these justifications, in contrast to a negative general world-view, is relevant to one specific sphere only.

Case-Study: Justifications for Employee Theft

These examples of situation-specific rationalizations, in this case for stealing on the job, were offered as justifications by some subjects interviewed by me and my colleagues:

'It was acceptable, so you did it. It was not by definition, but it was acceptable. That was one of the reasons you did it ... Everyone did it, so why should I be different and not do it.'

'When you see that other people do it, it seems to be no big deal. You think it's okay. As dumb as that sounds.'

'We are as good as management. They commit employee theft. Everybody does it. If I don't take it, someone else will.'

'I'd have to look at scamming as being more of something you do to gain for yourself; ripping off the restaurant for yourself as opposed to if you were kind of giving a friend of yours a free drink every once in a while. I don't think that's scamming; scamming is when you do it for your own gain.'

'It's on a smaller scale. It's nothing big.'

'Even though I've told myself I shouldn't be doing it, I justify it by saying it wasn't that big of a deal. I almost think I should do these people a favour when they come in to see me. I'm bringing in extra business ... I have a lot of friends that come in all the time to eat and drink. I give them a lot of free pop ... Maybe someone else who works here doesn't drink pop. I'm giving their free pop to someone else.'

'I've done it on purpose when I think that I deserve it because I work there maybe ten hours a day, which is illegal, so why shouldn't I get free food...We work long hours and we hardly ever get a break, so we deserve something extra.'

'For most people who scam, it's because they feel they're owed. They've lost money in another way that they feel wasn't justified and that the restaurant had some control over, but didn't do anything about it. Whether it's direct or getting a bad tip after you've done all this work and management says, 'This is customer prerogative; they don't need to tip you.' So you feel a little cheated 'cause you feel management should have done something about it. Anyway, you did it because of some wrongdoing against you.'

Thus, justifications that pertain to a specific job or milieu usually involve the contention that the perpetrator is being exploited by the victim (the employer in the case of employee theft); hence, it is really the perpetrator who has been victimized and he or she is just reclaiming what he or she deserves. Other common situation-specific justifications we have seen include the argument that many others, if not everyone, in that milieu are engaging in the misbehaviour, and that, therefore, it seems acceptable, and that the infraction was minor and would, therefore, not hurt the victimized establishment.

BLAMING THE VICTIM

Victim blaming is a common tactic in justifications as it attempts to transform an ignoble act into a noble one. Sociologists Sykes and Matza wrote about the tendency of delinquents to deny the existence of a victim deserving of respectful treatment. Thus, in some cases, the perpetrator makes the case that the victim, because of his or her behaviour or characteristics, 'had it coming.' In a sense, the perpetrator is arguing that he or she is settling accounts on behalf of society. Also, as we have seen, those admitting to theft at work often resort to blaming their employers for their behaviour. Employees claim to steal on the job because they are overworked, undercompensated, and unappreciated – they are just taking back perhaps only a small fraction of what their employers should have given them as compensation.

Non-human entities, such as organizations, are particularly easy to blame because they often are so amorphous they lack the ability to defend themselves (e.g., 'The system made me do it'). Inevitably, large organizations will fail to fully recognize the efforts of every individual working there or dealing with them, so there is no shortage of slights to which someone seeking to lay blame can point. Large bodies are also easier to victimize than are people as there is no tangible or clearly discernible consequence of the victimization. Probably the largest entity with which an individual can deal is the government and there is almost universal glee in victimizing governments through tax violations and other misconduct. Justifications bordering on the platitudinous are that tax rates are too high or that the political party in office is wasteful and corrupt. Quite obviously, one can find ample fault with any large bureaucracy and with the most effective and honest political leadership.

In his book *Blaming the Victim*, William Ryan reflects on the tendency of the middle class to blame the poor for their plight.[14] With respect to black Americans, for example, he states that even white liberals tend to lay the blame for poverty on the black family, the values of the black community, and other pathological elements within that community. Liberals, unlike conservatives, see a link between historical conditions and the deficits of the black population; however, the solution of these problems lies in the eradication of these deficits rather than in the transformation of society. This, Ryan contends, is a classic case of blaming the victim, as the focal point of the problems are the poor rather than the conditions (ongoing racism and exclusion from the power élite) that keep them in an inferior economic situation. Ryan describes the dilemma of white liberals and how they arrive at blaming the victim:

The highly-charged psychological problem confronting this hypothetical progressive, charitable person I am talking about is that of reconciling his own self-interest with the promptings of his humanitarian impulses. This psychological process of reconciliation is not worked out in a rational, conscious way; it is a process that takes place far below the level of sharp consciousness, and the solution – Blaming the Victim – is arrived at subconsciously as a compromise that apparently satisfies both his self-interest and his charitable concerns ...

The typical Victim Blamer is a middle class person who is doing reasonably well in a material way; he has a good job, a good income, a good house, a good car. Basically, he likes the social system pretty much the way it is, at least in broad outline ... On the other hand, he is acutely aware of poverty, racial discrimination, exploitation, and deprivation, and, moreover, he wants to do something concrete to ameliorate the condition of the poor, the black, and the disadvantaged ...

What intellectual position can he take, and what line of action can he follow that will satisfy both of these important motivations? ... They [middle-class liberals] cannot bring themselves to attack the system that has been so good to them, but they want so badly to be helpful to the victims of racism and economic injustice ...

Their solution is a brilliant compromise. They turn their attention to the victim in his post-victimized state. They want to bind up wounds, inject penicillin, administer morphine, and evacuate the wounded for rehabilitation. They explain what's wrong with the victim in terms of social experiences *in the past*, experiences that have left wounds, defects, paralysis, and disability ... They are most crucially rejecting the possibility of blaming, not the victims, but themselves.[15]

A similar dilemma presents itself when people concerned with maintaining their images (and self-images) as law-abiding, respectable citizens are contemplating the commission of illegal or otherwise dishonest acts. On the one hand, there is self-interest; the personal benefit to be gained through the act. On the other hand, their victimization of others may challenge their conception of themselves as morally upright. One solution to this dilemma is to derive the personal benefit by going through with the act, but to strip it of its negative connotation by casting it into a positive, or at least acceptable, light. One way of doing so is to devalue the victim as a person or to somehow make the victim responsible for his or her fate.

Case-Study: Victim Blaming in Unscrupulous Business Practices

Consider the following examples in which customers are cheated or conned by businesses or their employees.[16] In each case, the customer is depicted as stupid or larcenous in some way:

DRIVING SCHOOL INSTRUCTOR: 'When you see a lot of money coming in you get greedy. You take advantage of people. So if you can keep a student out an additional three or four hours, you get more money, and you justify it in your own mind by saying that the person really needed the extra lessons.'

SERVICE STATION ATTENDANT: 'A lot of guys who work at stations get into "hanging the pumps" ... Someone would come in and get $1 worth of gas and the attendant wouldn't turn the pump off – he'd hang the nozzle, but keep the pump running. Then someone else comes in and says, "give me $5 worth," and they'd keep that $1 on when they started pumping, so he'd end up with $1 less gas than he'd paid for. A lot of customers are really spacey. They'll look at the price and say they want so much gas, and go on talking to the person with them. They don't notice the $1 already on the pump.'

PARKING GARAGE ATTENDANT: 'You would overcharge the customers – anywhere from 75 cents to $1.50. It's kind of hard to add up the time when we're charging by the half-hour, and people don't pay any attention anyway. ... People leave their cars, go into a restaurant, have a few drinks, eat, are feeling good, come out, get in their car, and go. The only thing they're concerned about is going onto other things or that they have a long way to get to where they're going. People set themselves up. They'll be drinking, or they leave their trunk keys in the car, and when they come back, they expect it to be there.'

AUTO SALESMAN: 'I used to have a friend whose ads made us all laugh. They'd say, "Reprocessed cars. Assume payments." Well, people who have a mooch instinct read the word "reprocessed" and think they're reading "repossessed." "They took it away from some turkey who couldn't pay," they tell themselves, "and now I can assume the loan and take over the car." Literally, according to this dealer, the car was reprocessed, from the west end of the lot to the east end. Okay, maybe he washed a window. When the customer asks about the repossessed cars, the guy would say, "Oh, yes, come this way," and that was the last he would hear about the ad. From then on my friend was just sell-ing cars. ... Sometimes when a guy schlocked and mooched us [bargained] until we had no profit left in the deal, the sales man-ager would say, "I'll fix that son of a bitch." They might drill holes in the side panels to make it appear as if they'd drilled them to insert the rustproofing nozzles, but they were just holes. Or they might coat the underneath part of the car with some phony material that adheres, but which isn't even rustproof.'

COCKTAIL WAITRESS: 'At one place I worked, if a woman was drunk, they would ask her to leave, saying, "I really think you have had enough." ... At another place, though, it was just the opposite. We would never tell anyone they couldn't order another drink – instead, the bartender just gave her the mixer, and she was so drunk she could not tell the difference. The peo-ple were throwing around their money so fast that I don't think we felt any pity.'

MINIMIZING THE HARM CAUSED
BY CRIMINAL BEHAVIOUR

There are times when the perpetrator of criminal or other disho-nourable behaviour accepts responsibility and does not seek to exonerate himself or herself for the actions in question. He or she can resort to another tactic as a defence from the accusa-tions of others or the wrath of his or her conscience: the harm produced can be downplayed. The perpetrator is saying the behaviour 'wasn't so bad.' Delinquents, according to Sykes and

Matza, frequently use the defence that those they have victimized can afford the loss, because of their affluence or because they are insured for losses incurred from such actions as burglary, auto theft, and common theft. Citizens less frequently in contact with the law also use some techniques to soften or cushion the effects of their wrongdoings.

One tactic is to invoke the philosophy of *selective victimization*. Thus, ordinary citizens draw a distinction between legitimate and illegitimate targets of their aggressive or acquisitive actions. Two career armed robbers interviewed by a colleague stated the following about their code of ethics:[17]

ROBBER #1: 'We don't rob those poorer than ourselves; it doesn't make sense. It's like a form of valour.'
ROBBER #2: 'To rob working people is not right. Maybe these people make no more than $200 per week. Therefore, I want to rob those who have nothing to lose – the banks.'

Like these professional criminals, many ordinary people who violate the law distinguish between acceptable and unacceptable targets. In so doing, their behaviour (at least to them) becomes more acceptable. Studies of urban race riots taking place in the United States in the 1960s, for example, found that the looting of businesses was far from indiscriminate. Looters in many of the riots tended to victimize large businesses owned by people residing outside the ghetto. It was considered taboo to burn and loot an establishment owned and operated by a local ghetto dweller.[18]

Stuart Henry encountered the same phenomenon of selective victimization in his study of hidden-economy trading in England. One trader said the following about what he considered to be legitimate and illegitimate targets: 'It's important who we pick from. If we pick from our friends we deserve to get done. We certainly don't deserve to have any friends. If we pick from a big supermarket we're doing nothing wrong. It's a crime to steal from our brothers and sisters; it's a public service to help each other pick from millionaire companies.'[19]

A maintenance supervisor in a chemical plant expressed the following view to a member of my research team on the subject of employee theft, when commenting about an incident in which a fellow worker stole merchandise from a colleague who had just stolen it from the company: 'It's awful. It's all right to steal from the company, but it's a son of a gun whenever you steal from your own guy.' By considering certain targets out of bounds, the author of illegal activities feels he or she has a code of ethics and, hence, feels more comfortable about these activities.

A related way of minimizing the seriousness of behaviour is to point to behaviour that is more serious or offensive. Professional burglars will say that their activities are respectable relative to those of armed robbers because they use finesse rather than violence or the threat of it. Armed robbers might criticize burglars for the use of stealth rather than the honest confrontation of victims. Both burglars and robbers may be highly contemptuous of child molesters. Child molesters, however, may see themselves as having a 'problem' that is out of their control, but may view people who steal for a living as parasitical. Thus, even in the so-called criminal underworld, it is common for offenders to draw the line at certain types of criminality.

In the same way, citizens in legitimate jobs regard their illegal activities, such as employee theft, as different from those of burglars and robbers. They might claim that burglars and robbers are engaged full-time in stealing, whereas their own activities are mere sidelines or 'perks' of their otherwise legitimate occupations. The difference between 'respectable' citizens who steal and what we might call more 'chronic' offenders is rarely so clear-cut. Many burglars and robbers work at legitimate jobs (at least intermittently), and their profits may be more modest and their criminality less frequent than, for example, those of many hidden-economy traders. Nevertheless, the belief that the behaviour of others is more reprehensible makes people more comfortable with their own misdeeds.

Another device used to soften behaviour is the manipulation of language. The contract killer is often referred to as a 'hit man.'

Prostitutes frequently refer to themselves as 'working girls' and to their customers as 'clients' or 'dates.' Armed robbers may be referred to as 'heavies' and their crimes as 'hits,' 'scores,' 'heists,' or 'jobs.'

These forms of terminology are popular among those who are engaged in crime on a regular basis. Although a criminal argot may have evolved for a number of reasons, one purpose it serves is to downplay the seriousness or repugnance of a criminal act, thereby making it more palatable to its authors. By calling themselves 'working girls' and their customers 'clients,' prostitutes make their activities appear more mundane or routine and sound more like they are conducting a business than engaging in activity that is deviant and disreputable. By sharing a dialect, full-time practitioners of crime can promote the mutual delusion that their activities are those of a legitimate profession.

The use of euphemisms also facilitates the misbehaviour of more 'respectable' lawbreakers. In hidden-economy trading, people tend to use such terms as 'cheap goods' or 'bargains' rather than 'stolen goods' to make transactions appear more respectable. One 'trader' stated the following: 'If somebody came along and said to me, "This is stolen goods. Do you want it?" I wouldn't want to know. No thanks. I wouldn't take it. But, if they said "It's off the back of a lorry [truck]," I wouldn't mind. I don't think I'd like to know if they were stolen. I'd like to kid myself it was all right. I wouldn't like to know it was pinched. I wouldn't like it right out. It might enter the back of my mind but provided they didn't tell me straight to my face I would try to avoid the issue. I'd say, "I'd like it very much."'[20]

In the same way, tax violations are often referred to as 'finagling,' embezzlers sometimes claim they are borrowing from rather than cheating their employers, and waiters and waitresses talk of 'scamming' rather than stealing from employers and customers.

We have thus seen that rationalizations and other neutralization techniques are common among 'respectable' as well as more full-time lawbreakers. They are, in my view, a driving force behind crime and often precede specific episodes of criminality. One might argue that some explanations perpetrators offer for their conduct are not rationalizations at all, but accurate assessments of their predicament. Some employees who steal from their workplace, for example, may be treated as poorly and be as underpaid as they claim. In such a case, their justification does not qualify as a rationalization in the strict Freudian sense, because, in that context, rationalizations are considered false, though logical, statements.

Differentiating between false statements or 'thinking errors,' on the one hand, and legitimate justifications, on the other, is fraught with serious difficulties because justifications rarely refer to objective or factual standards. The claim that one is exploited by one's employer or is underpaid is not a factual one but an evaluative one (i.e., a judgment). Exploited in what way? Underpaid relative to whom? other workers in the same industry? in the same city? in the same province or state? in the same country? around the world?

Most justifications are thus inherently subjective and personal in nature. They relate to a person's values and life experiences. The task of distinguishing between legitimate and false justifications is often a Divine one. As such, I have steered clear of making judgments about the veracity or legitimacy of the justifications explored in this chapter. My concern has been to show how they are linked to behaviour because people violating society's rules (whether they are repeat or only occasional offenders) show a consistent tendency to justify their conduct when they are confronted with their own misdeeds. There is no doubt that some people resort more frequently to justifications than others. Whether this difference is attributable to the fact they simply have more misbehaviour to account for or exhibit some personality disorder is difficult to assess. Clinical psychologists and psychiatrists must wrestle with this issue.

One thing is sure: the world is imperfect and, by most standards, far from fair. People routinely encounter situations they consider to be injustices. We are not all faced with equal economic opportunities; we have not all emerged from harmonious families; few of us are treated benevolently by our employers; few of us are always satisfied with the fairness of our professional or business dealings; most of us could think about some complaint against local or national politicians. Thus, all of us have ample opportunities to cry foul about the treatment accorded us. We cannot completely eliminate these opportunities for justification, nor shed our tendency to justify. Justifications remain an integral part of the dynamics of criminality, and their persistence may be a powerful factor contributing to the persistence and universality of criminal behaviour.

As a way of ending this chapter, it may be instructive to look at the case of John E. List, a seemingly ordinary family man who, in 1990, was put on trial for killing his wife, three children, and elderly mother back in 1964. He was captured after eighteen years in hiding, during which time he started a new life and took on a new identity. The following are excerpts from the letter List left behind for his pastor before going into hiding:

I know that what has been done is wrong from all that I have been taught and that any reasons that I might give will not make it right. But you ... will at least possibly understand why I felt I had to do this.

1. I wasn't earning anywhere near enough to support us. Everything I tried seemed to fall to pieces. True we could have gone bankrupt & maybe gone on welfare.

2. But ... knowing the type of location that one would have to live in plus the environment for the children plus the effect on them knowing they were on welfare was just more than I thought they could and should endure ...

3. With Pat [daughter, 16] being so determined to get into acting I was also fearful as to what that might do to her continuing to be a Christian ...

4. Also, with Helen [wife] not going to Church I knew that this would harm the children eventually ...

At least I'm certain that all have gone to heaven now. If things had gone on who knows if this would be the case ... I'm sure many will say 'How could anyone do such a horrible thing' – My only answer is it isn't easy ...

It may seem cowardly to have always shot from behind, but I didn't

want any of them to know even at the last second that I had to do this ...
I'm only concerned with making my peace with God & of this I am
assured because of Christ dying even for me.[21]

This letter contains very little other than justifications for the
murder of List's family. The author is concerned both with
appearances and allaying his own guilt. The letter makes it clear
that List ruminated about his situation and contemplated
resolving it in a violent manner for a considerable period of
time. The many elements contained in his justification (his
financial situation, his daughter's acting, his wife's failure to go
to church, etc.), indicate this was a well-thought-out decision,
not an impulsive crime motivated by fleeting anger. Note the
use of terms and phrases suggesting he had little choice but to
commit the crime: 'I had to do this,' 'it isn't easy [to do such a
horrible thing]'; these represent classic denial of responsibility.

He also tries to cast his act in noble terms, as though he were
executing his family in order to protect them – 'knowing they
were on welfare was just more than I thought they could and
should endure'; 'At least I'm certain that all have gone to heaven
now. If things had gone on who knows if this would be the case';
'Helen not going to church I knew this would harm the children
eventually ...'; 'With Pat being so determined to get into acting I
was also fearful as to what that might do to her continuing to be
a Christian.'

One might conclude that it was *he* who felt inadequate for not
being a good provider; *he* who could not tolerate seeing his family on welfare; *he* who could not cope with his daughter's acting;
and *he* who could not deal with his wife's independence. He
probably felt worthless, and that his family was slipping away
from him. The only way he saw to regain control over what he
felt was a desperate situation was, paradoxically, to kill them. We
can see how his rigid value system, perfectionistic thinking, and
excuse making were an integral part of the crime. His justifications were formulated well in advance of the killings.

10

'Our Brother's Keeper?' The Commitment of the Public to Society's Rules

It is often assumed that the general public firmly subscribes to society's rules. It is believed that most people not only conform to these rules in their behaviour but believe in them as well, having internalized their inherent values during their development. Only a small fraction of the population is considered to be antagonistic towards the laws we are said to cherish.

One might be inclined to attribute the widespread involvement in criminal activity to momentary lapses on the part of people otherwise engaged in lawful activity. Thus, from time to time, even law-abiding citizens seize an opportunity to meet some goal illegally. A warehouse employee, for example, may spot an opportunity to steal a colour television set, something he has wanted for a long time but has been unable to afford. This type of characterization of the public's criminality views people as basically law-abiding, but occasionally prone to human frailties when exposed to extreme stress, deprivation, or a sudden opportunity.

It is also possible, however, that opportunistic crime does not always relate to a specific, pre-existing need. People may take objects home from work, a store, or a resort they are visiting that they had no intention of acquiring. The opportunity arises, and they seize upon it. Some incidents of looting during electrical blackouts and civil disturbances bear this out. In some of these incidents large numbers of people take as many objects as they can possibly carry, some of which simply have been in their path and which they have never considered purchasing. In a sense, opportunities can create their own 'needs,' rather than just fulfil existing needs. Behaviour can thus be driven by new incentives and not merely long-standing deprivation.

The response of people to unanticipated events, such as power failures, provides a good opportunity to observe their gut reactions. Often, but not always, these gut reactions show a disregard or, at least, an indifference to society's laws. If people in large numbers behave in a criminal or antisocial fashion when the usual deterrents to crime are neutralized, or fail to respond indignantly when observing others breaking the law, then one might reasonably conclude that support for the law is not as pronounced as we may like to believe. A lack of commitment to society's norms and values would constitute a powerful explanation for antisocial behaviour on a large scale. One way to gauge commitment to these norms and values is to see how people react to crimes in progress.

BYSTANDER BEHAVIOUR

In the early-morning hours of 13 March 1964, a young woman named Catherine Genovese was stabbed to death in front of her apartment in a middle-class neighbourhood in the Queens section of New York City.[1] Thirty-eight of her neighbours admitted later to having witnessed part of the attack or to having heard her screams, yet none went to her aid or even called the police until after the woman had died. Even then, the police were called in only after the man who placed the call consulted a friend.[2] Most of the witnesses, when confronted with their lack of involvement, showed little embarrassment or shame. Their underlying attitude appeared to be a fear of involvement of any kind. The justifications the witnesses gave for not intervening included: 'I was tired,' 'We thought it was a lovers' quarrel,' and 'I didn't want my husband to get involved.'[3]

The Genovese incident stimulated considerable interest

among social scientists in the behaviour of bystanders to crimes and other unexpected events. A substantial body of research corroborates the idea that people quite commonly turn a blind eye, failing to help those in need. In some cases, bystanders who do not intervene can claim, with justification, that intervention could have placed them in peril. In other cases, however, bystanders face no danger and, hence, one can only conclude that failure to help the victim of crime is attributable to a general indifference to the victimizations suffered by fellow citizens.

Much of the research stimulated by the Genovese incident has been of the experimental kind in which a crime or accident is deliberately staged and the reactions of passers-by are observed. A typical study in which a crime is simulated involves the staging of a shoplifting incident. The investigators, after gaining the cooperation of a store, pose as customers and pretend to shoplift in view of other customers. Other members of the investigative team observe and record the reactions of the real customers. Usually, only a small percentage of the subjects (the customers) seeing the incident report it to a clerk, and only a very negligible number intervene directly (for instance, by telling the 'thief' to return the item). These studies also show that the tendency to intervene is influenced by the characteristics of the 'shoplifter' and other conditions prevailing at the time of the staged incident.

Case-Study: Reactions to a Shoplifting Incident

A study conducted by Donna Gelfand and her colleagues at the University of Utah provides a good illustration of field experiments examining bystander behaviour.[4] One hundred and eighty men and 156 women shoppers in two Salt Lake City drug stores served as unsolicited subjects. To be selected as a subject, the shopper had to be an adult, unaccompanied, out of the visual range of a sales clerk, and in a position to observe the 'shoplifter' easily. The apparent shoplifter was a pleasant-appearing twenty-one-year-old coed whose actions were directed by means of radio communication with two observers concealed behind a one-way observation window that ran the length of the store. When a lone shopper approached, the shop-lifter, who carried a miniature radio receiver in her purse and wore a concealed earphone, was instructed to begin her shop-lifting performance. She first attempted to gain the customer's attention by dropping an article or reaching for an item located very close to the shopper. When notified by the observer that the shopper was watching her, the shoplifter blatantly placed sev-eral items into her handbag. After doing this, the shoplifter hur-ried to the front of the store and out the door without paying the cashier.

As subjects left the store, they were interviewed by the investi-gators to determine whether they had seen the incident and to obtain some personal information (e.g., the age of the subject and whether he or she was reared in an urban or rural environ-ment). The characteristics of the subjects were varied. There were male and female subjects of various age groups. The shop-lifter's appearance was also varied by the investigators: in half the cases she was dressed very professionally and in the other half she had an unkempt appearance.

Just 28 per cent of the customers who observed the shoplifting incident reported it to store employees. Male customers were twice as likely to report the incident as were females, and mid-dle-aged shoppers reported considerably more often than did either younger or elderly shoppers. Those from a rural back-ground were two and a half times as likely to report the incident than were shoppers brought up in a large city.

This case-study illustrates two points that have been consis-tently brought out in research dealing with bystander behav-iour. First, the reporting of crime incidents, even when they are directly witnessed, tends to be the exception rather than the rule. The aforementioned study found that 28 per cent of those witnessing the shoplifting reported it to somebody in charge of the store. Similar studies of staged crime incidents have found the rate of reporting to be substantially less than this figure.

Criminologists have known for a long time that much crime goes unreported. Although serious crimes are more likely to be reported than trivial ones, even many serious offences are not brought to the attention of the authorities. In Canadian cities, for example, about two-thirds of sexual assaults and over half of all robberies (hold-ups, muggings, etc.) are never reported to the police.[5] The staged shoplifting incidents are particularly revealing because the subject has the opportunity to intervene either directly or through notifying employees of the store with little danger posed to him or her. Also, unlike reporting crimes to the police, which may involve time and inconvenience to the victim or witness, there is little energy involved in notifying a clerk of a shoplifting incident. Thus, the cost to the subject of reporting such incidents is fairly minimal and, yet, people are reluctant to do so.

The second principal finding emerging from the experiments on bystander behaviour is that the specific circumstances of a crime or other emergency influence the responses of bystanders. Some of the situational factors that have been found to have such influence are:

1 / *Whether there are others around who are capable of intervening.* When one is alone in witnessing a crime or other emergency, one cannot shift the responsibility for acting to others. When more people are present, there is what is known as a *diffusion-of-responsibility effect*; that is, responsibility is spread over a number of people, and this situation tends to freeze behaviour. Each person thinks another has acted, can act, or should act. If others do not intervene, the individual feels that he or she need not do so either.[6]

2 / *Whether the witness receives encouragement or discouragement from others.* People tend to model their behaviour after that of others. They pay attention not only to behavioural cues, as in the diffusion-of-responsibility effect, but to verbal cues as

well. They are more likely to report an incident if they have been encouraged by others to do so.

3 / *The characteristics of the perpetrator.* The race and appearance of the perpetrator may influence the decision to report an offence. Some studies have found that where the offender is black (and the bystander white) or of 'lower status' attire (i.e., shabbily dressed), the bystander is more likely to report the incident.[7]

4 / *Victim characteristics and behaviour.* People are more likely to come to the aid of a victim of a crime or other emergency if they know the victim or if the victim is attractive, similar to them, or in dire need. People are less likely to get involved when they cannot identify with the victim (i.e., the victim is either very different from them or is an organization rather than a person). Even the friendliness of a clerk can influence the likelihood that people will report crimes they witness in a store.[8]

The importance of these and other situational factors shows that people do not automatically and spontaneously report crimes. Rather, their decision to do so is based on the particulars of a given crime incident. If they can empathize with the victim, lack empathy for the offender, are not endangered or likely to be inconvenienced, see the behaviour as serious enough, and cannot escape responsibility, they *might* intervene. The public as a whole, according to bystander studies, are thus far from being unconditionally bound to upholding the law at all costs.

Another factor of importance seems to be the background of the bystander or the setting of the relevant incident. People of a rural or small-town background are more likely to come to the aid of a victim. Also, intervention against the perpetrator is more likely in a small-town than in a big-city setting. It is believed that the anonymity prevailing in larger cities, together with the faster pace of life and increased stimulation, leads to a feeling of detachment from the plight of fellow citizens. This desensitization of people to the pain of others and to infractions against society as a whole might also account for the greater prevalence of criminality in larger communities.

In North America, unlike other countries such as France and Germany, there is no legal tradition requiring a person to intervene to assist a victim in need – what has been termed Good Samaritan legislation.[9] In fact, Anglo-American law warns bystanders that they face certain risks if they come to the aid of a victim and accidentally cause harm to the victim during their rescue attempt. They may face litigation in such an event. Our legal system thus discourages bystanders from getting involved. This non-interventionist leaning of our legal system reflects a dominant cultural theme in North America that one must defend oneself and is not one's brother's keeper. This ethic of individualism nurtures exploitative behaviour, including criminality. In this vein, the criminologist John Conklin has written:

Knowing that people are not legally obligated to help victims or to intervene in a crime may make potential offenders more likely to commit a crime. This will reinforce public fears and make Good Samaritan laws even more difficult to pass. Still, the absence of such laws is not the major reason that people do not respond to victims in distress, although such laws might occasionally influence behaviour. The presence of a law, even if unenforced and lacking strong impact upon behaviour, might create confidence that others would help. This could increase social solidarity and make people more willing to walk the streets at night because of the feeling that they could depend on others to help in an emergency. This view might be inaccurate, but it still could be self-fulfilling if it led people to spend more time on the street, since potential criminals might be less willing to commit crimes in the sight of others. For such an effect to occur, a potential offender would have to feel that there was some chance of being interfered with or reported to the police by witnesses.[10]

CRIMINALITY DURING CONDITIONS OF DISORDER

Another way to gauge the commitment of the public to society's laws is to observe behaviour when the formal mechanisms society relies on to keep people in line are absent or rendered ineffective. During power failures, police strikes, and natural disasters, for example, chaos may prevail as the police are either absent or performing duties other than crime control (e.g., evacuating citizens and handling traffic). During power failures, stores usually cannot function; hence, shopkeepers close down on a large scale, thereby leaving their businesses abandoned. Furthermore, power failures may trigger thousands of alarm systems in a community as they may be designed to become activated when power is cut. This situation leaves police departments and private security companies confused about which alarms are genuine and which are false. Large-scale natural or technological disasters can result in mass confusion when the affected population is mobilized. These events thus provide an excellent laboratory for examining the extent to which people are truly committed to upholding the law, as confusion may reign and those usually responsible for law enforcement may be unavailable.

Those who first studied mass phenomena such as riots, like the French scholar Gustave LeBon and Sigmund Freud, took the view that crowds brought out the most primitive side of human beings.[11] The person behaving in a group was considered very different from the same person acting in isolation. People in crowds were said to be highly suggestible and to allow their basest impulses to surface. They were considered to lack judgment and to be prepared to mechanically follow a leader. LeBon asserted that 'the mere fact that he forms part of an organized group, a man descends several rungs in the ladder of civilization. Isolated, he may be a cultivated individual; in a crowd, he is a barbarian – that is, a creature acting by instinct. He possesses the spontaneity, the violence, the ferocity, and also the enthusiasm and heroism of primitive beings.'[12] Freud, for his part, stated that behaviour in a group is driven by the unconscious: 'when individuals come together in a group all their individual inhibitions fall away and all the cruel, brutal, and destructive instincts, which lie dormant in individuals as relics of a primitive epoch, are stirred up to find free gratification.'[13]

This view, that beneath the surface of civility lies a barbarian in all human beings, is held not only by proponents of Freudian psychoanalysis but by some sociologists as well. (This perspective is discussed in the next chapter where the reasons for widespread public involvement in antisocial behaviour are addressed.) The early theorists of crowd behaviour also believed that because people in crowds are so easily influenced, moods and behaviour patterns spread from person to person much like a contagious disease.

Recent research tells us that crowds do not necessarily elicit nasty and brutish behaviour. There are many different types of groups and crowds, and even among gangs of youths it has been observed that there is a wide variation, from one gang to another, in the extent and seriousness of their criminality.[14] The degree of panic during natural disasters, for example, has been seriously exaggerated. This type of irrational response has been found to be a very rare occurrence.[15] Even looting, field studies tell us, is often not indiscriminate. In the civil disturbances of the 1960s in the United States, ghetto dwellers tended to be selective, looting only those businesses with a reputation for exploiting customers, those with white ownership, or those in which the ownership was considered to have anti–civil rights attitudes.[16]

Nevertheless, on occasion, the full fury of pent-up grievances comes to the fore when a sudden opportunity arises to vent anger and gain desired goods. Given the right set of circumstances, people not ordinarily in conflict with the law may become involved in criminal behaviour on a large scale. This is what happened in the New York City blackout during the summer of 1977. Fairly indiscriminate looting was also seen in the Los Angeles riot of 1992.

Case-Study: An Early Christmas in New York City

Just after 9:30 P.M. on 13 July 1977, about nine million residents of New York City lost electricity. Tens of thousands of looters plundered more than 2,000 stores in what *Time* magazine called an 'orgy of looting' (see figure 4). People poured out of their

Figure 4   Looting in New York City

homes to steal items ranging from clothespins to jewellry and automobiles. Others stuffed shopping bags with steaks and roasts, while baseball fans at New York's Shea Stadium amused themselves by singing 'White Christmas.' While the looters were concentrated among blacks and Hispanics, there was no evidence, as in many 1960s uprisings, that the looters were selective in choosing their targets. Stores owned by blacks and

Hispanics suffered the same fate as those operated by whites. Observers viewed looting during this crisis as an opportunistic response rather than as an expression of political and economic grievances as, for one thing, there was little evidence that the most needy were actually involved in the looting.[17]

During the more ideologically motivated riots of the 1960s, property destruction, including arson, tended to be more prevalent than looting. In the 1977 power failure, arson was less pronounced and was confined to a small number of areas – the desire to steal goods was the dominant theme.[18] One looter perhaps summed up the motives of participants best. 'Everyone's got a little thievery, a little wrong in them,' he said. 'It's nature. You're walking down the street and there's a store open, and there's TVs and stuff in there, and won't nothing happen to you if you go in and get it. You wouldn't go in and get one?'[19]

There were 3,776 people arrested for suspected looting during the blackout. A significant proportion of those arrested had no previous criminal record, so they were presumably ordinary citizens, albeit often impoverished ones, who were merely being opportunistic. These uninitiated 'thieves' did not get involved in looting until well into the blackout. There were different types of looters involved at different points or stages of the blackout.[20]

In the first hour or so of the blackout, the looting was undertaken primarily by those with a long history of criminal behaviour. These individuals, usually men in their twenties, were involved minutes after the onset of the blackout. In the second stage of the looting, occurring in the next three or four hours (between about midnight and about 3:00 A.M.), the hard-core criminal element was joined by alienated youth who were looking for fun and excitement, as well as an opportunity to gain free material goods. Also joining in at this stage were the chronically unemployed, poorly educated, ghetto poor under thirty-five years of age. The third stage of looting, occurring in the late morning and early afternoon of the next day, saw the community at large participating. There were the stable poor and working-class members of the community getting caught up in the near hysteria and the better-off neighbourhood residents moti-

vated by what appeared to be abject greed. The third-stage looters were encouraged by the early blackout situation, during
which there seemed to be little risk of arrest.

Enrico Quarantelli and Russell Dynes, two sociologists involved
in the study of many civil disturbances, have observed that looting and destruction are not indiscriminate, nor are they a way
purely of 'blowing off' steam.[21] They argue that new norms arise
during these incidents that legitimize these behaviours, as
ghetto dwellers expropriate goods they feel they have a right to
acquire. Widespread support emerges for the looting – as can be
seen by the fact that looters often work in groups and aid one
another. Thus, the prohibitions against theft are at least temporarily suspended, and people are encouraged and sometimes
even pressured to join in.

The Los Angeles riot of 1992 also showed how people from all
races and socio-economic groups can join in the looting when
opportunities to steal suddenly arise and disorder reigns. People
become aroused when they are exposed unexpectedly to profitable opportunities, while facing a minimum of risk. The involvement of countless others is an additional disinhibiting factor.
Consider the following account of some of the looting:

Looters of all races owned the streets, storefronts and malls. Blond kids
loaded their Volkswagen with stereo gear; a Yuppie jumped out of his
BMW and scrounged through a gutted Radio Shack near Hancock Park.
Filipinos in a banged-up old clunker stocked up on baseball mitts and
sneakers. Hispanic mothers with children browsed the gaping chain
drug marts and clothing stores. A few Asians were spotted as well.
Where the looting at Watts had been desperate, angry, mean, the mood
this time was closer to a manic fiesta, a TV game show with every looter
a winner. Toting a Hefty bag full of electronic calculators, a 13-year-old
black kid looked up dizzily and said, 'My mom's not gonna believe the
stuff I got today.'
    Richard Cunningham [a store clerk] ... ran 10 blocks from his home
to defend the Wherehouse, from looters who were swiping CDs and

videos ... [He said] 'They don't care for justice, they don't care for anything. Right now they're just on a spree ... They want to live the lifestyle they see people on TV living ... They see people with big old houses, nice cars, all the stereo equipment they want, and now that it's free, they're gonna get it.'[22]

VIGILANTE BEHAVIOUR

In the discussion of bystander behaviour above, I cited research showing that people are frequently reluctant to intervene when a crime is in progress, or even to report a crime to the authorities. On the other extreme are interventions in which citizens violate the rights of others by serving as judge, jury, and sometimes executioner.

The involvement of the public in maintaining 'law and order' has a long history in North America. In Canada as well as the United States, vigilante violence has not only targeted criminals, but has surfaced quite commonly to settle labour disputes and to control ethnic or racial minorities.[23] While classical vigilantism was a response to the lack of specialized, professional law enforcement agencies on the frontier, contemporary vigilantism is often a means to buttress police departments facing an onslaught of crime. Today there are organized groups, such as the Guardian Angels, that patrol subways and other hotbeds of crime in North American urban centres. More common, however, are less formal networks of private citizens who set up Neighbourhood Watch and Patrol programs, which are designed to render residents more vigilant about illicit activities occurring in their communities. These types of programs have been established in all major cities on the continent, as well as in many small towns and even in some rural areas.

Citizens are getting involved in law enforcement to augment existing police services, as there is a growing recognition, acknowledged by many major police departments, that crime prevention and law enforcement can no longer be handled exclusively by the police. Some dramatic incidents in the last few years illustrate the growth of this perception that the police are limited in their ability to control crime alone. These incidents also show the fragility of public order and the readiness of ordinary citizens to mobilize and engage in violent behaviour in order to protect themselves.

In December 1986, there were three shootings of robbers and burglars by shopkeepers in Quebec alone.[24] The convergence of these incidents in time – a few other incidents of vigilante violence by shopkeepers in other parts of Canada occured at about that time – may not be coincidental. Experience with assassination attempts against U.S. presidents and with riots, such as those in U.S. cities in 1967, 1968, and 1992 (to a lesser degree), indicates that these events often cluster in a relatively short span of time.[25] In the case of vigilantism displayed by shopkeepers, the occurrence of one shooting accords a form of legitimacy to such actions and leads other storeowners who are so inclined to be less reluctant to use force in similar incidents. The potential for this type of violence is ever-present; it just takes one or two incidents to make it more acceptable.

Just a few months earlier in 1986, in Montreal, bus drivers were arming themselves with billy clubs, brass knuckles, and cans of mace following a string of shootings, assaults, and robberies of drivers.[26] Many of these incidents occurred when passengers refused to pay the fare and were subsequently challenged by the driver. A study of the Montreal Urban Community Transit Commission has found that a quarter of all passengers fail to pay their fare.[27]

Perhaps the most dramatic incident of vigilante violence in recent memory occurred in New York City on 22 December, 1984, when a subway rider, confronted by four menacing youths, lashed out with a savage fury that provides insight into the psyche of millions of other North American urban dwellers who live in constant fear of victimization.

Case-Study: A Vigilante Becomes a Legend

Bernhard Goetz, a thirty-seven-year-old electronics expert, shot four black teenagers in a New York City subway car after the four youths approached him menacingly and asked him for five dollars. Goetz shot two in the back and stated he would have fired more shots had he not run out of bullets. The very lean, soft-spoken Goetz in no way resembled the tough vigilante of the type portrayed by Charles Bronson in '*Death Wish*.' The bespectacled Goetz appeared in every way to represent the hundreds of thousands of other white-collar New York subway commuters making their way to work.

The story that seemed to override the incident itself was the reaction of the public, particularly New Yorkers, to the shootings. Goetz, as soon as his identity was revealed, gained instant celebrity status. A poll of New Yorkers found that a large majority, including a majority of blacks, approved of the shooting. Some politicians spoke out on his behalf, songs were written about him, and he was celebrated on wall graffiti and T-shirts. Public collections were undertaken to raise money for his defence.[28]

The support for Goetz seems to reflect the public's sense of rage and impotence about the fear they must endure daily on the way to work in many North American cities. In the New York City subway system, it is not only the crime that engenders fear, anger, and indignation; it is the graffiti, vandalism, and constant harassment of passengers for handouts. There is a sense in such places that law and order have broken down and a cynical new order exists – an order in which violence, on the part of both villains and vigilantes, is the norm.

The blood-thirsty crowds present at most of the executions carried out in the United States provide another illustration of how the difference between the law-abiding and lawbreaker may be obscured. Perhaps the most graphic case took place in the winter of 1989 when serial murderer Ted Bundy was executed. A carnival atmosphere prevailed as about 300 people turned out at the institution in Starke, Florida the day the execution was to take place.[29] Members of the crowd guzzled beer, and vendors

'Civilized folk like us gotta be protected from animals like that'

Figure 5   The Bundy Carnival

sold electric-chair pins. Many people also carried tasteless plac-
ards bearing such messages as 'This Buzz is for You' and 'Roast
in Peace' (see figure 5). When prison officials indicated at 7:00
A.M. that the execution had been carried out, the crowd, which
had begun to assemble at midnight, cheered and set off fire-
works. This scene was repeated when the hearse carrying
Bundy's corpse pulled away from the prison grounds.

Such tongue-in-cheek celebrations underline the frustration
of many North Americans about the seeming inability of the
authorities to control violent crime. These displays also reflect
the streak of vengeance present in many of us. They also illustrate that ruthlessness is not confined to the predatory criminal.

11

Understanding the Widespread Criminality of the Public

The efforts to explain human criminality have been long-standing. In the Middle Ages, those violating the moral codes of European countries were often considered to be possessed by demons. A century ago, the first scientific studies were being conducted in criminology. Many of these initial studies supported the idea that criminals were constitutionally inferior beings or mental defectives. Early research also focused on the psychopathology of the offender, and this position remains part of the contemporary criminological landscape. In the past fifty or sixty years, criminologists increasingly have emphasized the environment of the offender: the family environment, the peer group, and the lack of opportunities available to some citizens to participate fully in society.

These different points of view about the roots of criminality have one thing in common: they assume that lawbreakers are in some way a distinct group and that society can roughly be divided into criminal and non-criminal camps. Many social scientists believe in showing compassion towards criminals because they feel that they should not be blamed for psychopathology or for having grown up in an adverse social environment. Nevertheless, even these more liberal scholars do not question the idea that criminals and law-abiding citizens can be clearly distinguished from one another.

In this book I have tried to show that the division of humanity into the two categories of 'criminal' and 'non-criminal' is artificial and must be seriously reconsidered. Research has shown that most people, at one time or another, violate the law, display dishonest behaviour, and/or engage in unscrupulous practices. To be sure, some are more deeply involved in criminality than are others; however, it is argued that criminal involvement is a matter of degree rather than of kind.

If we accept the proposition that virtually everybody violates society's rules, whether it is through violence, employee theft, tax evasion, or improper business practices, then the question 'What makes some people commit crime?' must be posed differently. Stated in this way, the question suggests that crime is an abnormal and unusual event, rather than a commonplace occurrence in everyday life. The question also implies that we need to identify those characteristics that distinguish criminals from the rest of society. In fact, much of the research concerning the causes of crime has tried to do just that. Typically, these studies have compared convicted criminals with civilians on some biological, psychological, and social factors. Most of this research has met with dismal failure.[1] Perhaps this failure to identify a set of characteristics that consistently distinguishes criminals from others is attributable, not to flaws in the research, but to a flawed assumption that there are clear-cut differences to identify. These failures in developing theories of crime suggest that criminality must be viewed in a different way.

I believe that two separate questions can be asked about crime causation. (It should be noted that some criminologists frown upon the term 'cause' and its variants because it suggests that human behaviour is automatic, with people viewed as unable to make choices or to act rationally. I share some of their concerns, as will be apparent later in this chapter. Therefore, I, too, generally avoid using the term.) The first question, and the one with which most of this chapter will be concerned, can be posed as: 'What accounts for the near universality of lawbreaking?' Thus, why is it that most people, in the North American context at least, participate in lawbreaking at some level?

A second question relates to that asked by many traditional criminological theorists. However, rather than asking 'What makes some people commit crime?' one might refine this question to take the following form: 'Why are some people more deeply involved in criminal or antisocial behaviour than others?' Posing the question in this way accepts the premise that criminality is virtually universal, but also recognizes that involvement is not uniform. Many of us are merely opportunistic lawbreakers, but there are those who pursue criminality more seriously and even as a vocation. Career criminals are not merely opportunistic; they are actively seeking out suitable targets for their crimes, whether these targets are banks to rob, women to rape, cars to steal, or citizens to cheat.

People differ not only in the intensity or frequency of their criminal activities, but also in the gravity of those activities. Some people kill and rape; others commit crimes against property only. While some armed robbers have no hesitation about mugging people, others limit their hold-ups to banks and convenience stores. While some employees take small items home from work, others may load up their cars with merchandise. While some business scams may victimize people for $100 or $200, others are designed to separate people from their life savings. Thus, our continuum of criminality must take into account the differential seriousness, as well as frequency, with which people commit their offences.

Efforts to provide answers to the two questions we have posed require very different approaches. The first question requires looking at human nature as well as the cultural values that may prompt large segments of the population to engage in lawbreaking. The second question inevitably requires that we distinguish between individuals and account for their differential behaviour. This does not mean, of course, that differences in criminality observed among individuals are attributable entirely to personality differences. Some of these differences may be explained by varying criminal opportunities.

The remainder of this chapter is concerned principally with the question of why most of us engage in lawbreaking or other unscrupulous behaviour. It will become apparent that part of the answer to this question lies in human nature itself – our imperfection and inevitable diversity. Another part of the answer can be found in those aspects of our cultural life that teach us that aggression and the exploitation of others are acceptable, if not commendable. Situational factors, I hope to show, are also important, as they can facilitate criminality, as well as provide the impetus for it through painful experiences or unexpected opportunities.

The final section of this chapter presents the view that human beings are far from passive actors who merely react to forces within or outside of themselves. People reflect (albeit to different degrees) on their choices and weigh the probable outcomes of their actions. At any given time, they may decide to act criminally if they feel that, in view of their capabilities, values, and the situation at hand, their goals can be met by doing so.

IS CRIMINALITY NATURAL?

The idea that all people are sinners has roots in religious doctrine as well as some prominent philosophical works. In Christianity there has been a preoccupation with Original Sin. All of humanity is said to be born in sin and lives in suffering and pain because the first human pair chose to disobey Divine injunction. Thomas Hobbes, a seventeenth-century English philosopher, echoed this negative view of humans, contending that people were basically brutes destined to pursue their own interests. It was their fear of one another that prompted people to form strong governments, as only in this way could society be prevented from descending into chaos.[2]

Adding another dimension to the argument that crime is inevitable was the French sociologist Emile Durkheim. Durkheim considered crime as a normal condition in society resulting from the inevitable diversity of its members.[3] All individuals, according to Durkheim, deviate to some degree from the rules of social behaviour set by society as a whole. He stated that, if there could be a society in which crime was completely eliminated, it would be so rigid as to eliminate the possibility of progressive social change. Durkheim further argued that crime is a necessary part of social life because the punishment of the criminal enhances the cohesion or solidarity of society's members. Failing to punish the transgressor may weaken the average citizen's overall commitment to the society and his willingness to make the sacrifices necessary to keep it intact. Durkheim asserted that, were crime in its existing forms eliminated, it would be necessary to designate other behaviours as criminal, as punishment serves an essential social function:

> Imagine a society of saints, a perfect cloister of exemplary individuals. Crime properly so called, will there be unknown; but faults which appear venial to the layman will create there the same scandal that the ordinary offence does in ordinary consciousnesses. If, then, this society has the power to judge and punish, it will define these acts as criminal and will treat them as such. For the same reason, the perfect and upright man judges his smallest failings with a severity that the majority reserve for acts more truly in the nature of an offence.[4]

Jeremy Bentham, a leading exponent of what is referred to as the Classical School of criminology, argued that human beings are rational creatures striving at all times to maximize their pleasure and minimize their pain.[5] People, according to Bentham, were hedonistic, and the only way they could be kept from committing crimes was to design a system of punishments such that the pain they could be expected to derive from the punishment would outweigh the potential benefit derived from committing a given offence.

The psychoanalytic perspective of human behaviour, pioneered by Sigmund Freud, also takes the view that people in their 'natural' state are criminals; that is, we are all antisocial and self-centred as infants. If we fail to develop adequate controls over our impulses, we risk leading a life of crime.[6] These controls are of two basic types: *ego control* – whereby a person learns to repress his or her urges when the failure to do so will produce painful consequences (e.g., the possibility of facing arrest and imprisonment) – and *superego control* – whereby a person develops a system of pro-social values that inhibit him or her morally from participating in behaviour that is hurtful to others.

Even a mature adult who has developed adequate controls of both types must constantly wrestle with the tendency of his basic biological urges and impulses to seek expression. Freud said that it was necessary for people to *sublimate* or transform their antisocial and aggressive tendencies into socially productive activities if society's cohesion was to be maintained. He wrote that 'civilization thus obtains mastery over the dangerous love of aggression in individuals by enfeebling and disarming it, and setting up an institution [the superego] within their minds to keep watch over it, like a garrison in a conquered city.'[7] Thus, psychoanalytic theory tells us that humans are not by nature social; they become so through learning to constrain their behaviour in light of the possibility of recriminations from others or themselves.

Harvard psychologist Lawrence Kohlberg has identified six stages of moral development.[8] According to Kohlberg, as people move from one stage to another in their development, they change in their moral orientation or judgment. The level of a person's moral development is said to be related to his or her moral behaviour. The six stages of moral judgment are:

Stage 1: Right is obedience to power and avoidance of punishment.
Stage 2: Right means to take responsibility for oneself, to meet one's own needs and leave to others the responsibility for themselves.
Stage 3: Right is being good in the sense of having good motives, having concern for others and 'putting yourself in the other person's shoes.'
Stage 4: Right means to maintain the rules of a society and to serve the welfare of the group or society.
Stage 5: Right is based on recognized individual rights within a society with agreed upon rules, a social contract.

Stage 6: Right is an assumed obligation to principles applying to all humankind, principles of respect for human personality and justice and equality.[9]

All people are located somewhere on this growth continuum, depending on where the person's development ceased. Kohlberg conducted studies in a number of countries and found that convicted delinquents, for example, usually fall at the first or second stage. Those who are at the first or second stage of moral development are very self-centred and their relationships and dealings with others are frequently based on power. By contrast, those who reach the sixth stage are highly principled individuals, who subscribe to abstract and general principles such as the Golden Rule and universal human rights. Kohlberg's investigations tell us that only 5 to 10 per cent of the population reaches Stage 6 in their moral development.[10] Theories of moral development, such as that of Kohlberg, indicate that people are likely to be egocentric and antisocial in their behaviour unless they have an enlightened moral education (from parents and other role models) and unarrested development.

Travis Hirschi, the American criminologist, has more recently developed a sociological theory, referred to as *control theory*, which shares some elements with psychoanalytic theory in particular. He, too, contends that 'we are all animals and thus all naturally capable of committing criminal acts.'[11] While the psychoanalyst focuses on the need to develop internal psychological controls (ego and superego control) to deal with antisocial impulses, Hirschi focuses on the social bonds between the individual and society. According to him, a person who fails to develop close bonds to family, school, and peer group is more likely to get involved in delinquency and criminality. These bonds take the form of attachment, commitment, involvement, and belief. Attachment refers to affection for and sensitivity to others. Commitment is the stake one has in conventional society and the risk one takes by engaging in criminal activity. Involvement refers to the extent to which one is involved in conventional (i.e., community) activities. Belief refers to the extent to which one subscribes to society's norms. The more one is attached to others, is committed to conventional society, is involved in conventional activities, and believes in society's norms, the less likely is criminal activity to occur because one has much to lose, has little time to engage in such activity, and simply is not motivated to become involved. Thus, social bonding can counter our 'natural' tendency to gravitate towards criminal behaviour.

We have seen in chapter 10 that there may be, in North America as a whole, a widespread indifference to law. We have shown that people are far from eager to intervene when a crime is committed or another is in trouble; that many take advantage of a state of disorder to meet their own needs; and that many even rejoice when somebody like Bernhard Goetz assumes the role of judge, jury, and executioner. It might be safe to say, therefore, that although there are undoubtedly differences from one community to the next, many people in North America are not closely bonded to society and, hence, are potentially indifferent to its laws.

CRIMINALITY AS LEARNED BEHAVIOUR

Psychoanalytic and sociological control theory suggest that criminality is natural and will occur if a person lacks adequate behavioural controls or bonding to society. Many of the offences discussed in this book, however, are not committed because a person is impulsive or insufficiently integrated into society. Scams by employees, tax evasion, hidden-economy trading, fraudulent business practices, computer crimes, political corruption, and corporate crimes can hardly be viewed as impulsive actions. Even many violent crimes, contrary to popular views, involve some element of planning. For example, one of the most comprehensive studies of rape revealed that over 70 per cent were at least partially planned.[12]

In the 1940s, the sociologist Edwin Sutherland argued that much crime, such as that of higher-status individuals, could not be adequately explained by inadequate controls, biological defects, or adverse social conditions. He suggested that people commit crimes simply because they subscribe to values and attitudes, as well as possess skills, conducive to criminal behaviour. Crime, to Sutherland, is normal, learned behaviour, just as is all other human conduct. People violate the law because they come in contact with more people who favour contravening the law than those who adhere to the law. Sutherland's propositions included the following:

1. Criminal behavior is learned in interaction with other persons in a process of communication;
2. The principal part of the learning of criminal behavior occurs within intimate personal groups;
3. When criminal behavior is learned, the learning includes (a) techniques of committing the crime, which are sometimes very complicated, sometimes very simple; (b) the specific direction of the motives, drives, rationalizations, and attitudes;
4. The specific direction of the motives and drives are learned from definitions of the legal codes as favorable or unfavorable. In some societies an individual is surrounded by persons who invariably define the legal codes as rules to be observed, while in others he is surrounded by persons whose definitions are favorable to the violation of the legal codes;
5. A person becomes delinquent because of an excess of definitions favorable to violation of law over definitions unfavorable to violation of law. This is the principle of differential association;
6. The process of learning criminal behavior by association with criminal and anticriminal patterns involves all the mechanisms that are involved in any other learning.[13]

Contemporary learning theorists have extended Sutherland's propositions as they contend that learning is not limited to the interpersonal relationships in which an individual is involved; that is, learning does not take place solely in the context of direct, face-to-face interactions with others. A great deal of experimental research shows that people may be influenced by what they read and see in the mass media. People are more likely to display aggressive or antisocial behaviour, for example,

if they witness others, on television and in the movies, participating in such conduct.[14]

Case-Study: The Impact of Live Models and the Media on Violence

Experimental psychologists have shown the extent to which
conduct can be influenced by what people see directly or in the
electronic media. A large number of experiments have shown
that antisocial behaviour can be learned through exposure to
live models, actors in a film, or cartoon characters behaving in
an aggressive manner.

In a classic study conducted by Albert Bandura and his colleagues, children were matched in terms of their interpersonal
aggressiveness and placed in one of five groups.[15] The first
group observed live adult models behaving aggressively towards
a plastic figure. A second group saw a film of the same models
performing the same aggressive acts. A third group observed the
model dressed as a cartoon cat enacting the same aggressive
acts on a television screen. A fourth group was not exposed to
any models during the experiment, and a fifth group viewed
filmed models behaving in a calm, non-aggressive manner. The
children in all the groups were then mildly frustrated and
brought to a room containing a variety of play materials. There,
the behaviour of the children was recorded.

The researchers found that the first three groups (that had
been exposed to aggressive models) displayed higher levels of
aggression when observed following the exposure. This difference between these three groups and the two control groups
(those not exposed to aggressive models – i.e., groups four and
five) held up for two types of aggression: *imitative aggressive
responses* – those forms of aggression in which the children
emulated the aggressive models (see figure 6) – and *general
aggressive responses* – other forms of aggression displayed by
the children, but not by the models. Thus, not only did the children who were exposed to aggressive models imitate the

Figure 6   Children imitating filmed model

aggressive acts of these models, but the exposure to aggressive models seemed to have what the authors have called a general 'disinhibiting' effect on the behaviour of the children. What they mean is that exposure to the violence of others leads the viewer to conclude that such behaviour is acceptable, particularly when no punitive consequences are incurred by the perpetrator. This situation then opens the door for all kinds of aggressive responses.

A corollary to this finding may be that the more we view others behaving violently with impunity, the more likely it is that our own inhibitions to behave accordingly will be removed. Not only do we come to realize that such behaviour is acceptable, but we also come to believe that there is no risk of punishment or loss of status associated with aggressive behaviour. It is interesting to note, as a final observation regarding the experiment just mentioned, that, of the two control groups, the group exposed to the non-aggressive model displayed less aggression than did the group of children who were not exposed to any model.

Learning theorists also distinguish between the reasons for one's original involvement in a certain type of activity and why it persists. One may shoplift initially to obtain approval from one's peer group. One may continue to shoplift regularly thereafter because one sees the ease with which the theft can be carried out. As the person succeeds in achieving his or her goals, the behaviour, in psychological terms, is *reinforced* and likely to continue as the success is gained without recriminations.

Antisocial conduct can therefore gather its own momentum as the perpetrator finds it rewarding and even habituating. This habituation of people to antisocial activities makes it difficult on a societal level to prevent crime through tackling the so-called root causes alone. It might be that more direct action needs to be taken to break the routine involvement in crime of many citizens by removing criminal opportunities, where possible, and increasing the negative consequences associated with criminal actions.

If criminality is largely learned, we can ask whether North American society provides a climate conducive to crime. The answer, I believe, is clearly in the affirmative. There are many elements in the mainstream culture that encourage antisocial behaviour. There are also some so-called subcultures, such as those found in some U.S. inner cities, in which violence and other forms of criminality are a part of everyday life.

Children growing up in North America learn the dominant cultural themes of their world from a variety of sources: their parents, peers, teachers, the media, political leaders, ministers, and even football or hockey coaches. They learn that the rights and interests of the individual often take precedence over those of the community. In the United States, for example, they learn that the right to bear arms is entrenched in the U.S. constitution and is protected by a very powerful lobby group (the National Rifle Association), even if this right is maintained at the expense of public safety. There may be over 200 million firearms in the hands of ordinary citizens in the United States, and the numbers are climbing in Canada.[16]

The pre-eminent theme of mainstream North American culture is the pursuit of material success: how one arrives at one's fortune or who is exploited along the way is less relevant. The fortunes of many renowned business tycoons have been made through unscrupulous means.[17] In our competitive society, people are taught that, to be successful, they must be aggressive, whether in business or on a football field. We pay mere lip-service to being a good sport, that is, being honest and acting with integrity. Vince Lombardi, the legendary football coach, perhaps expressed our obsession with success best when he stated that 'winning isn't everything, it's the only thing.'

In business, as we saw in chapter 6, dishonesty is a taken-for-granted component of everyday practice. Misrepresentations in advertising and deceptive sales techniques are commonplace. Worthless and even harmful products are marketed, without regard for their social value, through sophisticated promotional schemes. Many of us admire a particularly clever operator or business scam, in many cases identifying with the perpetrator rather than the victim.

Other aspects of the mainstream North American culture are especially conducive to criminality.[18] Although these may be more evident in the United States, they impact Canadian society as well.

Great inequities exist in terms of wealth and opportunities; however, these inequities, in themselves, do not explain high levels of crime. In feudal societies, for example, considerable order tends to exist, despite such inequities, because people learn to accept their position in the feudal order. In North America, however, the disadvantaged are not taught to accept their inferior social status. They are sold the American Dream and are constantly exposed to the conspicuous consumption of the affluent. Success does not merely bring material wealth; it furnishes status as well. The emphasis on success means that those who fail to achieve a measure of it become restless and frustrated, and may then seek out illegitimate means to achieve their goals.[19]

There is also a tradition of resistance to authority rather than blind obedience on this continent. Although more pronounced in the United States, the view that government should interfere only to a minimum in its citizens' affairs is pervasive in Canada as well. Many parts of both countries were settled before strong central governments were established. A tradition of resolving disputes and maintaining order at the grass-roots level emerged, without reliance on governments, armies, or the police. The violence and vigilantism that took hold during those frontier days are still with us. The statement has often been made that crime is 'as American as cherry pie.'

The hostility towards government we see in the emphasis on civil liberties, the existence of paramilitary groups (such as extremist Aryan supremacist groups), and vigilante organizations (e.g., the Guardian Angels) can be found in other realms as well. The tax revolts and general resistance to taxation underline the cynicism towards government initiatives. The very foundation of taxation has been questioned by some extremist groups in the United States. The view is pervasive that the government misuses and wastes 'our' money, and hence it is justifiable to withhold our money from the tax collectors. It is quite obvious that such a philosophy will foster tax evasion. Such individualistic sentiments undercut our ability to identify with other citizens. Once community bonds are undermined, it becomes easier to victimize others, whether such victimization takes the form of violence or business scams.

Yet another cultural element favourable to crime and violence in the North American context is the accent on 'toughness' for males. In U.S. inner-city neighbourhoods, the Southern states in general, and even in western and northern Canada, males are far more likely to be admired for their fighting ability and general physical prowess than, for example, in much of Europe. A boy interested in the fine arts risks ridicule as a 'sissy.' There is also a tradition, in these areas, of weapons possession.

Claude Brown, an African-American writer who grew up in the streets of Harlem, attests to the idea that there are virtual 'subcultures' of violence in the inner core of many U.S. cities.[20] In these communities, every male wishing to be respected as a 'man' must prove his willingness to fight when challenged. Whether he wins or loses is not as relevant as the fact that he defends his honour. In the same way, a man is expected, much as in Medieval Europe, to fight when the reputation of 'his woman' or family has been insulted:

Throughout my childhood in Harlem, nothing was more strongly impressed upon me than the fact that you had to fight and that you should fight. Everybody would accept it if a person was scared to fight, but not if he was so scared that he didn't fight.

As I saw it in my childhood, most of the cats I swung with were more afraid of not fighting than they were of fighting. This was how it was supposed to be, because this was what we had come up under. The adults in the neighborhood practiced this. They lived by the concept that a man was supposed to fight. When two little boys got into a fight in the neighborhood, the men around would encourage them and egg them on. They'd never think about stopping the fight ... Down on 146th street, they'd put money on street fights.

I remember they used to say on the streets, 'Don't mess with a man's money, his woman, or his manhood.' This was the thing when I was about twelve or thirteen. This was what the gang fights were all about. If somebody messed with your brother, you could just punch him in his mouth, and this was all right. But if anybody was to mess with your sister, you had to really fuck him up – break his leg or stab him in the eye with an ice pick, something vicious.[21]

Violence, in certain communities or regions, is a normal response to provocations and stresses, learned by males from their early years on. To demonstrate the extent to which violence is a commonplace phenomenon in some U.S. urban ghettos, Brown writes:

In any Harlem building ... every door has at least three locks on it. Nobody opens a door without first finding out who's there. In the early evening, ... you see people ... lingering outside nice apartment houses, peeking in the lobbies. They seem to be casing the joint. They are actually trying to figure out who is in the lobby of *their* building. 'Is this someone waiting to mug me? Should I risk going in, or should I wait for someone else to come?'

If you live in Harlem, USA, you don't park your automobile two blocks from your apartment house because that gives potential muggers an opportunity to get a fix on you. You'd better find a parking space within a block of your house, because if you have to walk two blocks you're not going to make it. ...

In Harlem, elderly people walking their dogs in the morning cross the street when they see young people coming. ... And what those elderly men and women have in the paper bags they're carrying is not just a pooper scooper – it's a gun. And if those youngsters cross the street, somebody's going to get hurt.[22]

It should not be surprising that criminal involvement is so widespread when our culture contains so many criminogenic (crime-producing) characteristics. Each generation assimilates these cultural elements through observing role models: parents, peers, celebrities, and society's leaders. The last-mentioned are profoundly influential because misbehaviour on their part has a disinhibiting effect on the rest of society. People feel that if society's leaders are dishonest and break the law, it is all right for everyone to do so. Members of the public become demoralized as they have no standards to aspire to with the ascendance of an 'anything goes' ideology.

Consider what *Time* magazine called the 'scandal-scarred' spring of 1987. The misbehaviour of leading political, corporate, and religious figures reached astounding levels. The convergence of scandals in that year could only lead an observer to believe that those involved were not mere 'rotten apples,' but a reflection of a deeper moral malaise. Within the span of several months, the American public bore witness to:

1 / The Iran-Contra scandal, in which the Reagan administration was involved in illegally bypassing Congress, obstructing justice by shredding documents, corruption, and dealing with hostage-takers (violating its most sacred principles).

2 / A leading presidential candidate, Gary Hart, was forced to withdraw from the race as a result of a high-profile, extra-marital affair. Photographs showing him in all kinds of compromising poses were featured in magazines from coast to coast. The young lady in question exploited the publicity by becoming a highly paid model, to the detriment of Hart and his family.

3 / The Bakker affair surfaced. Jim Bakker, leader of the Praise The Lord ministry, was found to have had an adulterous encounter, involving possible coercion, with a church secretary. This secretary eventually posed provocatively in a leading pin-up magazine. Bakker and his wife, Tammy, were also accused of enriching themselves and leading a lavish lifestyle at the expense of the church's followers.

4 / The Boesky 'insider-trading' scandal rocked Wall Street's financial community.

5 / A U.S. Marine guard at the U.S. embassy in Moscow was court-martialled for giving attractive female KGB agents access to highly classified information.

Such highly visible incidents can shake a society at its foundations and lead people to believe that no ethical standards for conduct remain. In such a state of suspended morality or norm-lessness, society becomes a battlefield where the only inhibiting factor is the fear of punishment, and this fear is often neutralized by the low certainty of punishment for most crimes. Widespread exploitation and lawlessness are the not-so-surprising results.

The idea that criminality is learned behaviour is not incompatible with the notion that crime is 'natural.' We have already discussed in this chapter the theories that describe people as being born antisocial and as driven by self-interest. Learning theories, by contrast, do not posit that people are inherently either prosocial or antisocial: people are seen as adopting the values and behaviour they are exposed to in the world around them.

These two very different perspectives can be reconciled much as any 'nature' and 'nurture' theories can be. Both our innate tendencies and our environment have an impact on our behaviour. Even if we subscribe to the idea that people are animal-like and innately motivated by self-interest rather than obedient to laws, there is still room for this tendency to be considerably modified by the environment. Probably the best example of self-interest being subordinated to the concern for the welfare of others is the kamikaze pilots of the Second World War. The very oppressive social pressure these men faced made self-destruction, on behalf of their compatriots, the ultimate noble act. In contrast, the mainstream North American culture I have just described tends to reinforce individualism. Hence, our natural tendency to make our own interests paramount is reinforced by the surrounding culture, providing a recipe for widespread law-breaking and exploitative behaviour.

THE POWER OF SITUATIONS

The susceptibility to crime arising from the forces of nature and nurture does not in itself guarantee that one will behave criminally. Triggering events, whether painful or rewarding, move the individual from a state of readiness to commit crimes to full action.

Human behaviour is not uniform in different situations. Even hard-core criminals are not dishonest or violent in every setting and circumstance. Conversely, those who are generally law-abiding, as we have shown, deviate from this tendency from time to time. An individual may be passive at work and among his friends, and be very abusive at home. A person who shoplifts might never think about stealing from family or friends. The owner of a small chemical company may be very irresponsible in the disposal of toxic waste by his plant, but may get very indignant when he sees his suburban neighbour defacing his street. People are often very selective in who they victimize and the circumstances in which they behave dishonestly or criminally.

In recent years, social scientists have given a greater emphasis to the situational influences on human behaviour. According to a situationist model, people are not viewed as merely responding to 'programming' in their formative years. Rather, their behaviour is seen as fluid and dynamic. Although they may be predisposed to act in a certain way, the circumstances they encounter will also affect the way they act. Some go so far as to say that situations override personality-related factors in their influence over behaviour. Research into the situational factors affecting criminal behaviour has yielded some of the following conclusions:

1 / Dishonesty is more likely when an object is valuable than when it is of low value.[23]

2 / People are more likely to cheat and steal when opportunities are more readily available and when the likelihood of punishment is low.[24]

3 / Cheating is more likely to occur when it is the means to an important goal and when other opportunities to reach that goal are limited.[25]

4 / Victim characteristics affect the likelihood of dishonesty. People find victims that are impersonal (e.g., large businesses) or remote easier to victimize than those with whom they have a face-to-face confrontation.[26] Those who are disliked, have lower social status, or are of the male sex are more likely to be victimized than are those who are liked, have high social status, and are female.[27]

As an example of studies examining the importance of situational or circumstantial factors, let us look at Leonard Bickman's research focusing on the characteristics of a potential victim.[28] In Bickman's experiment, 206 people using specified pay phones in New York City's Grand Central Station and Kennedy Airport were chosen as subjects. Forty-three per cent of the subjects were judged to be of low social status by the research team, and the remainder were judged to be of high status, according to some set criteria. Males and females of both high status and unkempt appearance served as stimulus persons or potential victims in the experiment.

The procedure called for a stimulus person to leave a dime on the shelf in a designated phone booth. He or she then left the booth and observed the behaviour of people (subjects) entering, making sure they noticed the coin. After the subject had been in the booth for about two minutes, the stimulus person approached the subject, tapped on the phone-booth door, and said: 'Excuse me, Sir [Miss], I think I might've left a dime in this phone booth a few minutes ago. Did you find it?' The stimulus person then recorded whether the dime was returned.

One finding was dramatic, illustrating the profound effect situational factors can exercise over dishonest or antisocial behaviour. When the stimulus person was dressed in low-status attire (the men were dressed as blue-collar workers and the women were unkempt), 38 per cent of the subjects returned the dime. However, when the stimulus person was dressed in high-status attire (the men wore suits and the women neat dresses), 77 per cent of the subjects returned the dime. This finding was highly significant statistically, indicating that a person's physical appearance and background can play a role in shaping the behaviour of others towards him or her.

In response to Bickman's study, and others reported in chapter 3, the sceptic might say that, while it is true that behaviour is governed by situations in the sense that people are selective regarding the circumstances in which they will be dishonest, the original impetus or motivation to act dishonestly comes from the person. The sceptic might argue that only those who are dishonest at the outset will respond dishonestly to situations favourable to such behaviour. (In the context of Bickman's study, subscribing to this position would imply that about 40 per cent of the population is dishonest!)

Many advocates of a situationist model of behaviour, however, do not merely argue that certain circumstances provide an outlet for those already motivated to commit crimes. They argue that opportunities or temptations can themselves motivate or stimulate people who initially had no intention of committing a crime. In chapter 10, we discussed looting in the New York City blackout of 1977. Thousands of people, including both those with extensive criminal records and those without any such background, never intended to engage in the looting in which they were eventually to participate. An unexpected opportunity arose, the risks were minimal, and the attitudes in the affected communities were favourable; hence, they were stimulated to act. There are many incidents in which neighbourhood youth, 'hanging out' on the street, are stimulated into action when they notice an opportunity, such as a key left in the ignition of an unoccupied car or a window open in an unoccupied home.

Thus, many crime prevention programs in recent years have focused on reducing the opportunities for crime, rather than on dealing with the 'root' causes. We are told to lock cars and fortify our homes, vandalism-proof materials are developed for buses, and surveillance levels are increased in subways, businesses, and housing projects through such means as short circuit television.[29] These types of programs are predicated on the assumption that opportunities create temptations that may be exploited by those lacking an initial intention to commit a crime (at least on specific occasions, if not generally). It is argued quite logically that, if adverse conditions can push people into crime, rewarding opportunities can pull them in the same direction. It only stands to reason that if negative environmental stimuli influence behaviour by raising the likelihood of criminality, positive (or at least rewarding) stimuli can similarly have an impact on behaviour.

In chapter 3, we discussed some field experiments, including my own, in which lying, cheating, and stealing were literally created or manufactured by the experiment. Subjects were given opportunities to behave dishonestly (without realizing that they were being observed) and often obliged the investigators by acting accordingly. Usually these studies have used members of the general public or college students as subjects, so we can contend with assurance that, as a whole, these subjects had no overpowering commitment to antisocial behaviour. They merely seized upon an opportunity to achieve some personal end (this could be very transient and brought to the surface by the opportunity itself) when one became available.

Case-Study: Ordinary People Following Orders

One series of experiments, relevant to the point that ordinary people can be induced to commit the most heinous acts, was that conducted by social psychologist Stanley Milgram at Yale University in the 1960s.[30] What distinguished his experiments from the field studies discussed in chapter three was that they dealt with more serious conduct than stealing or cheating. Also, while his experiments showed how situations could produce socially harmful behaviour, their focus was on the impact of stresses and pressures of situations, rather than on the criminal opportunities they afforded. A central part of his study was the impact of removing a person's responsibility for his or her behaviour; that is, will telling an individual that he or she is not accountable for any harm he or she causes to another make it more likely that he or she will inflict that harm? Milgram's principal concern was understanding what it was that turned ordinary people into vital cogs in the killing machines of totalitarian regimes such as Hitler's Third Reich.

Milgram advertised for people to participate in what they believed was a learning experiment. These subjects were to act as teachers who were to train 'learners' (these were actually actors) through the help of electric shocks. The 'learner' was strapped into a chair connected to electrodes. When he gave the wrong answer to a question, the 'teachers' were told to issue a shock to the 'learner,' using an elaborate instrument panel which had control switches ranging from 15 to 450 volts. The subject was told to start with a 15-volt shock and to increase the level of shock by 15 volts for each successive incorrect response.

In the initial experiment, 26 of the 40 subjects proceeded to the end of the shock generator (i.e., 450 volts). Many protested to the experimenter, as they escalated the shock levels, that the 'learner' was screaming, and they wanted to stop the experiment. At that point, the experimenter would intervene and command the subject to continue to administer the shocks. As the findings indicate, the subject would usually acquiesce. In reality, no shocks were administered as the contraptions used in the experiment transmitted no electrical currents. Here is an example of one subject's reactions:

150 volts delivered. You want me to keep going?
165 volts delivered. That guy is hollering in there [the next room]. He's liable to have a heart condition. You want me to go (*speech shows agitation*)?
180 volts delivered. He can't stand it. I'm not going to kill that man in there! You hear him hollering. He's hollering? He's hollering! He can't stand it. What if something happens to him? I'm not going to get that man sick in there. He's hollering in there. You know what I mean. I mean, I refuse to take responsibility. He's getting hurt in there. He's in there hollering. Too many left here [referring to shock buttons]. Geez, if he gets them wrong. There's too many of them left. I mean, who is going to take responsibility if anything happens to that gentleman?
(*The experimenter accepts responsibility*) All right.
195 volts delivered. You see he's hollering. Hear that. Gee, I don't know. (*The experimenter says*: The experiment requires that you go on.) I know it does, sir, but I mean-huh-he doesn't know what he's in for. He's up to 195 volts.
210, 225 delivered.
240 delivered: Aw, no. You mean I've got to keep going up with the scale? No, sir, I'm not going to kill that man. I'm not going to give him 450 volts! (*The experimenter says*: The experiment requires that you go on.) I know it does, but that man is hollering in there, sir ...

Despite his protestations, this subject continued to obey the experimenter, proceeding to the very end of the shock instrument. The experiment showed that ordinary people can do serious harm to others when the circumstances are right. In the Milgram studies, the subjects may well have been in awe of the setting (prestigious Yale University) and of the experimenter himself. In addition, many of them may have been influenced (as the subject in the transcript above was) by the statement that they would not be held responsible for whatever harm they caused to the 'learner.' Thus, people are more likely to engage in reprehensible actions if others bear the responsibility for it. They can then adopt the 'Nuremberg' defence, claiming that they had no control over the matter, they were only following orders.

Milgram conducted a number of variations of this experiment. In the original experiment, the 'learner' was in the next room; whereas, in later variations, he was in the same room as the subject ('teacher'). Milgram found, as other research has also shown, that the more remote the potential victim, the more likely we are to cause him or her pain. These experiments therefore show not only that certain circumstances can turn ordinary people into dangerous ones, but that slight variations of these circumstances can magnify or temper the extremity of behavioural responses.

It must be qualified that situations cannot be viewed in isolation but must be seen in interaction with different personality types. Not all of Milgram's subjects obeyed the experimenter. Different people respond differently to the same situation, although the 'average' person is more likely to act in a dishonest, unscrupulous, or violent way in some circumstances than in others.

Just as there are different types of people (e.g., some are more prone to aggression than others), situations similarly differ on a number of dimensions. Situations vary in their strength, that is, the degree to which they can elicit uniform reactions from people. Research has shown that powerful situations are those that lead virtually everyone to construe the relevant events the same way, induce uniform expectations regarding the most appropriate response pattern, provide adequate incentives for the performance of that response pattern, and require skills that virtually everyone possesses.[31]

A good example of such a powerful stimulus or situation would be a red traffic light. Everyone with a driver's permit discerns the colour of the light, and every motorist knows he or she is supposed to stop at a red light. Drivers are motivated to stop, as failing to do so carries strong legal and moral prohibitions and can endanger lives. Finally, every driver has the skill to stop at the light. Situations that are more ambiguous, carry weaker incentives, or require more advanced skills will evoke a wider variety of responses.

Case-Study: College Students in 'Prison'

A good criminological example of a powerful situation was the classic prison simulation experiment undertaken by Stanford University psychologist Philip Zimbardo and his colleagues.[32] The investigators set up a prison-like setting and recruited normal college students (none had a history of crime, emotional disability, physical handicap, or even intellectual or social disadvantage) to perform either as prisoners or as guards. The students were randomly assigned to the two groups, so that they were initially comparable, and their resulting patterns of behaviour were observed.

A 'mock' prison setting was created for the study and the 'prisoners' were placed in barred cells. Administrative procedure in the 'prison' as closely resembled that of a 'typical' prison environment as possible. The behaviour of the participants was recorded on video- and audiotape, through direct observations, daily 'guard' shift reports, interviews, and questionnaires.

The study, lasting almost a week, found that the simulated prison environment had a profound impact on the emotional states of both 'guards' and 'prisoners,' as well as upon the interpersonal interactions both between and within the two groups. The 'prisoners' and 'guards' became increasingly hostile towards one another. Also, as the experiment progressed, 'prisoners' more frequently expressed intentions to harm others. Both groups became more self-deprecating as time went on. Interestingly, the 'prisoners' tended to adopt a more passive response mode, while the 'guards' tended to be more active and to initiate interactions.

Although the experimenters did not permit physical violence to occur, less direct aggressive behaviour and verbal aggression were observed frequently. A number of 'prisoners' had to be released as they manifested extreme depression, crying, rage, and acute anxiety. When the experiment was terminated unexpectedly after six days, the 'prisoners,' who had agreed to participate for up to two weeks, were delighted by their good fortune. The 'guards,' by contrast, were distressed by the decision to stop the experiment because they appeared to have become so involved in their roles that they now enjoyed the control and power they exercised and were reluctant to give them up.

Here are a few representative comments of the participants following the experiment:

GUARD: 'looking back, I am impressed with how little I felt for them ...'

GUARD: 'Acting authoritatively can be fun. Power can be a great pleasure.'

PRISONER: 'The way we were made to degrade ourselves really brought us down and that's why we all sat docile toward the end of the experiment.'

PRISONER: 'I began to feel that I was losing my identity, ... that the person who volunteered to get me into this prison ... was distant from me, was remote until finally I wasn't *that* person, I was 416.'

PRISONER: 'I learned that people can easily forget that others are human.'

Thus we can see that, where there are powerful constraints in a situation, behaviour may change dramatically as people play out their prescribed roles. In an extreme environment, this type of adaptation may be a matter of survival. In everyday life, we still adapt our behaviour, although less fully, in order to achieve our goals.

CRIME AS GOAL-ORIENTED BEHAVIOUR

Most traditional theories of crime have seen the criminal as responding quite automatically to biological, psychological, or social needs or deficits. In this section, I argue that, while behaviour is certainly influenced by constitutional factors, social privations, and the like, criminality is ultimately a choice designed to achieve certain goals. It is not merely a response to past events. I see humans as active agents, giving meanings to and shaping the world, while at the same time being shaped by it. Before expanding on this view of criminality, let us review what has been said thus far.

First, some theories were introduced advancing the view that people are innately criminal. According to psychoanalytic theory and sociological control theory, for example, human beings are basically antisocial and will pursue their own interests unless internal or social controls are established. Thus, these theoretical perspectives hold that people by nature are potential lawbreakers.

It was then asserted that this potentiality is most likely to be realized if people learn, in interaction with others and from other role models, attitudes and skills favourable to criminal behaviour. In a society or milieu where individualism, violence, corruption, and anti-authority values are promoted, people will tend to incorporate these values and quite 'naturally' act accordingly. What they have learned will often be played out in their daily lives.

Also discussed was the manner in which situations can transform the person from a state of readiness to full criminal behaviour. Considerable evidence shows that people may respond criminally to temptations, opportunities, and stresses that are favourable to criminality. Whether that criminal response takes place depends on the individual's assessments of his or her chances of meeting some goal(s) – these goals may be quite fleeting. Such an assessment may take into account a whole host of factors: the expected gain derived from a given criminal act; the risks of punishment or danger involved; the degree of inconvenience; moral considerations; and many other situational factors.[33] Seen in this way, criminality is merely an extension of everyday decision making. While it is a problem for society, criminal activity represents a solution – occasionally a desperate and self-destructive one – to the perpetrator's problems or the attempt to achieve some fleeting objective.

This view of criminality is certainly compatible with the observation that virtually everyone is a lawbreaker, because it assumes that people will commit crimes when they feel it is in their interest to do so. It is also compatible with the theories we have reviewed. Psychoanalytic, moral development, and social control theory portray humans as driven by self-interest in their 'natural' state. Social learning theory tells us that people will persist in behaviour, including criminality, that results in rewarding outcomes. Situational theories stress the influence of situational factors on human behaviour.

Is criminality merely another problem-solving strategy, much like other decisions people make (e.g., to change jobs, re-enter school, or get a divorce)? Although the consequences may be very different, I will argue that there is one basic common denominator: all these decisions seek to achieve goals relevant to the individual. These goals may be ephemeral or long-term, well thought-out or poorly articulated. Whatever the case, they are a key to understanding the direction behaviour will take at a given time.

Seeing criminality as goal-oriented behaviour makes two assumptions that are at odds with many conventional theories of crime. The first assumption is that humans are decision makers, assessing their options and selecting the course of action likely to yield a favourable outcome. The second assumption of the perspective I am about to present is that people have some measure of control over their behaviour: they attach meanings to events, make choices after weighing options, and impact their environment with their actions.

Humans as Decision Makers

The view of criminals held by much of the public, many scholars, and even by many career criminals of themselves is that of a person who does not reflect on his or her actions and is highly impulsive, and basically out of control. In fact, many of the major theories in criminology and the social sciences in the last century have left little room for human rationality.

These theories, whether they have focused on the biological, psychological, or social factors underlying crime, have tended to view people as helpless organisms responding passively to forces around them. People have been viewed as essentially incapable of self-determination or rationality of any kind. Cesare Lombroso and Ernest Hooton believed that some people were lower-grade human beings destined for a life in crime by their genetic inferiority.[34] The orthodox Freudians believed, and some of them still believe, that criminality is an expression of neurotic conflicts of which the person may be largely unaware.[35] B.F. Skinner and the radical behavioural psychologists have taken the view that behaviour is largely under environmental control, governed by the extent to which it has been reinforced (there are rewarding consequences) during the person's life history.[36] The Marxists claim that capitalism and economic inequality inevitably lead to crime.[37] These and other models of human behaviour have left little room for personal choice.

By contrast, long before these theories were advanced, there was a widely held view that people were accountable for their actions; hence, society had the right to punish them. The 'social contract' writers of the seventeenth and eighteenth centuries, such as Hobbes, Rousseau, and Montesquieu, all subscribed to the notion of a free will.[38] There were, according to these writers, virtually no limitations in the choices a person could make.

Jeremy Bentham, the English philosopher writing in the eighteenth and nineteenth centuries, in some respects carried this idea of a free will even farther.[39] He argued that people were basically hedonistic, trying to maximize their pleasure and minimize their pain at every turn. To Bentham, the key to preventing crime was to raise the prospect of pain beyond that of the pleasure to be obtained from committing a criminal act. He argued that everybody makes rational choices and will refrain from a given crime if the expected punishment outweighs the expected gain from the crime.

Few criminologists today would subscribe to such an extreme

position. Very few people so rationally calculate the pros and cons of any action, particularly criminal conduct. Furthermore, the pleasure derived from a given criminal act and the pain accruing from selected punishments are very subjective. One person robbing a bank may enjoy not only the monetary gain but the sense of power the crime affords; another would derive pleasure or satisfaction from the monetary gain only, a third person would derive no pleasure at all from such an act and may even experience pain through remorse.

The view that behaviour has a rational element has made a comeback of sorts in contemporary criminology. The current view is that there is a middle ground between the belief that people are fully rational and the view that people merely respond to forces (biological, psychological, social, economic) beyond their control, without any reflection whatsoever of the options available or of the consequences. As I will show, the most extreme acts have a rational component. At the same time, few decisions that people make of any kind (e.g., career decisions, the decision to get married) are fully rational in the sense that they involve a careful weighing of all possible options and consequences. The middle ground between zero and full rationality has been termed 'limited rationality.'

Maurice Cusson, a criminologist at the University of Montreal, tells us that full rationality is rarely found in concrete situations because people do not always have clear objectives, situations limit choice, and full information is usually lacking.[40] In terms of objectives, people rarely have clearly defined goals. Considerable exploration is involved, and people often do things, including committing crimes, because others do them. In Cusson's view, people will do what will give them the most satisfying results, rather than move towards clear, predetermined goals. The idea that situations limit choice is obvious but must be stated: people cannot strive to achieve anything they want, and their circumstances and abilities limit the means available to achieve their objectives. These limitations, as we will discuss, will influence whether a person commits an offence at a given time and place, as well as the type of offence. As far as information is concerned, human behaviour is rarely completely rational, because to be so it would need to include a careful weighing of all possible means of achieving a particular end and the consequences of each of these means. Nobody knows, for example, the precise likelihood of succeeding or, conversely, of getting caught prior to a criminal offence.

Thus, criminality and other forms of human behaviour rarely approach pure rationality. At the same time, behaviour varies greatly in terms of the clarity of goals, options available, and the degree to which options and consequences are known and considered.

Cusson's bottom line is that, whatever the degree of rationality, criminality is chosen as a means to achieve certain results or meet certain goals rather than being a response to past experience:

> If we are to believe detective stories, when a detective is investigating a murder he first looks for the motive: what was the purpose of the crime? It is a natural bent of the human mind to start looking for the objective, the goal. What did the criminal want? – revenge? the victim's money? It is only later that the cause of the act will be investigated: psychological problems? poor upbringing? bad company?
>
> This is also what comes to the delinquent's mind when he is asked: why did you do it? His spontaneous answer will be: 'For kicks'; 'Because I needed the money'; 'In self-defence.' It is only after he has been in contact with psychologists, social workers, and criminologists that he will learn to reply: 'Because I was unhappy at home' or 'Because I had guilt feelings.'[41]

The idea that perpetrators of crime make conscious decisions has been shown in the experiments and research cited in this book. When contemplating crimes, people consistently show that they are responsive to situations: the potential profit, the degree of risk, the characteristics of the potential victim, the presence of others. As I have shown, even career criminals tend to draw the line at certain forms of conduct. Some armed robbers, for example, have told us that they will not take inordinate risks and will not hold up small businesses (see chapter 9). Nor will most of them molest small children. They have thus set certain decision rules about the circumstances under which and the manner in which they will proceed. Very few, if any, perpetrators commit crimes randomly and without any reflection. The planning of most crimes may not be extensive, but at least some hasty decisions are made about whether, when, where, and how to commit crimes.

Scholars such as Ronald Clarke at Rutgers University have just in the last few years begun the process of analysing offender decision making.[42] Clarke believes we must understand decision making at three levels. First, why people choose crime in the first place. Second, why a given crime is committed at a given time and place, as nobody commits crimes all the time. Third, why some people persist in crime while others never repeat their offences. Although my premise is somewhat different – I feel that practically everyone chooses crime at some point in his or her life – I agree with Clarke that crime is a choice and that it is important to unravel the factors that determine choices people make at the three levels mentioned. To say that crime is a choice is not to suggest that it is a fully rational one.

Thus crime, according to the perspective of limited rationality, is seen as a choice that people take, given their assessment of their circumstances, at a given time. This choice presumably can be made by anybody when the expected rewards of committing a crime outweigh the gains expected from other actions.

Humans Exercise Control Over Their Actions

To demonstrate that all human behaviour, including criminal behaviour, is designed to meet personal goals, we must show not only that people are capable of making choices but that they can orient their behaviour in the direction of these goals. The view that people react passively to inner needs and environmental stimuli, in some preordained fashion, is anachronistic. This view of humans as mere pawns, responding at every turn to forces beyond their control, is still implied by many biogenetic, psychological, and sociological theories of crime.

If people were mere pawns, at the mercy of their childhood environment or their genes, they would be able neither to overcome adversity nor to change. Humans have shown that they could blossom in the most oppressive conditions. In the most disadvantaged neighbourhoods, many residents grow up to be fairly productive members of society. As for change, studies of career criminals show that some do abandon entirely a life in crime.[43]

While it is true that we cannot do a great deal at this time to alter our genetic endowment, we can exercise considerable control over environmental forces that may lead us to engage in crime. This chapter has discussed some of these forces: cultural values, peer influence, the media, situational factors. Although people may have less control over some aspects of their environment, such as their family of origin – even here, many young people manage to remove themselves from highly dysfunctional homes – they exercise considerable control over others. We can choose the friends we associate with, the type of programs and films we watch, and many of the situations we encounter. Not all ghetto youth join violent street gangs. We also have a say in whether we watch Rambo and Dirty Harry movies, read romance novels, or spend our leisure time playing sports or a musical instrument.

Similarly, we have a choice in terms of the specific situations to which we are exposed. Although these choices are not unlimited, they are significant. Research over the last ten to fifteen years indicates that lifestyles affect one's likelihood of committing crimes or being victimized.[44] The more one is out at night, interacting with strangers, 'hanging out' in bars, and perhaps buying or selling illicit drugs, the more likely it is that one may be drawn into violent confrontations. While it is the situation that serves as the context for the instigation of the problem, it is the person who has chosen to enter the potentially dangerous context.

Thus, while an individual may be goaded into a fight in a particular bar, he has chosen both to enter the bar and to become involved in the fight. Entering any bar elevates one's risk of being provoked in some way and entering a tough bar with a history of violence elevates one's risk considerably. Similarly, the meaning one attaches to a provocation will shape one's response to it. A racial slur originating from an intoxicated patron can be taken as a personal insult or dismissed as the ranting of a degenerate. Somebody who perceives such a slur as an affront to his manhood or race is more likely to respond with force.

A perspective in psychology referred to as the 'cognitive approach' tells us that no environmental stimulus has the power, in itself, to evoke only one type of behavioural response. Cognitive psychologists tell us that we control the way we react, emotionally and behaviourally, to any event by the way we view it.[45] No event inherently and inevitably leads to only one type of reaction. The loss of a job can be seen as evidence of our worthlessness or as an opportunity to grow. A divorce can be seen as devastating or as providing one relief from a turbulent marriage. A physical handicap can be seen as incapacitating or as providing a challenge. Peer pressure to commit a crime can be viewed as irresistible or as reflecting immaturity and self-destructiveness on the part of our associates. Economic disadvantage can be taken as a sign of our hopelessness or seen as surmountable. Clearly, the way we view events will have a powerful impact on the way we respond to them.

People therefore exercise some choices over the environments in which they find themselves, and they give meanings to the specific situations they encounter. Rather than merely responding passively to the environment, they make choices and draw interpretations. This is the meaning of the term 'interaction.' The environment sets certain limits, and people shape it within those limits. In a similar way, people set limits about the situations they will encounter and define what these situations mean.

Case-Study: Rape and Suicide as Rational Acts

To demonstrate concretely that crime has a rational element

and is goal-oriented, let us take the most extreme examples: behaviours thought by many to be highly irrational – rape and suicide.

The popular conception of the rapist is of a person who is full of rage and is sadistic. Rape is usually viewed as a spontaneous or explosive act, in which the offender responds to his irresistible sexual impulses in a dramatic and brutal style. Actually, most rapes involve at least some hasty planning on the part of the offender.[46] In fact, serial rapists often stalk the victim for a considerable amount of time. They may also equip their cars and homes in such a way as to prevent the victim's escape.

Victim selection is also anything but a random process. Many studies have pointed out that the potential victim's dress, demeanour, language, reputation, and drinking may affect the likelihood of her victimization.[47] To say this is not to engage in victim blaming but to suggest that the offender is tuned in to cues emitted by the potential victim. In the eyes of the potential offender, the more provocatively a prospective victim is dressed, the more flirtatious her behaviour, the more she uses coarse language, and the more intoxicated she is, the more amenable to sexual relations and the less entitled to respect she will be perceived to be.

During the incident itself, the perpetrator is constantly evaluating the situation and is not in some crazed state. Most rape attempts begin with verbal threats or intimidating gestures. Studies tell us that, if the victim resists actively, the offender will either escalate the level of violence or flee the situation. This finding indicates that the offender takes into account the victim's behaviour and does not simply act on his own impulses. The goal is to succeed, but only if the risks are manageable.

Multiple rapes, or those in which there is more than one offender, tend to involve greater sexual humiliation and brutality against the victim.[48] One might speculate that the presence of their peers might lead the perpetrators to try to outdo each other in sexual prowess and sadism.

Thus, the victim's behaviour and characteristics, the presence of others, and other situational factors can affect both the likelihood of a rape and the eventual outcome. These factors are taken into consideration by the potential rapist; he is not merely driven by internal needs. Rape involves a whole process of planning and adapting to circumstantial factors, while achieving objectives such as dominance and status.

Suicide is perhaps the most extreme form of human behaviour, not only in view of its finality but because it violates the tendency of all living organisms towards self-preservation. Despite the extremity of suicidal behaviour, however, there are many indications that those who kill themselves do not do so without due consideration of the act and its consequences. Very few suicides are carried out on a whim. The fact that people who kill themselves have for long contemplated doing so is demonstrated by the fact that about two-thirds have, at least on one previous occasion, made a serious attempt to kill themselves.[49] In addition, most of those who have committed suicide have communicated this intention to others, whether openly or more subtly. Yet another indication that these people are very conscious about the implications and consequences of their behaviour can be found in the notes they frequently leave behind. These notes do not merely provide a reason for the suicide; they are usually designed to have some impact on the individual's survivors (e.g., to punish survivors or relieve them of guilt). Consider the following suicide note left behind by a thirty-eight-year-old woman:[50]

Bill,
You have killed me. I hope you are happy in your heart, if you have one, which I doubt. Please leave Rover with Mike. Also leave my baby alone. If you don't, I'll haunt you the rest of your life and I mean it and I'll do it. You have been mean and also cruel. God doesn't forget those things and don't forget that. And please no flowers; it won't mean anything. Also keep your money ... You know what you have done to me. That's why I did this. It's yours and Ella's fault, try and forget if you can. But you can't ...

Your wife

Suicidal people (both those who make attempts and those who are successful) often may be emotionally distraught, but their behaviour is designed to achieve certain goals other than their own demise. In the note quoted above, we can see that suicide was regarded as the best means of not only ending the woman's pain but, at the same time, taking revenge on her ex-husband.

In England and Wales, suicides dropped measurably from 1960 to 1975 following a program to remove carbon monoxide from the domestic gas supply. In 1960, about half the suicides occurred with the help of domestic gas, which at that time contained a lethal proportion of carbon monoxide.[51] By 1975, by which time carbon monoxide had been almost completely eliminated from the domestic gas supply, gas suicides had virtually disappeared. However, the overall decline in numbers of suicides shows that people did not simply substitute other means of suicide, probably because few were as accessible and painless as the domestic gas had been.[52] Thus, even people seemingly bent on killing themselves will weigh the relative discomfort of the different means available. Suicidal people, therefore, consider both the means available and the consequences of engaging in this ultimate act.

TOWARDS A THEORY OF UNIVERSAL LAWBREAKING

Why do most people violate the law and other social rules, at least on occasion? Figure 7 summarizes the underlying and situational factors, as well as decision-making processes involved in criminal violations. A person's degree of readiness to engage in criminal or other offensive behaviour is shaped by both natural and sociocultural factors. In some regions (e.g., where violent subcultures prevail) or in relation to certain forms of crime (tax crimes), a large proportion of the population may be highly susceptible to violating the law. This susceptibility can then be triggered or brought out by various situational stimuli. These stimuli can be aversive (provocation or stress) or rewarding

Degree of Readiness to Commit Crime	Situational/Instigating Factors
Susceptibility to crime shaped by: 1) *Natural Criminogenic Factors* – Innate antisocial and aggressive tendencies (people vary here) – Natural pursuit of self-interest – Criminalization of inevitable human diversity 2) *Learning of Criminal Behaviour* – Criminogenic aspects of one's immediate milieu and surrounding culture – Scandals and other events that desensitize and disinhibit behaviour – Habituation to crime	Criminality facilitated by: – Incentives/expected profits – Low risks – Provocation – Anonymity of offender – Stress/pressures – Altered responsibility – Victim depersonalization – Criminogenic social roles – Justifications

Decision/Action
Choice of crime influenced by: – Personal goals and anticipated success of achieving them through crime – Legitimate versus illegitimate means available to achieve goals – Appraisal of situation (meaning, profit-risk ratio, suitable targets) – Moral repugnance of act contemplated – Commitment to conformity

Figure 7   Factors contributing to widespread criminality

(financial incentives and low risks), or make the behaviour in question more acceptable (altered responsibility, victim depersonalization, and situationally induced justifications).

Both a person's readiness to commit a crime and the situation will influence the ultimate decision taken. This decision-making process, of course, is neither completely rational nor need it span more than a few minutes or even seconds. Here the person weighs such things as personal goals, risks, potential profits, alternatives available, the moral acceptability of the act, and what

he or she has to lose by engaging in it. Some of these considerations (e.g., personal goals and one's stake in conformity) are
more enduring elements and are not weighed on every occasion.

Put simply, people stray from a law-abiding path, on occasion
at least, because they feel that it is in their interest to do so, that
certain desired results will be achieved. Risk takers and outright
reckless individuals, of course, will spend less time evaluating
their goals, the means available, and the consequences of their
actions than will more prudent people. It is inevitable, however,
that even those who are stable and usually conform will find
that, from time to time, their interests clash with the law, with
society's interest, organizational rules, or community values.
How does the individual then respond?

Obviously, there will be a variety of responses. It will take
fewer incentives for the chronically antisocial individual to violate the law than for Joe Average to do so. Remember, though,
that we are trying to understand why middle-of-the-road people
break the law on occasion. Our concern is with the overwhelming majority of citizens, not the 10–15 per cent of the population
who are either extreme conformists or habitual rule-breakers.

Take the case of Grace, a salesperson at a large department
store. She would like a particular type of winter coat that is carried in the section in which she works. She cannot afford to buy
the coat and knows that, with a little bit of finesse, she could
wear it right out of the store following her shift. Does she steal
the coat?

Self-interest, I have argued, is a strong motivator for all
human beings (see the discussions of the Classical School, psychoanalytic, and control theories). But self-interest is complex
and is not removed from the social and cultural context in which
Grace lives. The coat has no inherent value, other than to keep
her warm, but Grace has other coats. Our materialistic culture
and, perhaps, the importance of fashion among her associates is
what makes the coat of value to her (cultural and learning theories). *Most property crime, in Western societies, at least, is not
motivated by some basic or essential need; it is motivated by a
perception of need and a sense of entitlement.*

Grace must weigh her desire for the coat against other considerations or interests. What is her stake in conformity; in other words, what does she have to lose by stealing the coat (control theory)? If she gets caught, she may lose her job and the esteem of her family and friends, and even suffer a decline in her self-esteem. The more important these are to her, the less likely it is that she will take the coat. Then again, the repercussions may not be severe if her employer tends to downplay such transgressions – providing no more than a verbal reprimand – or even ignores such conduct to avoid antagonizing employees or for other reasons. That type of posture, not an uncommon one, would have the effect of legitimizing theft (social learning theory) and reducing her risks (situational factors). Furthermore, the costs of getting caught would be further reduced if her family, friends, and/or work associates condoned or engaged in similar behaviour (social learning theory and differential association).

Social circumstances, too, may influence her decision (situational factors). If Grace has just been spurned by a boyfriend, she may desperately want to cultivate a new image to enhance her self-esteem. She may feel she is compelled to steal the coat because of this profound emotional need and her inability to purchase it. Given her readiness to commit the crime, her evaluation of her own skills and the probability of getting caught will be pivotal in her decision as to whether to commit the crime.

Situations, as discussed earlier in this chapter, can also serve as the impetus for crime. Occasionally we are confronted with an unexpected opportunity, quickly appraise the situation, and then seize that opportunity. John, who works in the warehouse of the store at which Grace is employed, may be unloading television sets from a delivery truck. Following his shift, he notices that one set, still in its case, has accidentally been left on the ground outside the warehouse. The store is closed, the truck is locked, and his car is parked only a few feet away. He thinks about how that set would look in his family room, sees no one present, drives his car around, and puts the set inside.

The types of factors mentioned in these examples are applicable in all kinds of crime, whether premeditated or fairly spontaneous, whether acquisitive or aggressive. We could apply the same analysis to domestic violence, armed robbery, or tax evasion. Even violent crimes and spontaneous offences, such as that of John, involve some hasty decisions and some awareness of means available and consequences. It is interesting to see how many wife batterers, whose behaviour is apparently out of control, suddenly gain control over their behaviour when they face criminal charges.[53]

People also make 'standing decisions' that apply across many situations. Most of us draw the line at certain behaviours and, hence, decision making can be quite rapid when we are confronted with a sudden opportunity. Some people will not take anything that does not belong to them. Others will take only things that fall into their laps. Still others will take only small items. There are also those who will take anything. We also have boundaries as far as the amount of aggression we consider acceptable, the permissable targets of our aggression or acquisitiveness, the circumstances justifying criminality, and so on. We will judge opportunities in light of the boundaries we have set. Having few or no boundaries is also a decision a person takes.

Virtually all human beings will decide, at one point or another, that it is in their interest to commit a crime. These decisions can still be influenced by social policy. Chapter 14 contains a discussion of how opportunities, social conditions, and attitudes favourable to crime can be modified in order to reduce participation in antisocial behaviour. Chapter 12 leads into that discussion by addressing how we can predict the extent of the public's involvement in a given crime at any particular time.

12

Predicting the Prevalence of Different Crimes in Society

In chapter 11, I explained why it was that lawbreaking was so widespread. In this chapter, I will show how a society can predict the prevalence or extent of participation in any crime, at a given time. Thus, the predictive model or system I will present can tell us what proportion of the population will engage in homicide, employee theft, tax evasion, computer crimes, and other crimes. Attempts have been made to forecast rates of crime, but that is very different from predicting the proportion of the population engaging in various offences. We may know that 1,000 burglaries have taken place in a community, and not know whether those burglaries were committed by 20 or 500 people. The implications for prevention and social policy will be dramatically different in the two cases. Few criminologists have thus far attempted to predict the extent of involvement in different crimes.

In presenting this predictive model, I will draw upon some of the theory already discussed, but will focus on predicting rather than explaining. I am not going to attempt to predict the prevalence or extent of involvement in various crimes to the nearest percentage point. I merely wish to present a system that can very roughly indicate whether the extent of the public's involvement in a crime will be very considerable, moderate, or negligible. Researchers in the future can, if they desire, work on refining these predictions.

According to my predictive model, four very basic conditions must be met in order for a crime to occur:

1 / The offence must meet some need or goal sought by the perpetrator.
2 / An opportunity to commit that offence must exist, along with an acceptable level of risk.
3 / The individual in question must possess the requisite skills to commit the offence.
4 / The individual's proclivities and attitudes, at the time of the offence, must be favourable to its commission.

I discuss these four elements of crime in detail below. They are relevant to all crime and disreputable behaviour and, hence, apply to criminality by the public at large. I will try to show that the more widespread the need to commit a given crime, the more prevalent the opportunities, the fewer the skills required to commit that crime, and the more favourable social attitudes are towards its commission, the more widespread involvement in that offence will be.

NEED

In chapter 11, I tried to establish that human behaviour is goal-oriented, even if the goals are often hazy and poorly articulated. Thus, people pursue their needs, whether these are biologically determined or influenced by our interpersonal relationships and the surrounding culture.

'Needs,' as referred to here, are those perceived by the individual. However perverse a person's behaviour or needs may appear to an observer, to understand the behaviour we must understand the person's needs from his or her point of view. Clearly, some 'objective' needs that apply to all human beings exist. Psychoanalysts talk about 'instincts,' some psychologists about 'drives,' and sociological control theorists about all humans being 'animals.' Most would agree that there is a strong innate tendency in people towards self-preservation, which entails obtaining enough food and shelter to survive.

There are also sexual needs and, some would argue, the need to propagate the species. Others would argue that there are still higher needs, such as those for intimacy and self-actualization. Food, shelter, and sex, however, are unquestionable biological needs. Although they apply to all humans, they are not uniform in the extent to which they motivate different people. People vary in the amount of food they need, in their shelter requirements (e.g., as determined by tolerance of extreme climatological conditions), and in the power of their sexual needs (as determined by health, hormone levels, etc.).

Even these basic biological needs are influenced by the surrounding social conditions and culture. People can show remarkable adaptability to shortages of food, for example, so long as others around them are in the same boat. Crime rates have frequently declined during wartime and economic depressions, indicating that people tend to pull together when they collectively face adversity.[1] Disaster research also shows that people tend to pull together and display all forms of altruistic behaviour in dealing with their common misfortune.[2]

These findings suggest that, beyond the subsistence level, needs in even these basic areas tend to be defined not by what people have, but by what others have and by what people feel they deserve. This is the idea of *relative deprivation*: we judge our plight relative to others. If others are similarly deprived, we may not be happy, but we will tend to accept our situation, at least temporarily. If, however, we perceive that our plight is the result of injustices and the monopolization of resources by some group in society, we tend to become restless. Studies of revolutions show that many occur when standards of living are actually improving, but these improvements are not commensurate with rising expectations.[3] Studies of countries with low crime rates show that the differences between rich and poor are less pronounced than in countries with higher rates.[4] Thus even basic needs are influenced by what others have and by that to which we feel entitled.

The surrounding culture also colours our needs along material and sexual lines. It has been said, for example, that materialism is paramount in the mainstream North American culture – ostentatious homes, cars, clothing, as well as the consumption of many other goods that could be considered luxury items or serve as status symbols. Individuals growing up in North America are more likely to assimilate these values than are those living in a less materialistic culture. People lacking easy access to highly valued goods through legitimate means may turn to crime to fulfil these needs.[5] This relativity of needs explains why most household burglaries involve the theft of stereos and other electronic equipment, alcohol, and other non-essentials, rather than basic food and clothing.[6] Although some burglars convert these items into cash, most do not belong to professional rings but are youngsters stealing items for their personal use.

In terms of materialism, I was struck by the number of my informants who attributed criminality to pure greed. My informants from Revenue Canada and the Better Business Bureau, on employee theft, the automobile-repair industry, and in the restaurant business kept alluding to greed as the primary motivating factor underlying illegalities in these different sectors. In my student days in criminology, I was taught to believe that people usually commit economic crimes in response to disadvantage and desperate need. Then, upon closer inspection of the facts, we discover that most tax crimes are committed by the well-to-do; that stealing by employees, not the unemployed, is probably the most common form of theft; that shoplifting cuts fairly evenly across all sectors of society; that dishonest practices abound in everyday business life; and that people who loot and burglarize, and even those committing armed robberies, usually take, or use the proceeds of their crimes to obtain, non-essential items.

Unlike raw need, greed is by definition insatiable. No matter what legitimate opportunities are available to him or her, the individual driven by greed will continue to commit crimes, and these crimes may even increase in magnitude as the person gains more power and affluence (the Helmsleys and the Marcos family are cases in point). The more a culture glorifies the unfettered accumulation of wealth and consumption, the more likely it is that people will be prepared to act criminally and unscrupulously, regardless of their employment opportunities and economic situation. Wealth, after all, is a symbol of status and power.

By contrast, some people subscribe to values that deviate from those of the mainstream culture. Rather than living a life of self-denial and hard work, some favour alternative lifestyles involving instant gratification. Many armed robbers, for example, use the proceeds of their crimes for recreational activities: drugs, parties, travelling, and the like, rather than to meet basic or even materialistic needs.[7] Whether these amount to alternative goals and lifestyles or merely a reaction to a sense of hopelessness is to some degree an academic question. One way or the other, people pursuing kicks and a life in the 'fast lane' are more likely to turn to crime regularly as a means of sustenance and of achieving their ends.

Cultural values can also moderate or magnify another biological need – the need for sexual relations. Some cultures promote more sexual exploration than others. Residents of some Islamic countries, for example, view North Americans as highly promiscuous, whereas North Americans tend to view the mores of strict Islamic countries as prudish. The more the popular images from which people take their cues promote sexual conquest rather than mutually satisfying relations, and the more sex is fused with power and aggression, the more likely it is that people of both sexes will use sex as a vehicle to some other end, exploiting others in the process. In some cultures more than others, for example, the worth of a man is closely bound to his ability to have sexual relations with a large number of women. He may also achieve status in some milieu for his ability to control women. In such contexts, the need to exploit women can be a powerful driving force, and such exploitation will be commonplace.[8]

Other needs also can lead to criminality: the need for action, vengeance, the release of aggression, and self-defence.[9] In the case of vengeance and self-defence, the need can be understood only in relation to others. Thus it is a fear of or anger towards others that can create the need to strive for revenge or engage in defensive aggression. Consequently, situations can create needs.

The example of blackout looting in chapter 10 illustrated how a sudden opportunity could generate needs for all kinds of items looters never contemplated acquiring. Anybody who has bought a house knows how obsessive the quest for a new house becomes when a family suddenly realizes that, because of a raise in salary or a drop in prices or interest rates, it can afford one. Needs cannot be seen, therefore, as preordained or fixed. People, as well as their circumstances, change, and their needs are consequently reassessed on an ongoing basis.

We may not even be aware of certain needs or may be loath to admit them. Many, if not all of us, have the need to assert our power and, perhaps, even to dominate others. In some cases, this power can be exercised in a benign way. A corporate executive, an army general, or a college professor can be easy-going because power resides in the position itself. Somebody lacking access to such positions may have to take more radical steps to achieve a sense of power and self-worth.

The quest for power and domination underlies much criminal behaviour, even if on the surface the crime appears to be motivated by other factors. Armed robbery, for example, would appear to be motivated purely by economic factors. Armed robbers, however, have told us the following when interviewed: 'when I have a gun in my hand nothing can stop me. It makes me feel important and strong. With a revolver you're somebody' and 'It's funny to see the expression of people when they have a .38 in their face. Sometimes when I went home at night I thought of it and laughed.'[10]

It is obviously impossible to put a numerical value on a sum total of a person's unmet needs. Some needs are natural; others are learned. Needs vary in the extent to which they motivate behaviour. Some are clearly recognized and defined, while others are not understood or recognized at all. What we do know from experimental research is that criminal and dishonest behaviour is more likely to occur when it is a means to an important goal and when other opportunities to reach that goal are limited.[11] Thus, a more powerful need is more likely to drive one to criminal behaviour than one that is viewed as less important by the individual. Need, however, is only one necessary element in crime. Another is a person's opportunity to fulfil a need in a legitimate fashion as opposed to through criminal means. It is to this issue of opportunity to which we now turn.

OPPORTUNITY

I have already discussed the role of opportunities in crime at length. I have discussed experiments in which people were given opportunities to act dishonestly and often acted accordingly. We have seen the dramatic behaviours elicited by the Milgram experiments on obedience, and the Zimbardo prison experiment conducted at Stanford University. Both showed that situations could be created in which normal human beings could be prompted to do serious harm to others.

The concept of opportunity can be related to crime in at least four ways. First, opportunities can themselves *influence needs and induce* an individual to commit a criminal offence. Second, opportunities can refer to the *availability of suitable crime targets*. Third, they can relate to the *relative accessibility of legal versus illegal means* of achieving personal goals. Fourth, opportunity can be seen as a function of the *degree of risk* to which a potential offender is exposed.

Above, we saw needs can be affected by opportunities, through the temptations created. People can be induced to commit an offence either through temptation or through adversity encountered in a situation. Temptations to steal, to use drugs, to take bribes, to deceive customers, to cheat on one's income tax returns are a few among many possibilities for committing infractions to which virtually everyone is exposed. Negative situations, too, may elicit a criminal response: a provocative comment by a stranger in a bar, abusive behaviour on the part of a spouse or other family member, maltreatment at work, a blatant act of discrimination, or a criminal attack by another. With respect to the last point, a classic study of criminal homicide found that, in about a quarter of the killings, the victim was the first to use physical force.[12]

Another example of provocation leading to crime was provided by an armed robber: 'The first time I did an armed robbery it was mainly for vengeance. My brother worked in a restaurant and the owner sold it to an Italian. He fired my brother so he could hire others of his own race. My brother and I robbed him to get revenge.'[13]

Not everyone, of course, will respond to provocation in such an extreme way. The claim can thus be made that the personality of the individual who has been mistreated, threatened, or exploited contributes to the commission of an offence. (I certainly agree and discuss this factor below, under 'Proclivities and Attitudes.' Notwithstanding the background of the offender (i.e., he or she may have killed, robbed, or assaulted before), the current incident can be understood only with reference to the situation at hand. The specific incident mentioned in the previous paragraph might not have occurred without the provocation involved.

The state of the physical environment itself can induce antisocial reactions. Studies of progressive vandalism show that an object or community that is decaying or in a state of disrepair is more likely to be further vandalized than one that is maintained properly. In one experiment, discussed in chapter 3, a car was left as though it had been abandoned on a New York street.[14] As the investigators secretly looked on, the car was stripped little by little until only a worthless frame remained. Progressively more people got involved as the car was increasingly reduced in value. Another study found that picnic tables with markings on them were more likely to be further marked or carved than those in the same area without markings.[15] Another general observation, corroborated by police officers, is that buildings with broken windows that are left unrepaired are likely to have their remaining windows broken.[16]

These types of findings have prompted environmental psychologists to argue that the environment provides cues as to appropriate behaviour in a given context.[17] The deteriorated physical condition of an object or building may encourage vandalism. Such environmental cues are called 'releasor cues' because they stimulate the release of otherwise inhibited behaviour. Releasor cues communicate that acts such as vandalism are acceptable in certain contexts because no one seems to care.

A second way in which opportunities are related to criminality is in terms of the *availability of suitable crime targets*. The word 'suitable' is crucial here because the only crime targets accessible to any given person are those within his or her means and capabilities to victimize. Another factor limiting potential targets is a person's moral standards. Take an armed robber. If he refuses to mug people, he is limited to commercial enterprises. If he lacks expertise, access to suitable weapons, and accomplices he can trust, sophisticated bank robberies, armoured truck robberies, and the like must be ruled out. He is thus left with simple targets, such as convenience stores and gas stations. If, at the time he wishes to commit a particular offence, he also has no access to a car, he may be limited in his selection of a target to only a few businesses that are within walking distance of his place of residence.

This factor of target availability is an obvious but important one in understanding both the occurrence of an offence and the form an offence will take. Target hardening and target removal are two strategies that have been practised on a large scale in efforts to prevent many different types of crime, ranging from airline hijackings and armed robberies to simple theft and vandalism. In the case of hijackings, a rash of these incidents in the late 1960s and the early 1970s was reduced significantly through the introduction of metal detectors at airports.[18]

Bank robberies in many jurisdictions (Montreal, for example) have been rendered more difficult by a variety of security procedures. 'Bandit' barriers, the removal of cash from tellers' drawers to more secured areas behind the counter, and drop-boxes equipped with timing devices, into which tellers drop large rolls of cash, are just a few measures designed to make the object of this crime – cash – less accessible.[19] Payroll thefts have become more difficult in many businesses, as salaries are more frequently issued through computer transfers to the employee's bank account. At the same time, electronic thefts and embezzlement have increased.

The shoplifting of movie videos provides another example of an area in which target removal has been extremely successful. Initially, VHS and Beta cassettes were placed on the shelves in video stores. Customers could determine whether a movie was available simply by looking for it on the shelf. Pilferage problems, forced many stores to replace the cassettes on the shelves with their original cases or plastic cards with some advertising material. Customers must obtain the video itself from a central desk.[20]

Patricia and Paul Brantingham, two criminologists with expertise in urban planning, describe how modifying the design of the environment can reduce the opportunities for crime. In the case of environmental abuse, they provide the following example:

A high school was located opposite a church. On the street behind the church there was a convenience store. As might be expected, students from the high school walked through the church parking lot to get to and from the convenience store. Lots of litter was left in the church parking lot, producing calls for police service and complaints. Church members were upset by the mess, but unable to stop either the trespassing teenagers or their littering ...

The crime prevention officer found an effective, low cost solution. He convinced the church to dig a ditch across the front of its property (except for an entrance way) and arranged a direct pathway from school to convenience store to be built along one edge of the church property. The new pathway had a tall cedar fence (2.5 metres) on one side to separate it from adjacent houses and a chain link fence on the other side. Low shrubs were planted by the chain link fence to enhance its appearance. The littering on the church grounds stopped and, perhaps surprisingly, the student pathway stayed clear of litter and graffiti. General research on litter and graffiti finds that keeping the area 'clean' is a deterrent to further problems.[21]

The availability of crime targets affects not only whether a crime will occur, but also the nature of a crime. If we look at employee crime, we see that the type of offences workers commit are closely related to the opportunities to which they are exposed. Blue-collar workers tend to take tools and materials from their workplaces and tend to steal time because they are often paid by the hour. White-collar workers tend to take stationery and office supplies, and to abuse telephone expense accounts. Accountants tend to embezzle because it is the type of crime they have access to. Professionals, such as doctors, commit fraud against clients/patients and medical plans, because that is where their opportunities for illegal activity lie.

Another way in which opportunities influence the commission of criminal acts relates to the means available to the potential perpetrator. The issue, essentially, is whether an individual can fulfil his or her needs or meet his or her goals in a law-abiding fashion or whether he or she feels it necessary to turn to illegitimate activities to achieve his or her ends. Put another way, what are the person's legal and illegal options?

Strain theory in criminology tells us that people engage in crime when the goals they have learned to pursue are unattainable through legal activities. Robert Merton, the leading exponent of strain theory, argued that, in U.S. society, the most prominent cultural goal was to accumulate wealth.[22] Everybody in the society is exposed to this goal and learns that it is paramount. At the same time, the culture specifies the means by which people should achieve this goal – the Protestant work ethic (i.e., hard work, honesty, education, and deferred gratification). Some people lack the skills or the access to employment and educational opportunities, and the resulting strain leads them to select illegal means of achieving their material goals. These people are most highly concentrated among the lower class and minority groups. The fact that social strain falls harder on these groups is the reason, according to strain theorists, why they are more heavily involved in criminal activity. Thus, the more a person sees his or her legitimate opportunities for success as blocked, the more likely it is that he or she will seek illegitimate means to achieve some measure of success.

Illegitimate means, like their legitimate counterparts, are not equally distributed in society. Some neighbourhoods offer greater access to the tools and the skills needed to commit crimes than others.[23] Guns used for armed robberies, burglary tools for breaking into homes, computer hardware and software for electronic crimes, insider information to commit stock market crimes, and power and influence to engage in corrupt practices are means not equally distributed in society. The companions one has, the position one holds, and the neighbourhood in which one resides influence the extent of one's illegal opportunities. It stands to reason that the more available these opportunities are and the less available legitimate opportunities at any time, the more likely a person is to commit crimes to achieve his or her goals.

A further dimension of criminal opportunity is risk. The idea that people are deterred from committing crimes when the risks they face are high is controversial. Some laypeople and scholars feel that because some people seem indifferent to risk (for example, those who keep returning to prison) and because some crimes appear not to be deterred by any sanction (e.g., certain crimes of passion), risk is not a factor in crime. While it is undoubtedly true that some people and certain types of crime are less influenced by the risk factor than are others, most people, including career criminals, are to some extent responsive to the risks they face. The fact that crime is very commonplace in no way negates the importance of risk. That Canadians commit thousands of crimes a year, despite the presence of legal sanctions, means only that their needs and opportunities, in a particular instance, overrode the dangers they perceived. The risk of punishment people are exposed to, for all but the most serious of crimes, is marginal. Although the possible sanctions one may face may be severe, the certainty that one will face these sanctions is usually very low. It is likely that people begin to take sanctions seriously when they are imposed with a sufficiently high level of certainty.[24]

The risks faced by people committing crimes do not merely take the form of arrests and sentences handed out by the justice system. A person committing an armed robbery or burglary faces being injured or killed by victims or the police. A person stealing on the job or embezzling company funds risks losing his or her job. A man beating his wife risks losing her and the children and, perhaps, even revenge. A doctor fraudulently billing a medical plan risks losing his or her licence. A person committing an act considered repugnant by the community risks, and puts his or her family at risk of, being harassed and ostracized by the community. Furthermore, any criminal conviction can result in a loss of stature within the community. Moreover, one risks self-recrimination in the form of guilt and shame.

I have already discussed how experimental research on honesty has shown that situational factors, including the risks to which subjects were exposed, had an impact on behaviour. People are more likely to cheat and steal, for example, when they remain anonymous; that is, they are either in a large crowd or disguised in some way. In one experiment, children 'trick-or-treating' during Hallowe'en were given an opportunity to steal money and candy at selected homes.[25] Those whose identity was known by the person in these homes (that person was actually an investigator), were less likely to steal than were those children who remained anonymous. This study also showed, as did the Milgram experiment, that subjects were more likely to engage in disreputable acts when they were informed that they would not be held responsible for these acts. As a professor, I have always been struck by the way disturbances in a classroom increase with the size of a class. People in large groups feel they are less likely to be caught and held responsible for transgressions than are those acting alone or in smaller groups.

Even long-term, violent offenders take risk into consideration in the timing of their offences. As already discussed, most rapists and robbers undertake some hasty precautions, at least, prior to their offences. Rapists try to move their victims to a place where they can avoid detection. Robbers, even if they are fairly impulsive and spontaneous in their crimes, spend at least a few minutes keeping their target under surveillance, trying to ensure that no police patrols are passing by and that few bystanders are available to intervene at the time of the offence. One armed robber told my collaborators in a previous study that 'the risks [are all important] because if you are likely to be caught, it doesn't matter if there is a lot of money there' Another robber said that 'sure there are places with a lot more money but it's impossible to do. You must think about the escape. It's better to go into a place with less money but where you have good chances of success.'[26]

Professional robbers will go to great lengths to avoid capture. They will steal cars, change licence plates, rent separate apartments to keep a target under surveillance and to divide up the spoils, study the routines of the personnel at the target, obtain weapons and disguises, plan an escape route, and run rehearsals. If 'professionals,' that is, criminals with the experience in crime and, perhaps, of prison, weigh the risks of a venture in crime, it only stands to reason that the general population, many of whom have much to lose by engaging in criminal activity, will also consider the risks.

Crime prevention programs, too, show the importance of risk in the decision to commit a crime. Bank robberies in Montreal and other centres have declined dramatically in recent years with improvements in security systems and changes in the physical design of banks, as well as increases in the certainty and length of prison sentences in some jurisdictions.[27] Hijackings, as already mentioned, have declined internationally with the introduction of detection devices that have elevated the risks of attempts. The Israeli airline El Al, perhaps one of the world's premier potential targets of terrorism, has been virtually immune from hijackings since instituting rigorous security procedures and putting armed sky marshals on every flight.

In a less serious vein, New York City officials found they could deter citizens from using slugs in city parking meters, a significant problem in the 1960s and early 1970s.[28] They merely placed a window on each parking meter, so that a traffic officer could see the coin used by the motorist currently parked next to the meter. In yet another example of the impact on crime of elevating risks, England, Holland, and West Germany have found that imposing mandatory helmet legislation for motorcyclists reduced motorcycle thefts.[29] It is believed that such legislation occasions a reduction in thefts because potential thieves, who are usually opportunistic and therefore do not carry helmets with them, know they will be quickly apprehended for not wearing a helmet.[30]

SKILLS

Even if the motive and opportunity are present, an individual still needs the requisite skills or capabilities to execute a crime. This truism needs little substantiation. One needs skills in accounting or financing to embezzle funds from an employer or to defraud stockholders. A personal computer and a modem are not sufficient to encroach illegally into various databanks: an individual must be able to break security codes to accomplish this. Sophisticated armoured truck and bank robberies require expertise in acquiring and handling weapons, overcoming resistance, auto theft, selecting appropriate targets, planning, and execution. Burglarizing hardened targets may require the acquisition of specialized tools, and expertise in using them. Interpersonal skills are necessary to commit certain frauds and confidence games, or to become involved in hidden-economy trading. Various organizational and social skills, as well as enforcement capabilities, are needed to engage in drug dealing, racketeering, and the like.

Many categories of crime, however, require few skills; not surprisingly, these offences are the most commonplace. Most thefts, including shoplifting and employee theft, fall in this category. Violent crimes, such as murder, sexual assault, and domestic violence, as well as most robberies, require only brute force or a weapon as an equalizer. The acquisition and use of illicit drugs require minimal skills that are easily acquired. Environmental abuse through littering, vandalism, and the dumping of toxic wastes, and cruelty to animals involve few skills. Making false claims about products or producing dangerous products also require little creativity (although making claims believable may require some ingenuity). Much fraudulent behaviour, such as issuing false cheques, cheating on exams, defrauding a medical plan, and cheating uninformed customers entail very little savvy. Accepting payoffs or illegal 'perks' on the part of police officers, public officials, or business people also involve little in the way of expertise.

Only a small percentage of crimes require extensive planning and skills in their execution. Most can be performed by people who are not schooled in the finer arts of cheating, stealing, and deception. Where some skills are necessary to commit a crime, these are usually acquired through simple learning, rather than through a long-term apprenticeship under professional criminals. Waiters and waitresses learn about scamming in restaurants through simple association with those who have more experience on the job. Hidden-economy traders, unscrupulous sales personnel, and auto mechanics likewise learn the techniques applicable to their illicit or dishonest activities from those with whom they work.

Others possess the necessary skills for crime by virtue of the requirements of their position. Embezzlers, for example, can use the same accounting skills necessary to perform their jobs to commit their offences. Public relations personnel can apply the same marketing skills needed in pursuing their careers to misleading consumers.

PROCLIVITIES AND ATTITUDES

The fourth component of my framework for understanding and predicting criminal involvement, at any given time, concerns the individual's disposition and his or her attitudes. 'Disposition' refers to more enduring behavioural patterns, to tendencies that surface across a variety of situations. Throughout this book, I have emphasized the sensitivity of human behaviour to situations, that is, temptations, pressures on the individual, opportunities, and risks. While I believe that very ordinary people often succumb to sudden opportunities and situational stresses by turning to crime, I have also stated at several junctures that this emphasis on the situation does not preclude or negate the importance of personality or dispositional factors in crime. A large part of the population commits primarily crimes of opportunity. There are others, however, who do not merely take advantage of opportunities that come their way; they actively seek to create criminal opportunities.

Some people show pronounced antisocial tendencies throughout their lives, disrupting the class in school, being truant, lying and stealing, drinking and abusing illicit drugs, having a poor work record, cheating on spouses, physically and sexually abusing family members, and so on. Those regularly breaking rules, acting impulsively, showing poor judgment, exhibiting callousness, and apparently acting without any ethical standards were once referred to as 'morally insane'; later as 'psychopaths,' then 'sociopaths'; and, more recently, by the psychiatric profession, as having an 'antisocial personality disorder.'[31] Whatever the terminology used to describe them, there are those – often regularly in trouble with the law – who show a disregard for rules and the welfare of others, or even themselves. Apart from career criminals, this group is said to include a mixed bag of individuals, such as 'unprincipled businessmen, shyster lawyers, quack doctors, high-pressure evangelists, crooked politicians, impostors, drug pushers, and prostitutes.'[32] The properties of the situation are not as relevant to understanding their rule-breaking or lawbreaking, because they are likely to lie, cheat, and steal in a variety of situations. Such people account for a disproportionate amount of crime, but, in their purer or more extreme form, account for only a small proportion of the population – perhaps, only about 2 to 5 per cent.[33]

Some people exhibit none of the traits attributed to the chronically antisocial individual. People can be viewed on a continuum, ranging from those exhibiting all or virtually all the characteristics of the antisocial person to those exhibiting few if any of these traits. As an example, there are many people who have a series of extra-marital affairs, but in no other way possess antisocial traits. They may otherwise be successful at work, be good parents, be generally law-abiding, and refrain from the abuse of drugs and alcohol. There are also 'con men' who, apart from their illegal schemes, have conventional family lives. Thus, it might be reasonable to say that people vary in degree in terms of their susceptibility to criminal and other antisocial behaviour.

Two factors affecting this susceptibility are a person's age and sex. Everything being equal, individuals in their teens or early adult years are more likely to be involved in a variety of criminal acts than are those at a more advanced age; likewise, the involvement of males exceeds that of females, particularly in the realm of violent crimes.[34] Thus, societies with a high proportion of young people, especially young males, will tend to experience a higher prevalence of many forms of criminality, by virtue of these demographic characteristics alone.

Attitudes favourable to crime derive from three basic sources: personality, culture, and situations. As far as personality is concerned, people with many antisocial traits of the kind just discussed are also known to blame others for their behaviour rather than accept responsibility for it. They are known for the many rationalizations they offer.[35] Thus, to varying degrees, people are predisposed to attitudes favourable to crime through the rationalizations they adopt. Some go through life feeling they never had a break or that others prevented them from becoming successful. Such people feel the world is unjust and they are therefore entitled to do whatever is necessary to 'correct' this injustice. As we have said in chapter 9, rationalizations are powerful guides to action.

Another source of attitudes conducive to criminality are the cultural values to which a person is exposed and which he or she assimilates. It is important to note that an individual may be exposed to different, and even incompatible, value systems in the mainstream culture, his or her neighbourhood, the workplace, and the family. I have already stressed that the mainstream North American culture places a heavy emphasis upon materialism and competitiveness, with success often taking precedence over the means one employs to achieve it. The mainstream culture itself promotes attitudes favourable to using unscrupulous means to achieving success. Anti-authority attitudes and individualism, values which further promote criminal and exploitative behaviour, are also fostered by the mainstream culture. The evidence presented in chapter 10 shows how weak the commitment of the population to the criminal law sometimes is.

Community and neighbourhood values, too, may encourage antisocial behaviour. Leading criminologists, such as Marvin Wolfgang and Franco Ferracuti, have written of the subcultures of violence prevailing in various regions of the world, including America's urban ghettos.[36] Disadvantage and hopelessness have made physical toughness the measure of a man in some neighbourhoods.

In chapter 11, we saw how young boys in the ghetto are often encouraged to fight by their elders. Unable to participate fully in U.S. society at large, residents of these areas develop some alternative values. Pimps, street fighters, and even dope pushers may gain respect in these areas, and their behaviour may be modelled by neighbourhood children. Thus, behaviour that is criminal and deviant in the wider society may become the norm in some areas. In these areas, heads of families are also more likely to be involved in crime, rackets, prostitution, drug abuse, and the like, thereby further promoting the entrenchment of antisocial values and behaviour.

Sociologists Maynard Erickson and Jack Gibbs have found a direct correspondance between the frequency of a given form of deviance within a community and the tolerance of the members of that community for that act. The greater a crime meets with disapproval in a community, the less frequent it will be.[37] Criminologist Maurice Cusson asserts that 'the intolerance of a community concerning a given deviant act inhibits its members from the tendency to commit such an act. In an intolerant milieu, a person hesitates to violate the law because he does not want his peers and friends to think ill of him.'[38]

Another environment that can promote attitudes conducive to criminal or dishonest behaviour is the workplace. Restaurant employees who engage in 'scamming,' hidden-economy traders, and dishonest automobile mechanics, for example, do not engage in these practices in isolation. These practices may be very commonplace and are learned in the work setting. Furthermore, employers who are aware of some of these activities may look the other way, not wanting to create a labour problem, or may use information about illegalities selectively to sack troublesome employees.[39]

In many settings, therefore, stealing and cheating receive at least tacit approval. In the case of ordinary employee pilferage as well, the theft of some items may be considered acceptable. White-collar workers, for example, may take home inexpensive office supplies, use office equipment to photocopy personal documents, and make a few personal long-distance calls at the office without facing severe reprimands, if detected. There may be an understanding, on the part of employers and employees alike, that such conduct is within the bounds of acceptability so long as it does not become excessive. These unofficial or informal norms tend to exercise a greater influence upon attitudes and behaviour than do the official company rules or the criminal law. These norms, however, do vary from one work environment to another. Not all companies experience the same amount of pilferage. Not all garages are equally dishonest. Not every police department condones, unofficially, the use of physical force by officers for the same reasons, and not all departments have the same policies with respect to 'perks' on the job. An individual's attitudes towards illegal practices will thus be influenced by the prevailing attitudes in the specific setting in which he or she works.

Beyond the setting itself, a host of situational factors is capable of fostering attitudes favourable to lawbreaking. Research on employee theft and some of my own interviews reveal that people are more favourable to victimizing their employers if they are dissatisfied with their jobs or feel they are being exploited. In general, we find it easier to justify harming those we dislike or do not know well than those we like. Similarly, those who are different from us by virtue of their race, ethnicity, or social class may also evoke less empathy from us than do those with whom we can identify. Feeling that we have been unjustly treated by another – provoked, struck, exploited, or humiliated – also helps us justify retaliation in some way, whether it takes the form of violence, theft, or deception. The sudden loss of a job or some other personal crisis may engender a sense of despair that makes us feel right about such acts as stealing or kidnapping our own children to gain custody of them. Alcohol in our bloodstream may make us feel particularly self-righteous about the actions of others and invincible enough to cause them serious injury. These are just some of the situational factors that may, despite their often transient nature, influence our perceptions long enough for us to commit criminal acts.

PREDICTING THE PREVALENCE OF CRIMINALITY

The factors of need, opportunity, skills, and proclivities and attitudes can both explain and predict the prevalence of a given form of criminality at a given time. I have summarized these four elements of my predictive model in table 6. All four components of the model must be present for a crime to occur. The offence must fulfil some perceived need of the individual; the opportunity to commit the crime must be available; the individual must possess the skill or capabilities required to commit that offence; and he or she must look favourably upon, or at least be able to justify, the commission of it.

It is hard to generalize about the relative importance of the different components of this model because on some occasions, one predominates, and, on others, the components are in balance. Take the case of a narcotics addict. He may have an overwhelming need to obtain cash as he begins suffering from severe withdrawal symptoms. His need to commit a robbery is so acute that he requires just the minimum of opportunity to strike. He may undertake the act even if the risks are very high. His need, as commonly occurs with addicts, overrides moral concerns, even though he may generally believe that theft and robbery are repugnant. His current state, however, lowers his moral standards, making him indifferent to the consequences of his actions. If he is suffering from withdrawal, his judgment and

TABLE 6
Elements of the Predictive Model

Need
- basic biological needs
- needs influenced by what others have (relative deprivation)
- culturally induced needs (e.g., materialism, machoism)
- needs for instant gratification
- other needs (action, vengeance, release of aggression, self-defence, power, and domination)

Opportunity
- opportunities can create needs through temptation, provocation, and other environmental stimuli (releasor cues)
- availability of suitable targets
- relative availability of legitimate versus illegitimate means of achieving goals
- risk

Skills
- expertise in the techniques of crime
- possession of pertinent equipment (e.g., burglary tools)
- interpersonal skills and networks (e.g., fraud and drug trafficking)
- education and intelligence (e.g., computer crime)

Proclivities and Attitudes
- antisocial personality is especially conducive to crime
- age and gender are related to crime
- one's milieu or surrounding culture can promote unscrupulousness, anti-authority attitudes, individualism, competitiveness, machoism
- situational factors can promote crime through job dissatisfaction, provocation, and lack of empathy for potential victims

---

skills are also impaired. In such a case, overpowering need lowers moral standards, capabilities, and the type of opportunity required to commit a robbery.

A professional, non-addicted robber, by contrast, may also have a strong need to commit a robbery – robbery is, after all, his vocation – but the need is not as overpowering and urgent as is the addict's. He will plan carefully and wait until a favourable opportunity arises. He will take advantage of his considerable skills to commit a robbery that maximizes his gains and minimizes his risks. His attitudes, too, are not entirely antisocial. The professional robber does not mug pedestrians and rob small-business people. He will be more selective in choosing a target as his moral standards are considerably higher than those of the addict. Thus, the professional robber tends to have, at any given time, a moderate to high need to commit a hold-up, has high standards as far as opportunities are concerned, possesses and employs a moderate to high level of skill, and is at least at a moderate level as far as moral standards are concerned. The professional is more balanced on the four elements, falling at a moderate to high level on each. The severely addicted robber commits far more crimes because of his overwhelming need, virtual indiscriminate selection of a target, disregard for risk, willingness to forgo any finesse or skills, and lack of virtually any compunction.

It is hard to determine which of the four elements of my predictive model is most important because they are of varying importance for different people and are subjective to some degree: one person will detect criminal opportunities where another will fail to do so, and two people may have very different views regarding the risks attached to a given act.

Consider two department-store clerks who consider stealing an article of clothing. One may perceive the likelihood of getting caught as very high, while the other may be far more optimistic about her chances. Their different personal situations, too, may come into play. One clerk may be a single mother with two young children, and the other a teenage girl with no dependents. The single mother would appear to have much more to lose, should she be caught: she faces the loss of her job, and perhaps criminal charges.

Needs and attitudes are, of course, also highly subjective. Even the same skills may be viewed differently by different people. One of the clerks might be confident about her ability to bypass store security and succeed in stealing the clothes, while the other, even if she is capable of similar stealth, may not believe she can succeed. The subjective nature of needs, opportunities, skills, and attitudes makes it difficult to predict how a person will behave in a given situation. Predicting the behaviour of individuals is also rendered difficult by the fact that needs, opportunities, and attitudes are very much influenced by the situations a person encounters, and predicting situations he or she will encounter is more art than science. For example, can we predict that John Doe will work, in the future, for a company where there are many temptations to steal, where the risks are low, and where he is so ill-treated by the company he has no compunction about carrying out thefts?

Obviously, we cannot predict the course of someone's life, and the needs, temptations, stresses, provocations, risks, and interpersonal influences he or she will encounter. Unless a person is very rigid, having clearly defined patterns of antisocial or morally 'upright' behaviour, prediction is very speculative. Even the extremely honest and dishonest are under situational influence, although less so than the population at large. In any case, it has been estimated that those who break rules in almost any circumstance and those who almost never break rules make up only about 15 per cent of the population.[40] Also, the purpose of this book is to understand the behaviour of the public at large, not that of specific individuals. Trying to predict how a given person will perceive a situation and react to it is an awesome task – that person may view the world in a very peculiar way. That one person may, for example, disregard risks or be paralysed by them, or may disregard moral considerations. If we focus our attention on society at large, individual peculiarities cancel each other out. If the chances of detection associated with a given act are high and that act is severely censured by society, as in an act for which a heavy sentence is prescribed by law, participation is not likely to be widespread. It is this prevalence of different illegal acts – that is, the degree to which participation in them is widespread – that we are seeking to understand.

In the remainder of this chapter and table 7, I apply the model I have presented to explain the prevalence or extent of public paticipation in various illegal acts. I begin with acts that are very prevalent and end with those in which very few people participate. As the objective here is to illustrate the application of the

TABLE 7 Applying the Predictive Model to Selected Crimes

Offence	Prevalence	Need	Opportunity	Skills	Favourable Attitudes
Tax evasion	High	High	Mod.-High	Low	High
Employee pilferage	High	Mod.	High	Low	High
Auto repair fraud	High	High	High	Mod.	Mod.-High
Shoplifting	Mod.	Mod.-High	High	Low	Mod.
Spousal assault	Mod.	Mod.	Mod.	Low	Mod.
Murder	Low	Low	Low	Mod.	Low
Computer crime	Low	Low	Mod.	High	Mod.

predictive model, I discuss only a small number of crime categories. I have already documented, in chapters 4–8, the extent of participation in the crimes to be discussed; thus statistics and other evidence are not reiterated here. The evidence on the prevalence of participation in the various crimes is far from definitive as most research looks at incidence or the volume of crimes, rather than the number of people participating in them. My estimates regarding the prevalence of the crimes to be discussed should be regarded as fairly rough. Let us now examine the model in reference to some concrete examples.

Tax Offences

One example of an offence that is extremely prevalent is that of income tax fraud or evasion (chapter 4). Non-compliance with tax laws, as indicated by my informant from Revenue Canada as well as by evidence from several surveys, can range up to 90 per cent in some professions. What is it that makes participation in this area so widespread? Looking at table 7, we observe that all the elements necessary for the commission of an offence, according to our predictive model, are favourable for this crime. There is a strong incentive to cheat on one's return: one stands to receive a larger cash payment from the government than one is entitled to, or one pays in less than one is required to do. Cash is the greatest incentive in property crimes because, unlike any item one might steal, cash does not need to be converted or disposed of. It can be applied for any purpose, that is, to meet basic or more culturally conditioned needs. The amounts one stands to gain in tax offences can be considerable.

The opportunity for the suppression of income and inflating deductions is also present for a large segment of the population. Anybody can manipulate the figures, but the risk for salaried employees and pensioners with no additional sources of income is quite high (although they can still claim they made an error in completing their forms). For corporations and the large number of citizens who are self-employed (either business people and professionals) or moonlight, there are ample opportunities for excesses and concealing income. The risk of being audited is very low. On the whole, therefore, a significant proportion of the population has considerable opportunity to cheat on their income tax returns. The skills required for most types of cheating are quite elementary. Income is simply concealed, or illegitimate expenses are claimed. Where greater sophistication in accounting is required, as in the case of corporations, accountants can be retained to provide advice. As far as social attitudes are concerned, few areas are more favourable to infractions. Surveys show that most of the public is receptive to cheating on their taxes as they tend to feel that they are merely withholding, from the government, money they have rightfully earned.

Employee Theft

Another very prevalent activity is employee pilferage or theft of small items. Such pilferage is the most common form of theft, committed by a majority of employees, and responsible for a significant proportion of all bankruptcies (chapter 4). Although not usually as lucrative as withholding taxes, the employee-theft incentive is at least moderate in strength as employees often steal basic items that they would otherwise have to purchase. White-collar workers take pens, stationery, office equipment, and the like; blue-collar workers take home tools, construction materials, and so on; employees in the food industry often pilfer food and beverages; those in the hotel industry take home silverware, furnishings, art, linens, and the like; those working in department stores might steal clothing or appliances. Opportunity is usually high, as employees are in the position to carry out such pilferage and are entrusted with their security. The risks tend to be low, and employees know that the company will rarely press criminal charges if they are caught. Dismissal is usually the most serious consequence an employee will face. Rarely are specialized skills required to carry out the types of pilferage mentioned.

As for attitudes, very few work environments, at least in North America, are so positive and concerned about the welfare of employees that they fail to provide some justifications for employee theft. Injustices experienced by workers are almost inevitable, whether these relate to remuneration, benefits, working conditions, opportunities for advancement, favouritism, or mere lack of respect. When none of these conditions prevails, the employee can still justify pilferage on the grounds that the article(s) stolen is small and the company can afford to lose it. Furthermore, taking home small items from work is often considered acceptable among co-workers and usually overlooked by employers. Thus, here again, all the elements necessary for extensive participation in the crime are present.

Fraud in Car Repairs

Next in line in terms of prevalence in table 7 is deception (padding bills) in the car repair business. Studies have found that as much as one of every three dollars spent on car repairs is lost because of fraud or incompetence (see chapters 3 and 6). Many other industries display equal levels of dishonesty in the repair sector; however, I have selected car repair as a representative example.

In terms of incentives or needs to deceive customers, large amounts of money are involved and earnings can be supplemented to a significant extent. Opportunities abound as the customer is usually poorly informed about auto mechanics and is usually not even present when problems are diagnosed and repairs undertaken. Furthermore, the vulnerability of customers is enhanced by their dependency on their car to get them home, to work, or to their next destination along the highway. This vulnerability makes them less likely to seek out other estimates and eager to get back on the road as fast as possible, regardless of the cost. Needless to say, the garage operator is aware of this vulnerability.

The garage operator also knows that his risk is minimal, owing to the ignorance, absence, or impatience of the customer. Customers from out of town pose a lesser risk, even if they were to discover an unnecessary repair, substandard work, or an overcharge. Furthermore, even if confronted by a customer for shoddy or unnecessary work, the operator can claim that an honest mistake was made. He can then offer to rectify the 'mistake' for free or, as has happened to many of us, can charge a second time for correcting the problem. Perhaps the reason such dishonesty is not quite as prevalent as is the case with tax offences and employee pilferage is that, in one area, risk is high. A garage can lose its reputation or certification with organizations such as the American and Canadian automobile associations.

Auto mechanics, of course, have all the skills needed to engage in countless schemes, whatever the problem a motorist is encountering. As for attitudes in the profession, there is widespread encouragement of customer 'rip-offs,' and admiration for clever schemes. There are also, however, some very honest small-time operators, as well as large chain stores, both of whom wish to promote their reputation. Furthermore, some large chains and dealers have adopted fixed prices for the various kinds of repair work. Such opposition and obstacles to dishonest practices on the part of a fair number of operators contribute to a lower participation rate in these 'rip-offs' than in tax evasion and employee pilferage, where support for theft and dishonesty is very high.

Shoplifting

One type of crime that is less prevalent than those discussed above, but still fairly commonplace, is shoplifting. Studies have found that up to a tenth of department store shoppers shoplift at any given time (chapter 4). The incentive for shoplifting may not be as great as that for tax offences and fraud in auto repairs, because the amounts taken are not usually as substantial. Still, people tend to steal those things they would otherwise need to purchase (e.g., clothing, groceries, candy, housewares). Whether in a small store or a large retail outlet with floorwalkers, cameras, and one-way mirrors, in many respects shoplifting is more carefully monitored than employee theft. Shoplifters are therefore more likely to be detected and, because they have no affiliation with the store, are more likely to be turned over to the police. Thus, while opportunities for shoplifting abound and the risk of being caught at any given time is fairly low, the risks are greater than for employee theft or for being audited on one's income tax return.

The increased risk may be one reason why there are fewer shoplifters than employee thieves. Another reason may be that, although most shoplifters are amateurs, greater stealth is normally required for shoplifting than for employee theft. Some people inclined to steal may feel they lack the skill for shoplifting. Attitudes, too, may play a major part in making shoplifting less popular than employee theft. Those with no previous association with a store have less reason to feel victimized by the business. It becomes more difficult to justify this behaviour (as a perk or as revenge for exploitation) and consider it as anything more than an attempt to get something for nothing.

Shoplifting may also be more difficult to rationalize because it tends to require more active participation, while employee theft is often quite passive. To shoplift, one has to enter a store, sometimes wear special (perhaps baggy) clothes and carry extra bags, look around to see if one is being watched, slip the item carefully in a bag or pocket without being noticed, and leave the store in such a way as to avoid arousing suspicion. Taking so many steps would make many people feel like thieves.

Employee theft is often more passive, as it occurs during the individual's routine functions. A blue-collar worker slips a drill he has been using at work into a bag; a waiter slips some silverware into his sports bag; a white-collar worker makes a personal long-distance call from her office. An employee may not only feel entitled to these 'perks'; these activities are also easier to justify because they are extensions of their jobs. The opportunities 'fall into their hands'; no special effort is needed to carry out the theft.

I would argue that the more passive the behaviour, the easier it is to justify. A good example is provided by the situation in which a customer receives an overpayment from a cashier. Many people keep the money in such circumstances because they feel it is an act of fate; they did nothing to bring about the situation – the money just fell into their hands. Shoplifting is fairly prevalent, but not extremely so, primarily because of increased risk, the fewer rationalizations available, and the more active participation necessary on the part of the perpetrator.

Spousal Assault

Spousal assault is another form of behaviour that falls within the middle range, between activities in which almost everybody participates and those in which only a fraction of the population takes part (chapter 5). Here, as is the case with all violent offences, there is a substantial difference in prevalence when one compares Canada and other Western countries with the United States. In Canada, the figure usually given is that domestic violence directed against a spouse occurs in about one of every ten households. In the United States, some studies show that spousal assault occurs in as many as 60 per cent of U.S. homes,[41] making it a highly prevalent activity. I will base the discussion here on the situation in Canada and other countries.

Spousal assault usually is a means of asserting power, as well as dominating and controlling. These issues of control are more pronounced in some marriages than others. Even where relationships are based on power, the partners can assert themselves through means other than physical aggression (e.g., verbal means and passive aggression). The lack of perceived alternatives to physical aggression in gaining control over a partner is found in a moderate number of families only.

The opportunity to batter a spouse is ever-present. In an era when extended family rarely share the same living quarters, husband and wife are frequently alone (along with, perhaps, the children) behind closed doors. However, the risks attached to spousal assault, while not inordinately high, are increasing. As society becomes more sensitized to this issue, women are coming forward and reporting the crime in greater numbers. Furthermore, more programs and shelters are becoming available for battered women, so that they are now able to leave an abusive situation more easily. As a result of this elevated risk, the overall opportunity for this crime is at a moderate level only.

The only skill required is that the perpetrator, usually the male, be physically able to strike his partner. Physical superiority is not a prerequisite. One further inhibiting factor, though, is the progressive change in public attitudes towards this type of behaviour. Legislation in many countries that used to permit wife-beating has been rescinded. Educational and media programs, too, have stressed the repugnance of old attitudes condoning such conduct. As such, I would say that attitudes among the public are, at most, moderately favourable to spousal assault.

Homicide

Homicide is an example of an offence with a low prevalence rate (chapter 5). Despite the high visibility of murder cases, even in the United States the national rate is only about 10 in 100,000 people. Since some kill more than once, there are fewer than 10 murderers per 100,000 people in any given year. The infrequency of this crime can be explained by the fact that none of the elements in our predictive model is highly favourable to homicide. Few people have a strong need or powerful incentives to kill. Control in a marriage can be achieved through other means and one can get out of an unhappy marriage or unsatisfactory business partnership. The incentive to kill may be greater for those involved in the trafficking of illicit drugs, where lucrative profits are at stake and no formal mechanisms exist to resolve disputes (i.e., a person 'ripped off' in a drug deal cannot call in the police to mediate). For the population at large, however, killing is rarely considered a viable solution in dealing with problems.

There is no shortage of opportunities to kill a specific target or at random (this is very rare), although killing is more difficult to achieve than simple assault, unless one also has access to lethal weapons. The risk component of opportunity, however, is very high. Murders probably have the highest solution rate of all crimes and also carry the most severe sentences. An individual killer, therefore, has a high probability of being caught, convicted, and sentenced to a long prison term or, in some countries, death. The likelihood of punishment is particularly high when the offender and victim have been acquainted with each other, as motive and the identity of the perpetrator can be more easily established. The dangers posed by the victim, too, are profound. The opportunity to commit murder, at a low level of risk, is consequently hard to come by.

A person's ability to commit a homicide cannot be taken for granted. The individual needs either to possess physical superiority over an adversary or to wield a weapon that can serve as an equalizer. Even with a firearm, success in achieving the demise of the target is not assured. As far as public attitudes towards homicide are concerned, there are strong moral and religious prohibitions against killing, unless sanctioned through declarations of war or committed by the state in the form of executions. None of the elements of our predictive model favours homicide, and therefore it is not surprising that the offence is committed by only a fraction of the population.

Computer Crime

Let us look at one final category of crime to illustrate our predictive model. Many forms of crime involve the use of computers: embezzlement, sabotage of a company by an employee, illegal use of another's computer account, and access to organizational secrets (chapter 8). It is to the last named of these that I wish to turn – the so-called 'hacker' who often playfully penetrates a corporate, military, or other databank and creates havoc, sometimes destroying vital information. Only a very small fraction of people engage in this type of activity.

Why is it that participation is so low? First, much of this behaviour is motivated by thrill-seeking, and there are many other more straightforward ways for young people to obtain kicks. Most kicks, whether they are petty delinquencies, taking drugs, or driving fast cars, are more readily available and require less skill. Many young people lack access to a personal computer and modem, let alone have the ability to crack security codes of major organizations. Although society does not take as strong a stand against these computer offences as it does in the case of murder (most people at this time are quite uninformed and indifferent to them), the lack of a strong incentive to engage in computer crimes, the limited opportunity, and the high level of skills required lead to only very limited participation in this realm.

From the application of our model, we can see that all the elements – need, opportunity, skills, and attitudes – must be favourable to the commission of a given offence if public participation is to be widespread. We have seen this in the case of tax evasion and employee pilferage. In contrast, where several elements are unfavourable, the public's participation rate will be low. As we will see in chapter 14, this model can be used not only to predict the prevalence of different offences in a society, but as a means to guide efforts to lessen the public's participation in a crime.

PART IV
DEALING WITH WIDESPREAD CRIMINALITY

13

'The Rich Get Richer and the Poor Get Prison'[1]: Why Most 'Respectable' Law-breakers Avoid Prosecution

After examining the evidence presented in this book, one might reasonably ask why it is that only a fraction of the population gets into trouble with the law if virtually everyone is violating it. First of all, although it is true that only a minority of people are subjected to criminal proceedings, this minority is not negligible. In Canada, for example, as we said in chapter 3, close to 10 per cent of the population has a criminal record. Evidence presented in that chapter also showed that males currently growing up in the United States and England have about a 50/50 chance of getting in trouble with the law during their lifetime. These figures are very striking, but, even so, many avoid prosecution, and even those who are charged for a criminal offence once or twice have probably managed to avoid punishment many times over.

One Canadian study has found that only 8.5 per cent of offences known to the police result in the imposition of a sentence upon an offender.[2] This study was not undertaken in a large city and does not take into account the fact that well over half of all offences are never reported to the police. Taking these factors into account, 3 to 4 per cent of crimes, at best, eventuate in the passing of sentence against an offender. In urban areas of the United States, well under 1 per cent of offences (reported and unreported) lead to the punishment of the offender.[3]

Such attrition of criminal cases is attributable to a number of factors, some of which are within the control of the justice system and some of which the system can do little about. The need for the system to filter cases out can readily be seen if we examine the capacity of correctional institutions. In Canada, the capacity of all federal and provincial prisons is slightly over 25,000, while the country's population is about 29 million. Thus, less than one in every thousand Canadians can be incarcerated at any given time. Leaving aside the ethical issues, simple practicality demands that prison be used very selectively. In the same way, police investigative resources, prosecutorial resources, the personnel and time of the courts, and the resources of community-based correctional programs must be rationed.

The filtering of criminal cases on the part of criminal justice system personnel is therefore a necessity. Members of the public, too, make decisions as to what warrants the involvement of the criminal justice system, although such decisions are based on factors other than resources.

A case must proceed through a number of stages for a criminal conviction to take place. First, the police must become aware of an offence, through either the reporting of it by a citizen or the detection of it through routine patrol. Next, where the police decide that a case is worth pursuing, they must identify and apprehend the suspect(s). Upon doing this, a decision has to be made, by the police and prosecutorial office, as to whether charges will be laid and the case prosecuted. Once prosecuted, some cases will result in a conviction, while others will end in the acquittal of the defendant(s). At each stage, cases will be lost and, ultimately, only a small percentage will end up in a criminal conviction.

I will now focus on a few of the key stages to show why people who fit the stereotype of the criminal – people with low social status who commit violent crimes (outside the family) and other conventional crimes, such as burglary and theft – are more likely to pass through the various stages of the justice system and why more 'respectable' lawbreakers committing other crimes are more likely to fall through the cracks. I will argue that whether someone makes it to the end of the road, by being convicted and perhaps imprisoned, may have less to do with the harm he or she has caused to society, as it does with his or her personal attributes, economic resources, and the type (not necessarily gravity) of offence he or she has committed.

Some scholars, such as Jeffery Reiman in his book *The Rich Get Richer and the Poor Get Prison: Ideology, Class, and Criminal Justice*, contend that economic leverage is the pre-eminent factor determining whether a person will ultimately be punished (and, in particular, face imprisonment) for his or her crimes.[4] Reiman points to the people who populate our prisons to support his position and, indeed, it is true that they are drawn overwhelmingly from the ranks of society's disadvantaged. Reiman states:

For the same criminal behavior, the poor are more likely to be arrested; if arrested, they are more likely to be charged; if charged, more likely to be convicted; if convicted, more likely to be sentenced to prison; and if sentenced, more likely to be given longer prison terms than members of the middle and upper classes. In other words, the image of the criminal population one sees in our nation's jails and prisons is an image distorted by the shape of the criminal justice system itself. It is the face of evil reflected in a carnival mirror, but it is no laughing matter.[5]

Reiman further quotes the late U.S. senator Philip Hart:

Justice has two transmission belts, one for the rich and one for the poor. The low-income transmission belt is easier to ride without falling off and it gets to prison in shorter order.

The transmission belt for the affluent is a little slower and it passes innumerable stations where exits are temptingly convenient.[6]

Although I agree that a person's economic resources are very influential in determining his or her likelihood of incurring legal sanctions, other factors exert influence as well. Even poor people are selectively punished. The poor people we find in prisons have been incarcerated for murder, robbery, theft, burglary, drug offences, and the like; they are rarely punished for assaulting their wives, abusing their children, or stealing from their employers. Thus, the type of infraction one commits, too, is important in the selection of people for legal proceedings. Other factors also determine one's susceptibility to such proceedings. I discuss below some of the key factors, at some of the principal decision points, influencing whether one travels on the transmission belt speeding towards prison or on the one with the many exits.

REPORTING CRIME

The first step involved in taking action following a criminal event is to notify the police, other than in corporate crimes, where local police forces are rarely involved in the investigation. Since the police rarely detect crimes themselves, it is up to victims, witnesses, or other concerned persons to come forward.[7] Only a small proportion of all crimes are ever reported to the police. Even very serious crimes often go unreported. In Canadian cities, for example, well under half of all sexual assaults, other assaults, and robberies are reported to the police, as indicated by crime victims.[8]

Why do victims fail to report so many crimes? First, a criminal act may never be uncovered. Victims of child physical and sexual abuse are usually discovered years later, or only accidentally, as family members tend to conspire to keep the secret or deny the presence of such abuse. Businesses are aware of inventory 'shrinkage' but rarely of specific acts of shoplifting and employee pilferage, as they occur. An organization may not be aware that its funds are being embezzled.

When they are uncovered, many crimes committed against companies by employees or customers are dealt with internally rather than through the legal system. The tremendous growth of the private security sector reflects this inclination of many organizations to become self-reliant in security matters and to handle their own problems without involving the police. It is easier and more economical for a hotel to increase the cost of a room than to report and testify against those who steal towels and linen. It is also better for business. As for employee theft, a company may avoid a crackdown on pilferage and may even look the other way, as it may not want to antagonize workers. We have seen that employees frequently rationalize their small thefts and scams on the basis that they are being underpaid. Perhaps employers rationalize modest salaries on the basis that their employees are permitted various 'perks.' A company may decide not to publicize victimizations against it for another reason. In the case of embezzlement. for example, it may not want to advertise its susceptibility to this crime to other employees.

People also frequently fail to report crimes they feel are trivial; it is perceived that the offence is not worth the effort of notifying the police and/or that the police would not regard the offence seriously.[9] Many petty thefts fall in this category, whether they are acts against individuals or small thefts committed against businesses (e.g., shoplifting).

People are also less likely to report crimes where it is not in their interest to do so. Victims or witnesses may fear reprisals to their reporting of an offence. A battered wife, for example, may fear that the beatings may escalate if she asks the authorities to intervene. Shame, dependency, and attachment to her abusive partner may also keep her silent. Workers witnessing fellow employees stealing on the job or police officers witnessing their fellows shaking down a burglarized establishment may face ostracism, reassignment, or even dismissal for 'blowing the whistle.' The fear that their own misbehaviour will be disclosed in retaliation for their revelations can also keep people mum.

A crime is more likely to be reported when a person has something to gain by so doing. Although battered wives rarely call in the police, one who feels her life is endangered may do so for protection. While a victim of a petty theft may not consider it worthwhile to involve the authorities, those losing valuable items will usually report the incident, even if they are sceptical about the ability of the police to recover their valuables. Such is the case because they wish to collect insurance. Auto thefts, for example, are among the most consistently reported crimes. Because most insurance policies contain deductibles of $50 or $100, a person may feel he or she has little to gain by reporting a theft of items falling within this range.

Some people may report crimes out of a desire for revenge. A rape victim may want to see her attacker caught and punished. She must weigh her desire to achieve this result against the embarrassment and humiliation she may experience as a consequence of reporting the crime.

Incidents will not be reported if victims or witnesses do not perceive the behaviour as criminal. A woman who is beaten by her husband after arguments have escalated gradually may not be aware that a potential crime has occurred when their interaction shifts from intense verbal arguments to the use of moderate physical force. Further, someone who has been abused for years may resign herself to that abuse, rather than regard it as criminal. She may be loath to admit to herself, let alone the authorities, that the person with whom she shares her life is abusing her in such a manner.

Similarly, the victim of a sexual assault may be more likely to report the act if it was committed by a stranger, than if the perpetrator was her boyfriend or a date.[10] She may feel more shame if she knew the offender beforehand. She may also be more likely to blame herself where a prior relationship existed, as she may reprimand herself for any encouragement she feels she may have given the offender in terms of the possibility of sexual relations. Having had a pre-existing (and perhaps sexual) relationship with the offender, the victim may not even conceive of the possibility that a crime has occurred. Also, seeing the event as an extension of their relationship, rather than as an aberration, may help her cope with the assault.

Illicit activity is also less likely to be reported when witnesses consider it justifiable or acceptable. Employee theft may be regarded, even by non-participants, as understandable when it is felt that the workers involved are underpaid. Kitchen staff in a hotel may remain silent when they see waiters stealing food because they may feel the waiters are poorly paid or fed. Witnesses to looting in a race riot may not intervene because they may feel that the looters have legitimate grievances and no reasonable means of obtaining the goods they are stealing.

An entire category of crime that tends to go unreported is that where no tangible victim is involved. Drug users and dealers, prostitutes and their clients, the consumers of pornographic material, those involved in illegal gambling, and related offenders are not likely to turn themselves in to the police. The parties to these 'victimless' crimes mutually consent to participate in the concerned transactions. On occasion, an indignant citizen or dissatisfied customer will inform the police about these activities.

In chapter 10, we observed that the characteristics of the offender and victim will affect the reporting of a crime. Experiments have shown that a bystander will be less likely to report an incident if the offender is of the same race, or if the victim is of another race, has an unkempt appearance, is unattractive, or is somehow different from the bystander. The existence of these types of prejudices shows that the stereotypes people hold about what criminals look like and their empathy towards the victim will influence the evaluation of the act itself. Calling in the police only when a member of a minority group or poor person is involved in illicit behaviour reinforces stereotypes held by the police and the public.

A final category of crime that tends to go unnoticed is that committed by society's élites and corporations. Whether it is embezzlement of a church's funds by a televangelist, the use of one's political position to gain personal profit, or the deliberate exposure of one's employees or the public to dangerous substances, we are dealing with harms which may have far more catastrophic consequences than conventional crimes. Yet they tend to go undetected longer and arouse less public indignation for several reasons.

First, the victimization is diffuse; that is, it is spread over a large number of anonymous people (contributors to a church, the taxpayer, hundreds or thousands of employees, the community surrounding a chemical plant, etc.). Somebody lying on the street or in a hospital emergency room, as a result of a mugging or rape, by contrast, is a very tangible victim.

Second, the harm caused by embezzlement or exposure to toxic materials usually unfolds over a long period of time; it is an insidious process. A company whose employees have unusually high cancer rates can claim that some outside factor was responsible. Even in the case of one of the most conclusive causal relationships – that between cigarette smoking and various illnesses – the tobacco industry maintains stubbornly that factors other than the smoking itself (genetic predisposition) are the principal causes of these illnesses. A mugging is far more dramatic and visible. Even where the perpetrator is not found, there is no need to quarrel about statistical nuances to understand how the victim incurred his or her injuries. Connecting the act with the outcome is straightforward: it is not an elusive and invisible process.

The perpetrator, too, is less tangible in corporate crime than in conventional crime. In a killing, mugging, or sexual assault, the offender has a human face. Specific people can be connected to specific acts.

Determining 'who done it' and who is ultimately responsible can be an overwhelming task in the case of a large corporation. Responsibility is very diffuse. Shareholders and upper-level management may set the general direction of the company and create a climate whereby fiscal restraint becomes far more important than the health and safety of workers. Such a direction may be reinforced by slack enforcement of regulations on the part of government departments and agencies. Perhaps the next level of management makes specific decisions relating to day-to-day operations. Furthermore, supervisors or foremen may be responsible for ensuring that the procedures outlined by management are adhered to. Company doctors might conspire to cover up illnesses brought about by hazards at work. Labour unions, too, might be more concerned with the fiscal health of the company and the size of paycheques than the physical health of workers. In the North American context, at least, organized labour has given priority to pay, economic benefits, and job security, rather than to working conditions. Workers, too, must take some responsibility for the fact that their representatives tend to take such a position and for their own naïvety and indifference to blatantly unhealthy working conditions.

Thus, where does responsibility lie for job-related illnesses in such an instance? It is also difficult to determine who made what decision and said what to whom. For these reasons, corporate crimes are very complex, time-consuming, and expensive to prosecute. Corporations, unlike muggers, are also seen as a constructive force in society, contributing towards the development of a country or to technology, not to mention their role in creating jobs. They also can have considerable political and economic clout, in so far as they contribute to the economy, have access to vast legal resources if prosecuted, and make contributions to political campaigns. The public is not in a position to detect corporate crimes. Local police forces are not charged with the responsibility of dealing with much more than conventional crimes. It is therefore up to government to detect most of these crimes and investigate them. The leverage of large companies and the modest resources available to those agencies responsible for regulating them ensure that corporate illegalities will not be in the forefront of people's minds when crime is considered.

We can see, then, that crimes committed by those with economic and political influence are less likely to come to light than are those committed by the disadvantaged. It has been said that the poor, due to the often crowded nature of their residences, are more likely to spend time on the streets; hence, their quarrels, drinking, and other socially devalued behaviour are more visible and troublesome to others than are the behaviours of those living within the walls of a single home. Apart from this factor, we have seen that offences are more likely to be reported to the police if: they are easier to uncover; they cannot be handled informally; they are not regarded as trivial; they occur among strangers; there is a tangible victim and offender; the victim has something to gain by reporting the crime; and the suspect fits the stereotype of a criminal.

It is not surprising, then, that apart from murder (which is the most extreme of crimes), among the most frequently reported crimes are robbery, burglary, and auto theft. These three offences are usually committed by strangers, so the victim has no stake in protecting the perpetrator. Having no prior relationship with the offender, the victim feels no sense of shame; nor is he or she dependent on or attached emotionally to the offender. An attack, intrusion by, or other victimization by a stranger is also more likely to be defined as a crime. Robberies and burglaries are rapid and dramatic acts that are likely to undermine one's sense of security. The loss of one's car, too, may be viewed as significant, both in terms of sentimentality and from a practical point of view. The recovery of losses in all three crimes or compensation for them entails the reporting of the incident.

Robberies, break-ins, and car thefts are difficult to deal with informally, in the way employee theft, for example, is dealt with, because the parties are rarely acquainted or affiliated in any way. In robbery, the paramount factors in reporting the offence are the intense fear and shock experienced by the victims. In addition, this crime is often committed by the poor, minorities, and addicted persons – groups that victims tend to associate with criminality. In burglary, the paramount factors in reporting tend to be the sense of shock at returning home following the incident and the vulnerability people feel when the environment in which they feel most secure has been invaded by people they do not know. In auto theft, the paramount concern is the value of the item stolen.

Members of the general public do not participate, in large numbers, in any of these three offences. Robbers are drawn principally from society's most disadvantaged, tend to have drug problems, and are usually repeat offenders.[11] Residential break-ins are usually committed by teenage boys and young men principally, although not exclusively, from less affluent neighbourhoods.[12] Auto thefts, other than joy-rides, are usually committed by professional rings, by individuals planning a robbery, and by highly impulsive people seeking transportation. If these three offences are any indication, it would appear that precisely those offences that more hardened and seasoned offenders commit have characteristics conducive to their being reported to the police. At the same time, crimes in which public participation is high (e.g., employee theft, domestic assault, tax crimes) tend to be those that are least apt to be reported. This fact serves to perpetuate the stereotype of the criminal as being a low-status individual who commits conventional crimes.

ARRESTING AND LAYING CHARGES

The same type of filtering processes apply in the decisions to arrest, lay charges, and prosecute a criminal case as in the decision to report a crime to the police. Here again, people of higher social status are more likely to be weeded out. There is much discretion in police work and in prosecutorial decisions. Police officers, as well as their departments, will employ similar criteria to those of citizens in deciding whether to pursue a case. They will not be overly concerned with petty or victimless crimes, and they will refrain from laying charges for behaviour that society, at least tacitly, supports.[13] For example, a group of college students who have been celebrating a football victory in the streets too boisterously will rarely be taken into custody and, if they are, they will normally be released without charges.

The police, however, tend to have their own preconceptions of what constitutes the 'criminal type.' A person who fits the mould is likely to be treated differently from someone considered to be law-abiding. A quarter of a century ago, the President's Crime Commission in the United States made the following observation:

A policeman in attempting to solve crimes must employ, in the absence of concrete evidence, circumstantial indicators to link specific crimes with specific people. Thus policemen may stop Negro and Mexican youths in white neighbourhoods, may suspect juveniles who act in what the policemen consider an impudent or overly casual manner, and may be influenced by such factors as unusual hair styles or clothes uncommon to the wearer's group or era ... those who act frightened, penitent, and respectful are more likely to be released, while those who assert their autonomy and act indifferent or resistant run a substantially greater risk of being frisked, interrogated, or even taken into custody.[14]

Other personal attributes, aside from race, age, appearance, and demeanour, influence the decision to press charges. The social status or power of a suspect is of particular importance. A number of studies have found, for example, that where young offenders are arrested, police are more likely to refer lower-class youths to juvenile court whereas, youngsters from wealthier homes are more likely to be dealt with informally – for example, by being handed over to their parents.[15] This type of diffential treatment may be partly attributable to prejudicial attitudes towards lower-class and minority youth held by police officers. Officers may also feel that the parents of an affluent youngster are more likely to discipline him or her than are parents of a youngster living in a disadvantaged neighbourhood. It has also been conjectured that the police principally arrest those with the least political power as such people are unable to focus public attention on police practices or to exercise political influence over the police.[16]

Mary Owen Cameron's classic study of shoplifting illustrates how economic status has a profound effect on policing, even in the private sector.[17] She found that detectives in a large Chicago department store tended to follow black people and adolescents more than other groups. Their greater vigilance with respect to these two groups was not merely based on the perception, on the part of the store detectives, that blacks and teenagers stole more often. The detectives feared wrongfully accusing an affluent or well-connected person. A person of high status can have access to first-rate legal counsel and initiate a lawsuit against such a store for false arrest. Such a suit is a public relations nightmare for a department store and anything but a boost to the career of a detective making such an error.

Where charges are laid, prosecutors must determine whether to proceed with a case. The leverage of the accused is again important at this level as influential persons can 'pull strings' behind the scenes to pressure prosecutors not to proceed with a case. Also, prosecuting an affluent person can result in long, laborious, and expensive proceedings that absorb valuable prosecutorial resources. Prosecutors may also feel more empathy for people of a similar background and for those committing white collar crimes. Reiman writes:

Not only are the poor arrested and charged out of proportion to their numbers for the crimes poor people generally commit – burglary, robbery, assault and so forth – but when we reach the kinds of crime poor people almost never have the opportunity to commit – antitrust violations, industrial safety violations, embezzlement, serious tax evasion – the criminal justice system shows an increasingly benign and merciful face: the more likely it is that a crime is the type committed by middle- and upper-class folks, the less likely that it will be treated as a criminal offence. When it comes to crime in the streets, where the perpetrator is apt to be poor, he or she is even more likely to be arrested, formally charged, and so on. When it comes to crime in the suites, where the offender is apt to be affluent, the system is most likely to deal with the crime noncriminally, that is, by civil litigation or informal settlement. Where it does choose to proceed criminally ... it rarely goes beyond a slap on the wrist. Not only is the main entry to the road to prison held wide open to the poor, but the access routes to the wealthy are largely sealed off.[18]

Reiman points out that the losses from white-collar crimes exceed by *250 times* the losses from bank robberies. He also notes that, although burglary, larceny, and motor vehicle theft cost the United States about the same as embezzlement, the number of arrests for those three crimes is about *133 times greater* than the number of arrests for embezzlement.

The brutal beating of Rodney King by Los Angeles police officers, described in chapter 1, is another manifestation of the differential treatment sometimes incurred by those in the hands of criminal justice personnel. Higher-status defendants seldom, if ever, are accorded such treatment – this type of treatment is usually reserved for the poor, minorities, and the intransigent.

CONVICTION AND SENTENCING

Although the only factor that should count in the determination of whether one is convicted or acquitted is the facts of the case, the economic means of the accused plays a major role at this stage of the legal process. Indigent defendants are less likely to be able to afford bail and, hence, are more apt to be in detention prior to their trial. It is difficult to interview witnesses and organize a legal defence when one is incarcerated. Also, whereas the affluent can afford first-rate legal counsel, the poor must rely on legal-aid lawyers or public defenders. Privately retained counsel are willing to fight a case to the end, introducing new evidence, bringing in expert witnesses, and causing delays, as their fee is related to the time and other resources expended in fighting a case. Publicly appointed counsel, in contrast, tend to operate on a fixed-fee basis; this fact, coupled with their high case-loads, serves as an incentive to wrap a case up in the shortest time possible. It is not uncommon for a legal-aid lawyer to spend only a few minutes with a client.

Somebody already incarcerated before trial and pessimistic about his or her ability to obtain an acquittal owing to the type of counsel available to him or her may well be willing to plead guilty so as to start being credited for the time served behind bars. It is also in the interests of overburdened prosecutors and public defenders to bring a case expeditiously to a close. Only a fraction of criminal cases in North America go to a full jury trial. Most cases end in guilty pleas. In many U.S. jurisdictions, over 90 per cent of guilty pleas are negotiated, whereby defendants are typically told by the prosecutor that some charges will be reduced or dropped in return for a guilty plea.[19]

Many innocent defendants plead guilty, feeling they have little chance to win a case with the resources available to them and fearing that they will incur the full wrath of the court if they are found guilty after forcing a full trial. In Canada, plea bargaining may be somewhat less common, although it is still quite a frequent practice. In a study of armed-robbery defendants in Quebec, my collaborators and I found that, in a sample of 515 accused, only 8 were tried in front of a judge and jury.[20]

Economic power therefore plays a major role in one's suscep-tibility to conviction, irrespective of one's guilt or innocence. The sentencing stage, too, tends to be more favourable to those of higher social standing. A large body of evidence tells us that the crimes that tend to be committed by middle-class people and the well-to-do (e.g., embezzlement, fraud, income tax eva-sion) usually earn lighter sentences than those more apt to be committed by the poor (e.g., robbery, burglary).[21] Furthermore, in instances of the same crime having been committed, the poor and minorities seem to have a greater susceptibility to longer prison sentences.[22] In the United States, close to half of all the inmates in correctional institutions are black, whereas blacks account for only about a quarter of all arrests in the country.[23] A similar situation prevails with respect to Native people in vari-ous regions of Canada.[24]

It should be noted that the issue of sentencing disparity is a complex one, as many U.S. states have adopted more determi-nate sentencing systems limiting the discretion of judges and parole boards. Limiting judicial discretion and limiting or abol-ishing parole, however, simply increase the leverage of prosecu-tors, as the decision to lay charges and the charges to be laid against a suspect become all important. Therefore, whatever biases prevail at the police and prosecutorial levels will have a profound effect on the selection of people for prison terms.

Other factors, apart from economic power and minority sta-tus, have an effect on sentencing and serve to weed out the more 'respectable' lawbreakers. Judges and parole boards often take into account whether a relationship existed between the offender and the victim prior to the offence: such a relationship is usually considered a mitigating factor and, hence, offences such as spousal assault or date rape, which are often committed by persons without criminal histories, frequently earn lenient treatment.

The prior criminal record of the individual up for sentence is a major criterion in the determination of the type and severity of the sentence to be imposed.[25] For the same offence, an individual with a long criminal record is likely to receive a heavier sentence than is one without such a record. Thus, an occasional offender getting caught once in a lifetime may receive a suspended or short sentence, unless he or she has committed a very serious crime. Even if the person has committed murder, an umblemished record up to that point may result in a modest sentence and will help his or her chances of receiving parole. Having a criminal record, by contrast, is self-perpetuating as one receives increasingly severe sentences and is subject to the close scrutiny of the police.

Yet another factor that may work to the advantage of 'respectable' citizens in the sentencing process is their demeanour. Judges frequently note, in explaining their sentence, that the offender's general attitude and remorse had a bearing on the penalty imposed. Experiments simulating courtroom situations indicate that people who appear attractive are dealt with more leniently than those deemed unattractive (see chapter 2). Other aspects of personal appearance, too, have been shown to affect our regard for and treatment of others; so it stands to reason that this factor may subtly enter into judicial decision making. Mannerisms, too, may be important. Defendants who are better attired, regarded as physically attractive, and with more finely tuned interpersonal skills may stand a better chance of impressing a judge or jury than those lacking these attributes, everything being equal.

As a way of concluding this section, let us look at the case of Ferguson Jenkins, the Canadian-born major-league pitcher and Hall of Famer. In 1980, near the end of his illustrious career in baseball, he was charged with being in possession of small amounts of cocaine and marijuana – the drugs were found in his suitcase as he entered Canada from the United States with his team. Edward Greenspan, the prominent Canadian defence lawyer who represented Jenkins, describes his submission on Jenkins's behalf to get an absolute discharge for his client (which means his conviction does not result in a criminal record) and the response of the presiding judge to it:[26]

There wasn't any question of demanding privileged treatment for Fergie for being a major-league star, only a recognition that even an ordinary penalty, such as a fine, would have been worse than ordinary consequences in his case. It was not a matter of punishing him less than anyone else, only of not punishing him more. 'I'm not asking for leniency,' I said to Judge Young in my final submissions. 'I'm asking for a just result ... To suggest that the consequences are irrelevant would be ignoring a reality of sentencing that ought not to be ignored ... It is not beyond the realm of possibility that if a conviction is imposed by you, then that would lead to a suspension [from baseball] ... it will amount in his case to a banishment from the game of baseball.

'He is thirty-eight years of age. Given what he has done with his life, given the records to which he's so close, he will be denied the opportunity for a place in the sun, for a place in the legends of baseball ... I'm not trying to put Mr. Jenkins above the law. I'm not asking for special treatment. I'm asking for the consideration of the law because the consequences that could flow to him would not be fair.'

'It seems to me,' he [the judge] said in his judgment, 'that a person who has conducted himself in such an exemplary manner that he is held in high account in his community, and indeed in his country, there comes a time when he is entitled to draw on that account. This is one of those occasions. Especially, and particularly, when the potential ramifications of a conviction would be so severe. I therefore find that it would not be contrary to the public interest to grant [an absolute] discharge.'

This case is an exemplar, *par excellence*, of the differential treatment that defendants may be accorded before the law as a result of their standing in the community. I am not arguing that Fergie Jenkins should have been treated more harshly than he was or that the appeal on his behalf was unreasonable (anybody making such an argument would incur the wrath of many Canadian baseball fans!). I am simply asserting that Jenkins, as a result of his celebrity status and respected standing in the community, received the type of consideration that would not have been extended to others committing an identical infraction. His being a celebrity and his ability to retain counsel as respected as

Greenspan certainly tilted the balance in favour of the discharge.

CONCLUSION

We have seen that every stage of the legal process, from the decision to report a crime to the sentencing stage, tends to weed out the powerful, as well as those who are generally regarded as being of 'good character;' that is, those who have no record of criminal behaviour. As a means of concluding, consider the following list of factors that may enter into the decision as to how society deals with a particular socially harmful act. The list contains those elements that increase the likelihood that an offender will face criminal sanctions. The more these elements are present in a case, the greater the likelihood that sanctions will be imposed.

- The offender has little political influence and few economic resources.
- The offender is unattractive and defiant, and has poor interpersonal skills.
- The offender is a member of a minority group.
- The offender has a *known* history of criminal behaviour.
- The offender is a person rather than an organization.
- The act is evaluated as a crime by victims or witnesses.
- The crime is not easily hidden.
- The crime cannot be dealt with internally by an affected organization.
- The offender and victim (be the victim a person or organization) have not been acquainted or affiliated prior to the act.
- The offence is not trivial.
- There is a tangible victim.
- The victim is displaying visible suffering.
- The victim, police, prosecutor, or some other relevant party has something to gain by pursuing the case (e.g., insurance, revenge, or protection for the victim, public confidence for the police, reputation for the prosecutor).

- The victim feels no shame or need to protect the offender.
- The behaviour is not regarded by observers and other relevant parties as justifiable or acceptable.

It is therefore clear that crime is dealt with very unevenly. We might even go so far as to say that that the public and the criminal justice system are not concerned with crime as such; only with selected crimes under particular circumstances. We can see that law enforcement is determined very much by the situation at hand: the attributes of the perpetrator, the nature (not simply gravity) of the act, victim characteristics, and the relationship between offender and victim. The *extent of social harm* is often secondary to these other considerations. Furthermore, the factors influencing the fate of an offender seem to be systematically tilted in favour of the powerful, those with a good reputation in the community, and the offences these 'respectable' people tend to commit.

14

Dealing with Crime by the Public

This book does not present a neat and simplified view of crime as an undertaking of isolated individuals at the fringes of society. Conservative-thinking people have seen the criminal as a degenerate of some sort – the product of heredity (a 'bad seed'), of a family failing to instil discipline, or of an inferior social group. Liberal-minded individuals have taken a more compassionate stance towards the criminal, seeing him or her as coming from an economically deprived background, a broken home, or persecuted minority group.

Yet both these perspectives of crime, as divergent as they may be, share the assumption that participation in crime is limited to only a fraction of the population – generally, the poor, uneducated, chronically unemployed, mentally ill, and minorities. Liberals and conservatives have also tended to focus on conventional crime: brutal murders and assaults, rapes, robberies, common thefts, and burglaries.

This book has shown that, even when we examine these conventional crimes, participation in many of them is fairly widespread and not just limited to a small 'criminal element'; that is to say, while most people do not kill, if we examine those who have, we find a substantial percentage without a criminal record or a known history of antisocial behaviour.

I have also tried to show that there are many types of offences other than those that immediately come to mind when the topic of crime is discussed. Employee theft, tax evasion, misleading advertising; illegal copying of videos and computer software; fraud in auto, television, and other repair businesses; corrupt practices by politicians, criminal justice personnel, and professionals; and environmental abuse are just a few of the crimes that proliferate. Yet, these categories of crime are rarely studied by criminologists or are seldom thought of by ordinary citizens in the context of crime.

There are also many types of dishonest and unscrupulous behaviours that may not violate a law technically, but are substantially similar to crimes in the harm they produce, the violations of trust they engender, and the cynicism they breed. Deceitful sales techniques may be one example of such acts. Although misleading customers about the true quality or value of an item may be as old a practice as entrepreneurship itself, it is erroneous to think that there is no connection between dishonesty of this kind and criminally exploitative behaviours. After all, that is what crime is: the exploitation of others physically, sexually, emotionally, economically, intellectually; the violation of their trust; or the destruction of the environment.

Exploitation breeds further exploitation as experiencing victimization in one sphere may lead one to victimize others in another sphere.[1] When an individual is deceived in the purchase of a car, he or she may take this experience as further evidence that the world is corrupt and that such behaviour is acceptable. We saw in chapter 9 how repeated victimizations may lead victims to adopt global justifications that clear the way for their own wrongdoings. The considerable evidence showing that violence in the family of origin often leads victims to abuse their own children and spouses in adulthood represents just one example of how criminal victimization is self-perpetuating.[2]

The problem with the view I have taken is that a very complex and unsettling picture of crime emerges. Rather than attributing crime and all that is evil in society to a relatively small group of people, I am saying that criminal and socially harmful behaviour is widely (although not evenly) dispersed in society. Similarly, rather than focusing on a handful of crimes, I am arguing, that at some level, despite their different characteristics, all types of crime are interrelated. Developing solutions is easier when we can focus our attention on a limited number of crimes and criminals. But, is it surprising that many conventional efforts to prevent crime that have assumed a small criminal element have not succeeded?

The image of crime I have presented is that of apparent chaos. Most, if not all, members of society are seen as committing at least some crime, some of the time. In this chapter, I hope to make some sense of this apparent chaos. I would like to present an orderly and simple picture of crime, but to do so would do more to meet our understandable need to see the world as just and orderly than it would conform to the reality of crime, at least as I see it. I believe we have to view criminal involvement as a matter of degree, as the real world does not easily accommodate the classification of people into simplistic good and evil, criminal and non-criminal categories. We have to accept that there are different shades of dishonesty, different degrees of commitment to crime, and different levels of seriousness of crimes.

To further confound things, these gradations are difficult to measure as they are largely subjective. People have varying views as to what dishonesty is, and only the person whose behaviour is under consideration really knows his or her true intentions.

When a political leader conceals some information from the public, is he doing it for the good of the country or to save his political skin? When a waitress hands out free drinks to friends without permission, is she doing it out of noble motives, to gain approval from her peers, or to get back at her boss? We might argue that the issue is irrelevant because she engaged in unauthorized behaviour and that is all that counts. The boss, however, might have given her latitude to offer free drinks under certain circumstances, for example, when a customer has already paid for several drinks. Thus, to classify the behaviour as dishonest, we really have to get inside her head, and even she may not be totally aware of what motivates her. Even in law, behaviour itself does not qualify an act as criminal; in most cases, the intentions and mental state of the perpetrator are taken into account.

Measuring the seriousness of criminal acts is likewise a daunting task. Although public-opinion surveys indicate that there is more agreement on the seriousness of some crimes than others, there is still considerable variation in the way people rate different crimes. Even if we look at a crime that most of us agree is very serious, such as murder, when we examine a case concretely, the opinions begin to vary. Most, if not all of us, consider murder in the abstract as reprehensible. But, in any specific case, there are many circumstances which individuals would assess differently. The perpetrator may have been under great emotional stress or have faced extreme provocation, to the point where his or her judgment was impaired. The offender may have been under the influence of drugs or alcohol. The perpetrator may have felt extremely threatened by the victim. He or she may have struck the victim with the intention of hurting or intimidating the latter and may have inadvertently killed the victim instead. There are many other circumstantial factors that will elicit very different reactions from us. Every criminal act is rich in detail, which is why assessing the seriousness of it is such a complex task.

DEALING WITH WIDESPREAD CRIMINALITY

Recognizing the complexity of crime and the widespread involvement in it does not mean we are powerless to deal with it. Although no two criminal acts are identical, we can identify categories of roughly similar offences, although these should not correspond to the legal categories. In Canada, the Criminal Code recognizes two categories of theft – theft under $1,000 and theft over $1,000. In this book, we have referred to the more meaningful terms 'shoplifting,' 'employee theft,' 'hidden-economy trading,' and the like. Even these categories can be further subdivided.

Once crimes are classified into more sensible categories (incidentally, to my knowledge, no criminologist has ever proposed a comprehensive classification of crimes, beyond creating such crude categories as 'violent offences,' 'sex offences,' 'property offences,' etc.), strategies tailored to each category of crime can be developed. It would be ludicrous to suggest that offences as different as tax evasion, mass murder, and computer crimes can be dealt with through identical measures. Developing specific measures for each offence does not contradict my earlier point about the interrelatedness of all crimes. Certainly, we can alter cultural and social conditions to create a general climate in society that is less favourable to all crimes. I will have more to say about these measures later in this chapter.

The first thing that needs to be established is the prevalence or extent of involvement in a given category of crime. Traditionally, our focus has been on the incidence or rate of criminality, that is, the amount of crime occurring in a given area. This information, however, tells us very little about who are committing the crimes. Take tax evasion and robbery (hold-ups and muggings). Both may occur quite frequently in a country, but that is where the comparison ends. Tax crimes, as shown in chapters 4 and 12, are committed by a large segment of the population. Involvement in robbery is far more confined to a limited group in the population – almost always young males, frequently with drug problems. The reason why the rates of robbery may still be high is because many robbers commit a large number of offences in a year. Studies have found that some addicted robbers commit *thousands* of offences a year.[3] The large number of tax crimes is attributable to the participation of literally millions of people in a country like Canada; whereas, much of the robberies may be the undertaking of a few thousand highly active offenders.

Clearly, the implications for preventing these crimes are different. To demonstrate the potential for prevention, I will apply the predictive model developed in chapter 12 to the crimes of tax evasion and robbery. I have argued that the four preconditions for crime are need (or perceived need), opportunity (which includes the consideration of risk), skills, and attitudes/proclivities favourable to the commission of an offence.

Preventing Tax Crimes

As far as need is concerned, many people have much to gain from misrepresenting their true income: they can receive sizeable cash refunds or pay in considerably lower sums than they would be otherwise required to do. It is hard to say whether that need can be altered through improving economic conditions in society, as the evidence suggests that the well-to-do are as active, if not more so, in cheating on their taxes as are those with more modest incomes. Need in this context can be influenced, theoretically, by trying to alter the value people place on money, although this would entail monumental attitudinal changes in any society.

Reducing the opportunities also does not offer much promise in the prevention of the widespread involvement in tax offences. The system in place in countries such as Canada and the United States is that of self-reporting, whereby taxpayers prepare their own tax statements and a very small percentage are audited. For the government to reduce opportunities in this domain, it would have to either change the entire self-reporting procedure or increase dramatically the number of audits it performs. The cost of either would be astronomical and, in North America at least, would be regarded as a major encroachment of the government in the population's private affairs. In business, where many deductions are allowable, auditors would virtually have to follow business people around on a daily basis to verify that their claims are legitimate. Such measures are unthinkable. However some measure of success can be achieved through closing various tax loopholes.

As for skills, cheating on one's taxes does not ordinarily require a great deal of skill, just dishonesty and 'aggressive accounting.' Where skill is required, . accountants can be retained to provide advice. Perhaps we could raise the risk to accountants for preparing fraudulent returns, but accountants are not always involved and, where they do provide advice, they can be misled by their clients.

The final recourse is to change the public attitudes that are so favourable to cheating the government. The experimental evidence presented in this book indicates that people find it easier to victimize large, impersonal concerns, such as governments and big businesses, than to victimize individuals with whom they come into contact. This fact, together with the prevalent view that withholding money from the government is not really cheating but holding on to what rightfully belongs to one, makes tax offences particularly commonplace.

These attitudinal obstacles are very hard to overcome. We do know, however, that underground economies are more likely to flourish when shortages prevail, planned economies stifle incentives, and the tax burdens on ordinary citizens are perceived as unreasonably high. It is also probably true that a government that is regarded as illegitimate or corrupt is more likely to elicit tax crimes than one that is held in high regard. Therefore, favourable economic and political conditions can at least minimize the volume of tax crimes.

Preventing Robbery

We have seen that tax offences are very difficult to eradicate and that the few measures that are available may entail large-scale cultural, economic, and political changes. Robbery, by contrast, can be combatted to some degree through more focused measures.

As far as need is concerned, most of the public does not have a need to commit the offence, and that is one reason why participation in hold-ups and muggings is not widespread in the population. Robbery, after all, is not just a property crime, but one involving force or the threat of force. A person needing money can select from many other illegal activities. Robbery achieves two principal goals for its authors: a sense of power and instant cash. Most people do not have to resort such an extreme measure to achieve a sense of power and self-worth. They also do not have such a desperate and immediate need for cash as addicted robbers, addiction and robbery being very closely linked. The need for robbery among this relatively small group of citizens can be dealt with in a significant way by addressing those social factors responsible for drug use and predatory violence. Drug use and robbery tend to proliferate when large numbers of young people (often members of a minority group) are marginalized in society and experience a sense of hopelessness. Robbers are often angry young men who come from disorganized neighbourhoods and feel their opportunities for entering society's mainstream are blocked. Combatting drug abuse directly, and perhaps even the legalization of many prohibited drugs, may lessen the desperate need for cash now seen among many drug abusers.

Unlike tax evasion, a fair amount can be achieved by limiting opportunities for robbery. Successes in dealing with hold-ups have been achieved through limiting the cash available in stores, making targets more difficult to holdup (hardening targets), and raising the risks robbers confront.[4] These risks can be raised by posting security guards at banks, decreasing the response time of the police to the robbery site, increasing the conviction rate, and increasing the length of sentences robbers receive. These measures can be particularly effective when the number of people committing this offence is quite small. Increasing conviction rates and sentences becomes more difficult when the number of robbers is large enough to overwhelm the criminal justice system. Thus, a hard-line, punitive response can be effective in relation to certain crimes, particularly those in which only a relatively small number of people are involved.

Most robberies do not involve a great deal of skill and only specialized targets, such as banks and armoured carriers (Brinks, Wells Fargo), have the resources to raise the skill level required of robbers. As far as attitudes are concerned, there is very little social support for robbery in the general population; therefore, changing societal attitudes is not relevant to this crime.

SOME ALTERNATIVES TO THE TRADITIONAL APPROACHES TO FIGHTING CRIME

Our examples of tax evasion and robbery show how different

crimes respond to different preventive strategies. My position is that one of the principal factors determining the appropriate strategy is the prevalence or extent of participation in an offence. When involvement is very widespread in society or some milieu (an organization), the attitudes of the people therein need to be examined. We might even have to live with the possibility that some crimes are very resistant to elimination. Tax offences, it might be argued, are endemic to contemporary, bureaucratized societies where the population feels alienated from an impersonal and remote government. Even in this case, however, we are not at a complete loss for solutions as there are more localized forms of government, such as that existing in Switzerland, where the population feels they have more input into political decision making.

The traditional approach to fighting crime has been to call in 'specialists' such as the police or private security personnel. Allied with this approach is the temptation to mete out stiffer sentences to convicted persons. This traditional approach is now regarded by the law enforcement community itself to have a very limited effect in suppressing most crimes.[5]

An alternative strategy to that of delegating the responsibility for law enforcement to professional 'crime-fighters' is to include the concerned population in crime prevention. Giving people greater responsibility, in both developing and implementing a prevention plan, may be a worthwhile strategy, not only in crimes against the state, but in many crimes committed against organizations. Waiters and waitresses who scam in the restaurant business indicate, for example, that a significant reason for their actions is that they are poorly paid and not respected by their employers. Although such behaviour cannot be eliminated completely even in the most positive work environment, the presence of an adversarial climate of 'us' versus 'them' is likely to exacerbate dishonesty on the job.

Stuart Henry's research in relation to hidden-economy networks (chapter 4) revealed that such thefts and bartering for goods were justified by employees on the grounds that 'it's a public service to help each other nick from millionaire companies.'[6] Traditional preventive strategies can facilitate the deterioration of the relations between employees and their employers. The conventional response of large companies in dealing with employee theft and illegal trading has been either to ignore the activity or to employ private security personnel. The temptation to ignore small-scale thefts and to write losses off as 'shrinkage' is great because reporting such incidents to the police or firing personnel is embarrassing, costly to the company, and not conducive to positive labour relations. Ignoring such activity, however, is read as resignation or even acceptance of it. By 'turning a blind eye' the company sets no standards.

On the other extreme, a company can try to take a hard-line approach by using private security personnel to crack down on internal theft. The problem is that such theft is so pervasive that only the 'tip of the iceberg' is uncovered. The return for enforcing a small fraction of crimes may be the creation of precisely those conditions companies wish to avoid. Management, by unilaterally taking responsibility for enforcement, conveys to workers that they cannot be trusted and bear no responsibility for enforcing company norms. They thus succeed in antagonizing workers and creating a climate whereby employees feel no responsibility for upholding rules. The worker's attitude is more likely to become that of 'They don't trust us anyway, so what is there to lose' and 'Let's see if they can catch us.' By taking an authoritarian stance, the company therefore makes sabotage and theft more probable.

It has been suggested that companies enlist their employees in enforcement activities. As Henry has pointed out, informal norms setting limits on what employees can take from work already prevail in many environments.[7] After all, workers know that if some among them take items of great value, the company may crack down on all unauthorized activities. As a result, workers may ostracize an overzealous thief. They have even been known to steal the merchandise the 'outlaw' has stolen.

Companies have the option of taking advantage of the informal controls already existing among their personnel to create a system of theft control that both respects workers and is more effective than traditional controls. Perhaps, a more democratic and egalitarian framework can be established in which management and employee representatives reach a consensus on broad company goals. This should not be so difficult because all parties have a stake in the company's well-being. Worker's committees may then be given the responsibility for ensuring that approved policies and practices are enforced. Empowering workers by giving them a say in a company's overall direction, as well as in rule enforcement, accords them more of a stake in the company's performance and might lead them to recognize that dishonest activities on their part are ultimately detrimental to themselves.

The recent trend towards community policing shares similar goals. This model of policing, which has been implemented in a number of North American cities, puts the citizen at the forefront of many law enforcement and service functions that have been traditionally the exclusive domain of sworn police officers.[8] According to the community policing philosophy, residents no longer play a passive role, as in the past, when they merely served as witnesses to crime and, perhaps, set up a Neighbourhood Watch program under the guidance of their local police department. Rather, they play an active role in both operations and setting the priorities of a department.

Citizens staff small storefront (mini) police stations that handle more minor, day-to-day problems. Community police officers work with citizens to solve problems, such as neighbourhood conflicts, disorder, and fear of crime, before they escalate. They play a facilitating role, helping citizens solve their own problems and improve their quality of life, rather than act as authority figures who are either benevolent or intimidate the public.

This new model of policing is based on the finding that the militaristic, 'law enforcement' posture of policing has been largely ineffective in preventing crime. At its best, the technologically driven, 'professional' police force has been able to handle just a small proportion of crime. At the same time, the impersonal, authoritarian style of policing it promotes is more likely to alienate the population it serves and to result in insufficient cooperation from the public. Such cooperation as reporting crimes and serving as witnesses is now recognized to be vital to law enforcement. By giving people a say in crime prevention and by concerning themselves with the quality of neighbourhood life, the police are more likely to elicit respect and cooperation from the public.

By joining forces, the police and the public avoid an adversarial relationship that breeds disrespect for the law. Furthermore, the police are more apt to regard the community as an ally rather than as a threat. It is the feeling among police personnel that they are isolated from the community that produces hostility towards citizens and the creation of a subculture that fosters corruption and cover-ups.

The cases of employee theft and policing crime in general suggest that mobilizing people and allowing them to assume greater responsibility in crime prevention may be far more effective than trying to impose order on them. Breaking down apathy and the unencumbered pursuit of self-interest are, as I have tried to show in chapter 10, a community's best defences against crime. Apathy keeps people from contributing positively to a community and from responding when problems arise. Much crime and other exploitative behaviour could be avoided if people regarded fellow citizens as allies rather than as potential adversaries who are to be regarded with suspicion.

In the sphere of labour relations, Japanese corporations, unlike their North American counterparts, demonstrate loyalty to their employees and give high priority to job security. In return, employees, even in the largest companies, take a personal interest in the welfare of the company because they and the company are perceived as one. I remember shopping in one of the massive department stores in the Ginza district of Tokyo and the pride that each employee took in the merchandise being sold. These workers, I thought, are not going to be chronically absent from work, use drugs and alcohol on the job, or steal from or sabotage the company.

Professionalism and specialization have helped alienate people and create the climate of indifference so conducive to criminality. Just as we have learned in medicine that the front line in dealing with disease is the patient and his or her lifestyle rather than the physician, we are beginning to discover that the front lines of crime fighting are the potential victims and perpetrators themselves.

The traditional response to employee theft has been to call in security consultants and personnel. The response to shoplifting has been to hire floorwalkers (detectives) and to introduce a variety of electronic equipment. The response to crime in general was to 'leave it to the police.' The police became highly professional crime fighters with specialized training, weapons, and tactics. They have worn distinctive uniforms and have patrolled in 'souped-up' patrol cars that have distanced them from the community they serve. Senior police officers take management courses for executives. Sophisticated computerized dispatching and crime analysis systems, as well as identification techniques, have been acquired. Specialized tactical and other squads have been established in larger departments. And, all the while, crime levels have not been affected significantly as a result of these developments.

The failure of this professionalization of the police to lower crime levels is, in part, attributable to the fact that ordinary citizens have seen no role for themselves in crime prevention. The traditional model of crime fighting sees criminals as some alien, parasitical group of predators who, with good police work, can be plucked from society, allowing the rest of us to live in peace.

In reality, crime usually originates in the community in which it occurs. Many violent crimes take place in the home, and among those who know one another. Thefts on the job are frequently a result of the working conditions in that environment. Burglaries, rapes, assaults, and robberies also usually take place within a mile or two of the perpetrator's residence.[9] Thus, crime cannot be dealt with adequately by parachuting professionals onto the scene – the basic dynamics of crime and the moral malaise that often underlies it must be addressed if significant inroads are to be made.

The same realization has occurred in the mental health field where peer counselling, through countless self-help groups, has to some degree supplanted intervention by professionals. Groups as diverse as alcoholics, overweight individuals, the physically disabled, gamblers, and crime victims' groups sometimes provide a combination of support and insight that can compete with individual, one-to-one counselling. The emphasis increasingly is on empowering individuals and having them take responsibility for themselves, instead of a passive stance.

Similarly, entire communities have sometimes taken matters in hand to deal with the crime problem confronting them. One example was the prevention program established in the Asylum Hill section of Hartford, Connecticut, in the 1970s.[10] The program, funded by both public and private organizations, targeted robbery and burglary, two offences arousing particular concern in Asylum Hill. The goal of the program was not only to reduce the incidence of these crimes but, at the same time, to reduce levels of fear in the neighbourhood.

A multidisciplinary team of specialists (urban planners, criminologists, police) designed a program which included physical changes of the neighbourhood, changes in policing, and the cooperation of residents. Since some of the perpetrators of these crimes were from other communities, and Asylum Hill was becoming highly transient, urban designers, in collaboration with local residents, developed a plan whereby the neighbourhood would be less accessible to outsiders. Cul-de-sacs (dead ends) were created at some critical intersections, the entrances to some streets were narrowed, and other streets became one-way routes. These changes not only reduced the flow of outsiders into the community but increased the sense of security of residents, resulting in their greater use of parks and streets. Rather than avoiding the streets, residents were now in a position to exercise a stronger deterrent effect through heightened surveillance levels.

The involvement of community organizations in the neighbourhood design changes, too, gave residents who had become
very apathetic a greater sense of control over the crime problem
and stimulated the development of the type of informal bonds
necessary in dealing with burglary and robbery. The program
increased the cohesiveness of the neighbourhood and, with it,
the ability of local residents to recognize strangers and suspicious activities.

To make full use of this increased guardianship of citizens
over their community, the Hartford Police Department assigned
a decentralized team of officers permanently to Asylum Hill,
rather than rotating personnel, as was their usual policy. In this
way, communication could pass back and forth between residents and the police, each supporting the efforts of the other.

The program appeared to have had a short-term impact on
the burglary and robbery rates in Asylum Hill. More important,
the program seemed to affect residents' fear levels with respect
to these crimes. Residents also were less likely, three years after
the program's implementation, to regard these offences as con-
stituting a serious neighbourhood problem. Moreover, they
were more likely to regard other residents and the neighbourhood as a whole in a positive way.

What do we do about crime by politicians and business people?
As already shown, research indicates that the more estranged we
become from others, the easier it is to justify victimizing them. In
the same way, I believe that the more removed politicians
become from their constituents, and business people become
from their customers, the more likely it is that these constituents
and customers will be regarded as faceless masses to be exploited
and even abused. As a very general principle, therefore, I believe
that overly centralized political systems that tend to alienate
leaders from the population at large may be more prone to corruption and atrocities. Leaders who are more directly accountable to a specific community or region and who can identify with
the population they are representing will tend to show more
empathy towards the public, everything else being equal.

The same situation undoubtedly holds in the business world, where large multinational corporations and chain operations will have little concern for the welfare of a given community. The selective looting and burning of businesses owned by persons living outside the ghetto during the civil disturbances in the 1960s in the United States showed the antipathy prevailing between ghetto dwellers and these outsiders. The rioters felt that these business people, much like the 'slumlords,' had no compunction whatsoever about exploiting inner-city blacks. Executives setting policies at corporate headquarters are unlikely to be sensitive to the concerns of consumers living in communities possibly thousands of miles away. Even organized-crime bosses may subscribe to the idea of selective victimization. This was illustrated poignantly in the movie *The Godfather* when the heads of various New York crime families agreed to distribute heroin only in black neighbourhoods.

By contrast, businesses operated by local residents are less likely to extract profits at any price. They will tend to have more empathy for neighbourhood residents, who are likely to be of a similar social class and ethnicity, and to have shared similar experiences. Also, various pressures to which entrepreneurs from the outside are more immune can exert an influence on a local business operator. An unscrupulous local entrepreneur may face ostracism by the community. His family may face harassment. If a corner grocery-store owner is perceived as hostile to the neighbourhood, his business may be more prone to shoplifting, vandalism, and even hold-ups. There is thus a vested interest in maintaining good relations with the surrounding community.

The localization of businesses and governments may therefore make them less prone to certain forms of victimization – victimization which usually goes both ways; that is, more remote governments and businesses are more likely to victimize and to be victimized by the population they serve. Where politicians or businesses do abuse their offices or endanger employees, consumers, or the environment, we may have recourse to measures that are more effective than in the case of other crimes.

Criminologists John Braithwaite and Gilbert Geis have argued that the type of punitive sanctions that are less effective for conventional offenders, such as robbers and assaulters, may be more useful in dealing with corporate crime.[11] They assert that corporate crimes (and, perhaps, many political crimes) may be easier to deter through legal sanctions because they are more apt to be calculated rather than impulsive acts. Also, political and corporate criminals have far more to lose than most conventional criminals if they are subject to criminal sanctions. The cost of a conviction may include the loss of their reputation in the community, their job, and a comfortable home and family life.

One of the most important assets of a corporation is its reputation. Highly visible legal sanctions can serve as a powerful deterrent to corporate misconduct. As it stands now, penalties imposed on companies tend to be low profile and usually take the form of fines that are very modest in relation to their assets. Corporations are often prepared to absorb these periodic fines: they are not deterred by them. In the case of the Pinto, for example, Ford executives calculated that even paying out $50 million in lawsuits for deaths and injuries resulting from the faulty design of the car's gas tank was preferable economically to altering the design of the tank.[12] More visible and harsh sanctions, such as the incarceration of company executives, would be something a company would want to avoid because of the hardship the individuals involved would be forced to endure, as well as the loss of the standing in the community the company would experience.

One type of measure that may well serve as a deterrent to business crime, whether perpetrated by a large corporation, car dealership, or repair shop, would be publicizing the names of companies convicted of infractions. Labour unions and consumers' groups could work with and even finance a regular column in local newspapers devoted to publishing the names of businesses that have been convicted of violating codes relating to the health and safety of workers, environmental laws, and laws protecting consumers.

Another type of punitive measure would be to revoke the charter of the corporation or to place it into receivership. A less draconian measure would be to limit the company's charter so as to force it to discontinue those aspects of its operations that were deemed to be in violation of the law.

Shaming is a practice that has been undertaken for centuries in many parts of the world. It can be an effective vehicle of social control with respect to infractions committed by individuals, as well as corporations. In recent history, community or workers' courts have been used in China and the Soviet Union, whereby the accused was judged by his other colleagues and could be required to issue an apology and self-denunciation. Such systems, although potentially highly repressive, have in some contexts been found to effectively deter theft in the workplace, as few deterrents are more powerful than the disapproval of one's peers.[13]

REFORMING VALUES AND SOCIAL CONDITIONS CONDUCIVE TO CRIMINALITY

Having offered some specific recommendations for preventing crime in various spheres, I would like to briefly address some of the larger social and cultural issues underlying crime. Some of these were alluded to in chapter 11, but bear emphasis, as they are fundamental in shaping a community's crime problem. The prescriptions I am providing are of a general nature and are based on my understanding of the international crime situation. It is important to note that research comparing the crime situation in different societies is not only lacking in abundance, but fraught with numerous difficulties. Foremost among these are the many different legal systems and codes, and the diverse procedures for collecting crime data around the world. To make things worse, no country collects information on the issue discussed in this book – the prevalence or extent of involvement of the population in different crimes.

Therefore, the recommendations I am about to make are hardly based on irrefutable fact. Rather, they are grounded on my reading of the comparative criminological research that does exist, as well as on some sociological and criminological principles to which I subscribe. I therefore urge the reader to examine the proposals with a critical eye; if discussions can be provoked on some of these larger issues, we may at least move towards some agreement on the social forces that can build a community's resistance to crime. For too long, in my view, much criminological theorizing and research have been driven by ideological dogma, narrow-minded self-interest, or a preoccupation with isolated issues rather than broader social concerns. In these proposals, I am trying to steer clear of any political allegiances and am rather attempting to identify those societal reforms that hold the promise of preventing crime in a given country, region, or community.

Combatting Social Inequality

The conclusion is unavoidable that large gaps between rich and poor or between a dominant social group and minorities provide fertile ground for serious crime and social unrest. Countries like the United States and Brazil, with pronounced differences in standards of living among their citizens, tend to have higher levels of crime and other forms of social pathology (e.g., drug addiction) than countries, such as those in northern Europe, where social policy guarantees decent minimum standards of living for all citizens.[14]

The large gaps between the poor and affluent are likely to engender the greatest frustration and sense of injustice where the disadvantaged have not been taught to accept their situation, but rather have been told that they are both entitled to and have access to the means to achieve success. The sense that legitimate avenues of success are blocked creates hopelessness and despair, which are conducive to predatory crime and civil disturbances. Where the underclass is concentrated in specific areas, such as the U.S. urban ghettos, an entire different way of life or subculture may emerge to adapt to the seemingly hopeless economic situation.

Much of the population may, out of discouragement, take up vices such as substance abuse, gambling, and prostitution. Becoming an entrepreneur in, say, the drug traffic, may provide a ghetto dweller with an identity and a measure of status, apart from its economic rewards. The kingpins of these vices may be the only tangible role models for the young, and, therefore, these patterns of behaviour are transmitted intergenerationally. It comes as no surprise that such a high percentage of non-white, inner-city dwellers in the United States come into contact with the criminal justice system (see chapter 4).

Any policy preventing the formation of a large underclass and a sense of despair among a significant proportion of the population can prevent the formation of such a critical mass of serious offenders. Reasonable minimum income and wage policies, anti-discrimination programs, incentives for investment in lower income communities, support for families under stress, educational opportunities, vocational training, and enlightened urban planning are just a few of the measures that can avoid the type of monumental social problems that make the crime problem in certain areas seem insoluble.

Developing Allegiances to the Community without Stifling Individual Rights, Ambition, and Creativity

Some forms of crime, as discussed above, are fostered by a sense of despair about reaching one's goals. Such alienation can be created not only in situations where opportunities for success are blocked, but also in those environments where individual rights and interests are totally subordinated to that of the community and society at large. In totalitarian regimes where a central government has set political, economic, and social policies unilaterally and has disallowed or set limits on private ownership, the lack of input into political decision making and of economic incentives creates deep resignation. In the former Soviet Empire, crime and social pathology often took the form of suicide, alcoholism, sabotage at work, and black-market activities. In chapter 4, we saw how the inefficiency of the centrally planned economy of Poland, under the communist regime, virtually forced peasants to sell their goods and conduct other business through illegal channels.

At the other extreme are societies that establish a cult of the individual, whereby communal rights and respect for authority figures are totally subordinated to the welfare and interests of the individual. Probably nowhere is this cult more pronounced than in the United States. There are many ramifications for a society centred on the individual. Governmental intervention is minimized, which means that tax rates are low, and support is minimal for public works, the poor, education, parental leave, working mothers, and many other spheres that foster some of society's basic institutions (e.g., family and education).

An individual-centred society is also bound to be one in which relationships between people (whether at work or even in the family) are likely to be highly competitive, rather than supportive. Overly competitive environments create winners and losers, rather than a balance in which compromises are worked out and the dignity of all parties remains intact. Hostility and vindictiveness are the result when people are rejected without compassion, whether they are cast aside by their employers, dumped by their spouses, or abandoned by the educational system.

An overly competitive society is also one in which profits are pursued without regard for the welfare of employees, customers, and business ethics in general. When corporations act irresponsibly, violate acts protecting the health and safety of workers, use deceptive marketing techniques, and produce dangerous or useless products, how can their employees be expected to refrain from theft on the job, and the unemployed to restrain themselves from committing conventional crimes? Because criminality is, in a sense, contagious, it is vital that the most visible members of society, such as political and business leaders, be held to a high standard of behaviour. Societies founded on a strong ethic of individualism are not likely to promote such ideas as corporate social responsibility.

Another implication of radical individualism is the pervasiveness of anti-authority attitudes. Individuals who break the rules and act unconventionally are often revered for 'bucking the system.' The state and the legal system are regarded as intruding upon the sovereignty of the individual. In such a climate, shady entrepreneurs such as Richard Sears, founder of Sears, Roebuck, are held out as role models to other business people. Outlaws, too, may be regarded with considerable admiration. When Jesse and Frank James robbed the Kansas City Fair in broad daylight in 1872, their audacity was held in admiration by many citizens. A reporter of the *Kansas City Times* described the robbery as 'so diabolically daring and so utterly in contempt of fear that we are bound to admire it and revere its perpetrators.'[15]

Certainly, individualism and anti-authority attitudes, when taken to these extremes, do not encourage law-abiding behaviour and social responsibility on the part of individuals or corporations. At the same time, stifling authoritarian rule creates its own forms of social pathology and crime. It may not be coincidental that countries such as Japan and Switzerland, which leave room for individual initiative and creativity, while teaching communal values and social responsibility, have been among the most successful in dealing with crime.[16]

Avoiding the Adverse Effects of Urbanization, Urbanism, and Mobility

The experience of many societies indicates that the processes of urbanization and industrialization create their share of social problems. People who have lived in rural areas and small towns may flood in large numbers to an inhospitable urban environment without the skills required to compete in that setting. If urbanization proceeds too quickly, the employment and housing opportunities required to accommodate the migration of large masses of people are simply not present. In such an event, the city is confronted with a large number of people with adjustment problems, perhaps concentrated in one district, who no longer have the support (emotional, material, spiritual) they could count on in the smaller communities from which they have come.

To make matters worse, most newcomers from rural areas and foreign countries move into lower-income and, often, disorganized neighbourhoods that already have their share of crime and social problems. With all the vulnerabilities of and stresses on families in these situations, it is not hard to see why the offspring often succumb to the temptations of these neighbourhoods. Studies at the University of Chicago in the 1920s and 1930s showed how each successive wave of immigrants tended to have among the highest levels of crime in the city.[17]

The high level of mobility of the population in North America also undermines community life. Highly transient people are less likely to have a vested interest in their community and, hence, to participate in various aspects of community life. Neighbourhoods containing many highly mobile residents cannot become cohesive or stable, or develop some shared values, informal controls on behaviour, or directions for the young. It is not surprising that transient areas, such as Canada's northern forestry and mining communities, experience so much violence and substance abuse.

Urban life itself may be conducive to criminality for a number of reasons. In chapter 11, I discussed research showing that people find it easier to victimize those unknown to them or different from them. Both of these conditions are more likely to be found in large urban settings than in small towns. One's behaviour is also less likely to be detected in a large community; even if it is one is less likely to be identified and held accountable for criminal conduct than one would be in a small community. Large cities, because of their multicultural nature and divergent lifestyles, do not promote the consistent set of values and conduct norms that may be present in smaller communities. In urban environments there is a greater tolerance of behavioural diversity and a general abandonment of traditional norms.[18] Pluralism is more likely to promote innovation, but it also provides a favourable environment for non-conformist behaviour of a destructive nature.

Some scholars have asserted that the fast pace, noise, overcrowding, and various other stresses associated with large cities create a form of stimulus overload with which urban dwellers must deal. It is argued that this hyperstimulation is dealt with by shutting off one's emotions, and hence decreasing one's sensitivity to the plight of others. This phenomenon might help explain the finding, reported in chapter 10, that urbanites are less likely than those raised in a rural community to help fellow citizens in need or to report a crime in progress. Altruism is the opposite of crime and other forms of exploitation. Presumably, where there is less altruism, there will be more crime.

Another feature of urban life is the emphasis on external appearances and material possessions. The wide range of activities brings people in contact with large numbers of other persons, thereby increasing the superficiality of these contacts. Intimacy is often replaced by a focus on status symbols, such as high salaries, luxury cars, and designer clothes.[19] The lack of closeness can lead to a sense of social isolation, as well as a lack of concern for the well-being and transgressions of others.

What do we do about the criminogenic effects of urbanization, mobility, and urbanism? Obviously, a democratic society must wrestle with the conflict between allowing total freedom of movement within its borders and contending with the adverse effects of the unrestricted mobility of its citizens. It is a question of civil liberties versus a potential catastrophe. Perhaps one example of such a catastrophe is the case of Mexico City, where thousands of people pour into the city weekly from the countryside. The result is a social and environmental disaster. No form of social or political organization could absorb such a large-scale invasion of needy people. If governments do not wish to intervene to halt such mass migrations, it would appear that social policies ought to address the regional inequities and deprivation that lead to such desperate uprooting of a large segment of the population.

The same holds for immigration policies that do not consider the social impact of very liberal levels of immigration. Although multiculturalism may well be a desirable objective, this process can occur at different speeds. Any form of immigration, particularly that involving many different ethnic, racial, and national groups, involves adjustments by both the newcomers and the host society. The lower the level of immigration, the more support (educational, vocational, economic, housing) immigrants can receive and the less threatened the indigenous population will feel. Overly liberal policies produce numerous adjustment problems on both sides, creating a situation that is ripe for crime, as well as interethnic and racial conflicts.

As far as urban life itself is concerned, zoning laws can limit the growth of cities or at least physically separate communities so they can become somewhat self-contained. Localized political structures can also give the residents of a large city a greater sense of involvement in the decisions affecting their lives. Furthermore, neighbourhood organization of the type that occurred in the Asylum Hill section of Hartford can help build community cohesion.

Changing Attitudes Conducive to Violence and Other Unlawful Acts

As discussed in chapter 10, there is a myth that society in general stands firmly behind its laws. In reality, attitudes and values promoting violence and other unlawful behaviour are found in many societies. Physically abusive behaviour towards children is considered by many to be the sovereign right of parents. The right to hit one's spouse, even in Western countries, was enshrined in law up to the beginning of this century. There are still many men who feel that they have the right to control their wives in this way.

Machoism is still very much alive in many communities and even societies as a whole. Males may learn from a young age that the proof of manhood is the willingness to fight in response to provocations and insults. One reflection of this accent on 'toughness' can be found in the level of gang activity in a given community. In Los Angeles, for example, it has been estimated that there are more than 70,000 street gang members. Another reflection of machoism is the level of aggression found in popular sports. In North America, one need look no farther than the nearest hockey rink or football field to appreciate the value our society places on aggression.

Yet another indication of machoism is the presence of a gun culture or mania surrounding firearms. The evidence from countries such as Switzerland, where many households possess a firearm, suggests that it is not gun ownership *per se* that contributes to violent crime. Rather, it is the glorification of weapons and their irresponsible use. A culture in which there is a fascination with weapons and where the calibre of a firearm is a measure of one's manhood is one in which conflicts are more likely to involve the use of guns to settle scores. The countless publications and associations devoted to gun lovers in North America is testimony to this worship of guns.

There is no quick and easy solution to changing social values and attitudes favourable to crimes of violence. Public education at all levels is certainly one step. The public should be informed of the cost of gun worship. At present, the loudest voices are those of organizations, such as that of the National Rifle Association in the United States, with a vested interest in the glorification of firearms. Changes in social attitudes promoting violence that have prevailed for centuries cannot be expected to occur overnight.

Investing in Families

No discussion about preventing widespread or hard-core criminality would be complete without mentioning the role of the family. Research in criminology has shown consistently that family dynamics and stresses are related to crime. Children who are physically or sexually abused are more likely to engage in such behaviour themselves as they grow older than those not subject to such abuse.[20] Families instilling discipline are more likely to promote conformist behaviour than those that encourage impulsive, non-reflective behaviour.[21] Economic strains on families are also important. Families in perpetual conflict and those living in chronic poverty are less able to provide sufficient nurturing and are more likely to be abusive than more stable and financially secure families.[22]

There are a number of ways in which society can invest in families in order to strengthen familial bonds, minimize abuse, and enhance the promotion of pro-social values. One way is to provide for parental (maternity and/or paternity) leaves that are of a duration long enough to develop a close bond between parent and child. In the United States, there is no national statutory parental leave policy, whereas in Sweden, such policies call for extended leaves. Accessible and affordable daycare, too, can ease the stresses facing working parents. Here again, North America lags behind many European countries where day care, regardless of one's income, is accessible even for very young children.[23]

Also important are programs that can detect and reach out to families that are at high risk of producing offspring particularly predisposed to antisocial behaviour. Physically abusive families, families in conflict, those with substance abuse problems, and those headed by young single parents are especially at risk. Although the resources needed to provide these families with financial, educational, and psychological support may be extensive, these expenditures must be weighed against the long-term social and economic costs of not acting decisively in these areas.

ARE WE EXPERIENCING A MORAL DECLINE?

Does the widespread involvement in crime documented in this book reflect some form of moral decline and the ascendance of an 'anything goes' morality? I have tried to show that many forms of criminality are widespread in all sectors of society, including the elite. Commentators, such as the influential U.S. public policy analyst James Q. Wilson, suggest that, since the 1960s, there has been a significant shift in the fundamental values pursued in U.S. society. Wilson contends that some of society's basic institutions – the family, the church, and the school – have been weakened in terms of their ability to exert authority and influence over the lives of the young. He asserts that recent decades have seen the triumph of 'self-expression over self-control as a core human value' and we now 'exalt rights over duties, spontaneity over loyalty, tolerance over conformity, and authenticity over convention.'[24]

Unfortunately, it is hard to measure such shifts in values or to determine whether, in fact, criminality is considerably more widespread at present than was the case a half-century ago. The type of standardized data now being collected in many countries simply weren't available at that time.[25] The data that are available – primarily in the form of archival sources – suggest that medieval England and America during its settlement were very violent places. Then, with the exception of a few brief turbulent periods, rates of violence declined until the post–Second World War period. Since then, a fairly gradual increase has been experienced in these two as well as many other countries.[26]

In any event, no records have been kept on the question of the extent of the public's involvement in crime. So, we can only speculate, from the anecdotes of older generations, that more people engage in violence today, that employers are more callous, employees less trustworthy, politicians more corrupt, and the young more unruly than in the past. We have no means of verifying definitively whether these represent the nostalgic observations of society's elders or whether they reflect a genuine decline in our moral standards.

It may be the case, in part, that we are becoming more self-critical and taking more notice of flaws in society and its institutions than might have been the case several generations ago. Since Watergate, the media in many countries have placed politicians under a microscope and have uncovered increasingly more corruption, abuses of power, and peccadilloes. The professionalization and expansion of police departments has also contributed to greater vigilance in detecting, reporting, and recording crime.

At the same time, the criminal justice system and the media may have contributed inadvertently to *real* increases in antisocial behaviour. By expanding and professionalizing the justice system, we have in a sense removed the responsibility of dealing with socially disapproved behaviour from the community and shifted this responsibility to specialized agencies. Rather than encouraging the community to reflect upon and, perhaps, develop constructive solutions to its problems, we have turned over social control to agencies that are primarily punitive–agencies that tend to react after the fact instead of developing long-term solutions to persistent problems.

We therefore have the community, on one side, and those monitoring it, on the other. Inadvertently, we have set up a polarized 'us–them' situation, with a fair amount of mutual distrust. The police subculture in North America is testimony to the isolation of the police from the community. Police officers have often felt pitted against the community, waging war against the 'bad guys' often with little cooperation and gratitude from the public. Citizens, at the same time, have felt they had little say in law making and enforcement. To many citizens, rule-breaking has been regarded as an action not against the community but against those in control; i.e., 'getting one over on the system.'

The media, too, may have played a role in fostering antisocial behaviour. The electronic media are often criticized for their glorification of violence and sexual exploitation. They may also be accused of promoting the values and lifestyles of a marginal group of eccentric and Bohemian individuals based in Los Angeles and New York. Media celebrities frequently flaunt their unconventional, self-indulgent behaviour, glorify the use of illicit drugs, make light of their marital problems, and communicate the idea that superficial witticisms and physical appearance are more important than genuine wisdom, empathy, and personal integrity.

The media also promote contradictory messages. While many films, soap operas, and talk shows titillate viewers with accounts of life in the fast lane, educational programs tell viewers not to use illegal drugs, to avoid driving while impaired, and to engage in safe sex. Routinely exposing the public to contradictory messages undermines the credibility of those messages designed to cultivate pro-social behaviour. To the young, contradictory messages are read to mean that there are no moral absolutes, that all of society's rules are negotiable.

One of Stuart Henry's informants cited in his book, *The Hid-*

den Economy, sums up well the belief, frequently expressed, that law-breaking is pervasive, and society essentially corrupt. Sarah, a Birmingham, England, factory worker had the following to say about how most people respond to an opportunity to steal: 'Every single person on this earth has received something that's fell off the back of a lorry [truck]. Nobody could say they don't do it because they do. I don't know anybody who hasn't had furniture, washing machines, kitchen things. I don't know anybody who would say, "Oh, I don't want it." They'd all say, "Ooh, can you get *me* one?" I tell you what – if you was to pinpoint all those who had had stuff and put them in a circle, you'd get 95 per cent of the population in that bloody circle.'[27]

Stan, another of Henry's informants, states that 'no one is honest,' providing the example of the vicar who 'dips his hands in the collection box.' Stan, a stonemason who had performed restoration work on a number of churches, goes on to say, 'Now you can't get much closer than a vicar for being honest, can you?'[28]

Both Sarah and Stan, in all likelihood two ordinary working people, get to the heart of the issues covered in this book. They justify their dishonest behaviour by saying that 'everybody does it.' I have shown that there is more than a little truth to this observation, although there is also distortion and hypocrisy. While it is true that most – not all – people act dishonestly and illegally on occasion, there are wide differences in the frequency and seriousness of such behaviour. Those involved regularly in criminal activity or in the theft of large items cannot equate their behaviour with that of the many people who commit the occasional petty offence.

What is hypocritical is that, while most people resort to the justification 'Everybody does it' to excuse their own behaviour, they take a very different stance towards crime in more general terms. The public tends to take a hard line towards crime and regards only a fraction of the population as criminals. When their own behaviour is in question, however, people resort to the argument that criminality is commonplace.

What are we to make of this contradiction? We can see that

people very readily use the misbehaviour of others as justifications for their own misdeeds. Self-interest is always a strong driving force of behaviour, as is the tendency to justify its pursuit. Society, however, can try to avoid adding more fuel to burning self-interest. Respected and influential persons, such as vicars and politicians, must be held strictly accountable for their actions. Cover-ups in all spheres, from police departments to the medical profession, need to be prevented.

Gary S. Green, in his book *Occupational Crime*, writes that illegal and immoral behaviour must be consistently censured if society's laws are to be respected. He also points out that moral education is a life-long process that begins in the family and continues well into adulthood, at which point an individual will be influenced by employers, colleagues, and friends. He calls for the validation of society's norms to be undertaken at all levels:

Parents, for instance, can teach their children to pay all income taxes due and to respect the property of others. Teachers in business schools can demonstrate to their pupils that it is legally wrong, and therefore morally inappropriate, to fix prices, misrepresent products, pollute the environment, manufacture unsafe products, and exploit labor. Teachers in medical schools can demonstrate that it is legally and professionally inappropriate to split fees, double-bill patients, and commit unnecessary surgery. Correctional officers can be taught that they have a sacred duty to respect citizens' rights. Legal-moral education, then, should not stop in the home, it should continue throughout one's formal education and occupational socialization. Occupational legal morality must be constantly reinforced by educators, firms, industries, and immediate work groups.[29]

Society cannot eradicate all unscrupulous and criminal behaviour, but through placing a strong emphasis on honesty and integrity at all levels – in the home, school, business, professions, political circles – we will all have more reason to pause when confronted with specific opportunities to exploit others. When momentary self-interest is allowed free expression, it loosens the inhibitions of others to act likewise. The foremost cause of crime and other socially harmful behaviour, perhaps, is crime and immoral behaviour itself, as socially harmful behaviour is self-perpetuating. Crime by the vast majority of citizens – people without criminal identities – would be harder to justify if people felt more isolated in their lawbreaking. The fear of the condemnation of others and of self-reproach is great. However, criminality will continue to be widespread as long as there is more than a grain of truth in the refrain that 'everybody does it.'

Notes

CHAPTER 1

1 Canadian Centre for Justice Statistics, *Canadian Crime Statistics 1991.* (Ottawa: Statistics Canada 1992)
2 Julian V. Roberts, 'Public Opinion, Crime, and Criminal Justice.' In Michael Tonry, ed., *Crime and Justice: An Annual Review of Research,* vol 16, 99–179 (Chicago: University of Chicago Press 1992)
3 Daniel J. Koenig, 'Conventional Crime.' In Rick Linden, ed., *Criminology: A Canadian Perspective,* 351–88 (Toronto: Harcourt Brace Jovanovich Canada 1992)
4 Solicitor General Canada, *Canadian Urban Victimization Survey: Victims of Crime* (Ottawa 1983)
5 Melvin J. Lerner, *The Belief in a Just World: A Fundamental Delusion* (New York: Plenum 1984)
6 B. Roshco, *Newsmaking* (Chicago: University of Chicago Press 1975)
7 These and other facts about the public's participation in criminality will be documented in chapters 3–8.
8 Maurice Cusson, *The Social Control of Crime* (Montreal: International Centre for Comparative Criminology, University of Montreal 1986)
9 Albert Bandura, *Aggression: A Social Learning Analysis* (Englewood Cliffs, NJ: Prentice-Hall 1973)
10 Fred Bruning, 'The Enemy Is Us, Not the L.A. Police,' *Maclean's,* 15 April 1991; 'Gate's Hell,' *Vanity Fair,* August 1991, 103–8, 168–73

11 Neil Boyd, *The Last Dance: Murder in Canada* (Scarborough, ON: Prentice-Hall 1988)
12 Quoted in Ysabel Rennie, *The Search for Criminal Man* (Lexington, MA: Lexington Books 1978), xiii
13 Thomas Gabor, Micheline Baril, Maurice Cusson, Daniel Elie, Marc LeBlanc, and Andre Normandeau, *Armed Robbery: Cops, Robbers, and Victims* (Springfield, ILL: Charles C. Thomas 1987), ch 3
14 Cusson, *The Social Control of Crime,* 71–3
15 Allen H. Barton, *Communities in Disaster: A Sociological Analysis of Collective Stress Situations* (Garden City, NY: Anchor Books 1970), ch 5
16 Don C. Gibbons, *Society, Crime, and Criminal Behavior,* 6th ed. (Englewood Cliffs, NJ: Prentice Hall 1992), 7–9
17 Ronald V. Clarke and Derek B. Cornish, 'Modeling Offenders' Decisions: A Framework for Policy and Research.' In Michael Tonry and Norval Morris, eds., *Crime and Justice: An Annual Review of Research,* vol 6, 147–85 (Chicago: University of Chicago Press 1985); Howard S. Becker, *Outsiders* (New York: Free Press 1963)
18 See, for example, Edwin Lemert, *Social Pathology* (New York: McGraw-Hill 1951)

CHAPTER 2

1 Walter Lippmann, *Public Opinion* (New York: Harcourt Brace 1922)
2 D. Katz and K. Braly, 'Racial Stereotypes in One Hundred College Students,' *Journal of Abnormal and Social Psychology* 30 (1933), 175–93
3 Paul F. Secord and Carl W. Backman, *Social Psychology* (New York: McGraw-Hill 1964), 70–2
4 Edwin Lemert, *Social Pathology* (New York: McGraw-Hill 1951)
5 Ysabel Rennie, *The Search for Criminal Man* (Lexington, MA: Lexington Books 1978)
6 Cesare Lombroso, *Crime: Its Causes and Remedies* (Monclair, NJ: Petterson Smith 1972)
7 Jessica Mitford, *Kind and Usual Punishment* (New York: Random House 1974), 61–2
8 Michael Saladin, Zalman Saper, and Lawrence Breen, 'Perceived

Attractiveness and Attribution of Criminality: What Is Beautiful Is Not Criminal,' *Canadian Journal of Criminology* 30 (1988), 251–60

9 Karen K. Dion, 'Physical Attractiveness and Evaluation of Children's Transgressions,' *Journal of Personality and Social Psychology* 24 (1972), 207–13

10 Donald Shoemaker, Donald R. South, and Jay Lowe, 'Facial Stereotypes of Deviants and Judgments of Guilt or Innocence,' *Social Forces* 51 (1973), 427–53

11 Alvin G. Goldstein, June E. Chance, and Barbara Gilbert, 'Facial Stereotypes of Good Guys and Bad Guys: A Replication and Extension,' *Bulletin of the Psychonomic Society* 22 (1984), 549–52

12 S.E. Goldin, 'Facial Stereotypes as Cognitive Categories.' Unpublished doctoral dissertation, Carnegie-Mellon University, 1979

13 Gideon Fishman, Arye Rattner, and Gabriel Weimann, 'The Effect of Ethnicity on Crime Attribution,' *Criminology* 25 (1987), 507–24

14 Eliezer Jaffe, *Ethnic Preferences Among Israelis* (Tel-Aviv: Cherikover 1984)

15 Colleen Ryan, 'The Typical Criminal.' Unpublished manuscript (Ottawa: University of Ottawa 1988)

16 Richard Lacayo, 'Anatomy of an Acquittal,' *Time*, 11 May 1992

17 John P. Reed and Robin S. Reed, 'Status, Images, and Consequence: Once a Criminal Always a Criminal,' *Sociology and Social Research* 7 (1973), 460–72

18 Research Group on Attitudes Toward Criminality, *Attitudes of the Canadian Public Toward Crime Policies* (Ottawa: Solicitor General of Canada 1984)

19 Ibid., 257

20 Julian V. Roberts and Nicholas R. White, 'Public Estimates of Recidivism Rates: Consequences of a Criminal Stereotype,' *Canadian Journal of Criminology* 28 (1986), 229–42

21 M.G. Efran, 'The Effect of Physical Appearance on Judgment of Guilt, Interpersonal Attraction, and Severity of Recommended Punishment in a Jury Task,' *Journal of Research in Personality* 8 (1974), 45–54

22 Arye Rattner, 'Convicted but Innocent: Wrongful Conviction and the Criminal Justice System,' *Law and Human Behaviour* 12 (1988), 283–93

23 Gordon W. Allport and Leo J. Postman, *The Psychology of Rumor* (New York: Henry Holt 1947)

24 Doris A. Graber, *Crime News and the Public* (New York: Prager 1980)

25 J.R. Dominick, 'Crime and Law Enforcement in the Mass Media.' In C. Winick, ed., *Deviance and Mass Media* (Beverly Hills, CA: Sage 1978), 105–28

26 L.G. Barrile, 'Television and Attitudes about Crime.' Unpublished Ph.D. dissertation, Boston College, 1980

27 'Prime-Time Violence,' *Maclean's*, 7 December 1992, 41

28 Thomas Gabor and Gabriel Weimann, 'The Coverage of Crime by the Press: Reflection or Distortion?' *Criminologie* 21 (1987), 79–98

29 Kevin N. Wright, *The Great American Crime Myth* (Westport, CT: Greenwood Press 1985)

30 R. Sherrill, 'Murder Inc. – What Happens to Corporate Criminals?' *Utne Reader*, March/April 1987, 48–56

31 A-T-O Inc., *The Figgie Report Part Two: The Corporate Response to Fear of Crime* (Cleveland: Research and Forecasts, Inc. 1980), Preface

32 Ernest A. Hooton, *The American Criminal: An Anthropological Study* (Cambridge, MA: Harvard University Press 1939), 309

33 The work of Philippe Rushton of the University of Western Ontario in Canada is particularly noteworthy in this context. Using more sophisticated statistical techniques, he is promoting the idea that criminals are inferior and are disproportionately drawn from the black 'race' due to innate racial differences. My colleague Julian Roberts and I identified what we believe are many flaws in his ideas in a debate with Professor Rushton. This debate is contained in the *Canadian Journal of Criminology* 32/2 (April 1990), 291–343

34 Emile Durkheim, *The Rules of Sociological Method*, trans. by Sarah A. Solovay and John H. Mueller; ed. by George E.G. Catlin (New York: The Free Press 1965)

35 Robert M. Bohm, 'Crime, Criminals and Crime Control Policy Myths,' *Justice Quarterly* 3 (1986), 193–214

36 Melvin J. Lerner, *The Belief in a Just World: A Fundamental Delusion* (New York: Plenum Press 1984)

37 Ibid, 9

38 Nelson R. Cauthen, Ira E. Robinson, and Herbert H. Krauss, 'Stereo-
    types: A Review of the Literature 1926–1968,' *Journal of Social Psy-
    chology* 84 (1971), 103–25
39 Susan T. Fiske and Shelley E. Taylor, *Social Cognition* (Reading, MA:
    Addison-Wesley 1984)

CHAPTER 3

1 Charles E. Silberman, *Criminal Violence, Criminal Justice* (New
   York: Vintage 1978)
2 Ibid, 50–1
3 Ibid, 31
4 Personal communications with officials of Correctional Services
   Canada. The figure of two million was originally published in *Basic
   Facts About Corrections*, a Correctional Services Canada pamphlet
   that was issued in 1982.
5 Thomas Gabor, The Dangerous Offender and Incapacitation Policies,' Ph.D. Dissertation, Ohio State University, 1983; Marvin E. Wolfgang and Paul E. Tracy, 'The 1945 and 1958 Birth Cohorts: A
   Comparison of the Prevalence, Incidence, and Severity of Delinquent
   Behaviour,' paper presented at a conference on Public Danger, Dangerous Offenders, and the Criminal Justice System, sponsored by the
   National Institute of Justice at Harvard University, 1982
6 The reader should note that these figures are very rough estimates.
7 R. Christensen, 'Projected Percentage of U.S. Population with Criminal Arrest and Conviction Records,' in President's Commission on
   Law Enforcement and Administration of Justice, *Task Force Report:
   Science and Technology* (Washington, DC: Government Printing
   Office 1967), Appendix J
8 J. Belkin, A. Blumstein, and Elizabeth Graddy, 'Recidivism as a
   Feedback Process: An Analytical Model and Empirical Validation,'
   Journal of Criminal Justice 1 (1973), 7–26
9 Alfred Blumstein and Elizabeth Graddy, 'Prevalence and Recidivism in Index Arrests: A Feedback Model,' *Law and Society Review*
   16 (1981/2), 265–90
10 David P. Farrington, 'The Prevalence of Convictions,' *British Jour-
    nal of Criminology* 21 (1981), 173–5

11 J.A. Wallerstein and C.E. Wyle, 'Our Law-Abiding Law-Breakers,' *Probation* 25 (1947), 107–12

12 James F. Short and F. Ivan Nye, 'Extent of Unrecorded Juvenile Delinquency, Tentative Conclusions,' *Journal of Criminal Law, Criminology, and Police Science*, 49 (1958), 296–302

13 Martin Gold, *Delinquent Behaviour in an American City* (Belmont, CA: Brooks 1970), 4

14 Wolfgang and Tracy, 'The 1945 and 1958 Birth Cohorts'

15 Paul E. Tracy, Marvin E. Wolfgang, and Robert M. Figlio, *Delinquency Careers in Two Birth Cohorts* (New York: Plenum Press 1990), ch 5

16 Eugene Vaz, 'Delinquency among Middle-Class Boys,' *Canadian Review of Sociology and Anthropology* 2 (1965), 514–15

17 L. MacDonald, *Social Class and Delinquency* (London: Faber and Faber 1969)

18 Marc LeBlanc and Marcel Frechette, *Male Criminal Activity from Childhood Through Youth: Multilevel and Developmental Perspectives* (New York: Springer-Verlag 1989), 60

19 Lincoln J. Fry, 'Drug Abuse and Crime in a Swedish Birth Cohort,' *British Journal of Criminology* 25 (1985), 46–59

20 Gwynn Nettler, *Lying, Cheating, and Stealing* (Cincinnati, OH: Anderson 1982)

21 H. Hartshorne and M.A. May, *Studies in Deceit* (New York: Macmillan 1928)

22 Walter Mischel, *Introduction to Personality* (New York: Holt, Rinehart, and Winston 1971)

23 Jack Henry, 'The Employee Theft Triangle,' *Canadian Security*, August/September 1988, 26–7

24 R.W. Riis, 'The Watch Repair Man Will Gyp You if You Don't Watch Out,' *Reader's Digest* 39 (1941), 10–12

25 Roy E. Feldman, 'Response to Compatriots and Foreigners Who Seek Assistance,' *Journal of Personality and Social Psychology* 10 (1968), 202–14

26 C.B. Merritt and R. G. Fowler, 'The Pecuniary Honesty of the Public at Large,' *Journal of Abnormal and Social Psychology* 43 (1948), 90–3

27 David P. Farrington and B.J. Knight, 'Two Non-Reactive Field Experiments on Stealing from a "Lost" Letter,' *British Journal of Social and Clinical Psychology* 18 (1979), 277–84

American Society
for Industrial Security

1655 North Fort Myer Drive, Suite 1200, Arlington, VA 22209
Telephone 703-522-5800

3 November 1995

Mr. Shropshire -

For a current catalog of Training Sessions
offered by the DoD Security Institute contact
the following:

> DoD Security Institute
> 6000 Jefferson Davis Hwy
> Richmond, VA 23297-5091
>
> tel: (804) 279-5593

Call if there are any questions

TRACY F. LOPEZ
Library Assistant

AMERICAN SOCIETY FOR
INDUSTRIAL SECURITY

1655 North Fort Myer Drive, Suite 1200   Arlington, VA 22209
(703) 312-6372   (703) 522-5800   Fax: 703-243-9385

28 Thomas Gabor, Jody Strean, Gurnam Singh, and David Varis, 'Public Deviance: An Experimental Study,' *Canadian Journal of Criminology* 28 (1986), 17–29; Thomas Gabor and Tonia G. Barker, 'Probing the Public's Honesty: A Field Experiment Using the "Lost-Letter" Technique,' *Deviant Behavior* 10 (1989), 387–99

29 Philip G. Zimbardo, 'A Field Experiment in Autoshaping.' In C. Ward, ed., *Vandalism*, 85–90 (London: Architectural Press 1973)

30 Ibid, 87–8

31 '40% of Students Cheat,' *The Ottawa Citizen*, 8 February 1986

32 'Hey Ma, Get Me a Lawyer,' *Newsweek*, 30 October 1989, 10

33 Charles Gordon, 'Lies We Tell Ourselves: Does the Truth Really Hurt That Much?' *The Ottawa Citizen*, 30 April 1991, A11

34 Ilana Stein, 'Academic Fraud,' Unpublished manuscript, Department of Criminology, University of Ottawa, 1992

35 'Can You Pass the Job Test (Validity or Honesty Tests)?' *Newsweek*, 5 May 1986, 46–52

36 P. Shaikun, 'Private Security Nabs More Business Amid Growing Fears,' *St Petersburg Times*, 28 June 1987, 1–I, 4–I

37 Floyd H. Allport, 'The J-Curve Hypothesis of Conforming Behavior,' *Journal of Social Psychology* 5 (1934), 141–83

38 Ibid

39 Karen Ells, 'Degrees of Conforming Behaviour.' Unpublished paper, University of Ottawa, 1989

40 Allport, 'The J-Curve Hypothesis'

41 Ells, 'Degrees of Conforming Behavior,' 3

42 H. Lawrence Ross, 'Folk Crime Revisited,' *Criminology* 11 (1983), 75

43 Howard S. Becker, *Outsiders: Studies in the Sociology of Deviance* (Glencoe, IL: Free Press 1963)

CHAPTER 4

1 Chok Hiew, 'Prevention of Shoplifting: A Community Action Approach,' *Canadian Journal of Criminology* 23 (1981), 57–68

2 Claude L. Leger, 'Employee Theft: Thievery from Within,' Master's thesis, University of Ottawa, 1990

3 Steve Allen, *Ripoff: The Corruption that Plagues America* (Secaucus, NJ: Lyle Stewart 1979)

4 Ibid, 26
5 Neal Hall, 'The Crime that All Shoppers Pay For,' *The Vancouver Sun*, 28 November 1988, D6
6 Abigail Buckle and David P. Farrington, 'An Observational Study of Shoplifting,' *British Journal of Criminology* 24 (1984), 63–73
7 Hall, 'The Crime that All Shoppers Pay For,' D6; Mary Owen Cameron, *The Booster and the Snitch: Departmental Store Shoplifting* (New York: Free Press of Glencoe 1964)
8 Hall, 'The Crime that All Shoppers Pay For,' D6.
9 Don Lamontagne, 'Understanding Retail Theft,' Master's thesis, University of Ottawa, 1989
10 Don C. Gibbons, 'Mundane Crime,' *Crime and Delinquency* 29 (1983), 213–27
11 S. Irini and R. Prus, 'Doing Security Work: Keeping Order in the Hotel Setting,' *Canadian Journal of Criminology* 24 (1982), 61–82
12 D.M. Horning, 'Blue Collar Theft: Conceptions of Property Attitudes Toward Pilfering and Work Group Norms in a Modern Plant.' In E. Smigel and H.L. Ross, eds., *Crimes Against Bureaucracy*, 46–64 (New York: Van Nostrand Reinhold 1970)
13 NBC *Nightly News*, 20 June 1991
14 Leger, 'Employee Theft'
15 Ibid
16 Lisa Leduc, 'Scamming in the Restaurant Industry.' Unpublished paper, Department of Criminology, University of Ottawa, 1989
17 S. Leininger, 'Internal Theft Investigation and Control,' *Security World*, 1975, 102
18 '415 Ways to Steal,' *New Haven Register*, 26 December 1976, 42a
19 P. Bullard and A. Resnick, 'SMR Forum: Too Many Hands in the Corporate Cookie Jar,' *Sloan Management Review*, Fall 1983, 51–7
20 D. Merriam, 'Employee Theft,' *Criminal Abstracts*, September 1977, 375–406
21 Leger, *'Employee Theft,'* 25
22 Ibid
23 Ibid, 26
24 Stuart Henry, *The Hidden Economy: The Context and Control of Borderline Crime* (Oxford: Martin Robertson 1978)

25 Gerald Mars, 'Dock Pilferage.' In P. Rock and M. McIntosh, eds., *Deviance and Control* (London: Tavistock 1974), 216

26 Merriam, 'Employee Theft,' 379

27 Maria Los, *Communist Ideology, Law and Crime: A Comparative View of the USSR and Poland* (London: Macmillan 1988)

28 Ibid, 212

29 Greg Barr, 'The Irresistible Lure of Hotel Linen Lifting,' *The Ottawa Citizen*, 14 May 1988, H3

30 J. Coleman, *The Criminal Elite: The Sociology of White Collar Crime* (New York: St Martin's Press 1985), 83

31 R. Willis, 'White Collar Crime: The Thefts from Within,' *Management Review*, January 1986, 27

32 Leger, 'Employee Theft,' 21–4

33 This case appeared in *The Practical Accountant*, June 1981, 63–4.

34 Donald Cressey, *Other People's Money: A Study in the Social Psychology of Embezzlement* (Belmont, CA: Wadsworth 1953)

35 K.D. Deane, 'Tax Evasion, Criminality, and Sentencing the Tax Offender,' *British Journal of Criminology* 21 (1981), 47–57

36 Neil Brooks and Anthony N. Doob, 'Tax Evasion: Searching for a Theory of Compliant Behaviour.' Toronto: Centre of Criminology, University of Toronto, 1990.

37 Alan Murray, 'IRS in Losing Battle Against Tax Evaders Despite Its New Gear,' *Wall Street Journal*, 10 April 1984, 1

38 Brooks and Doob, 'Tax Evasion'

39 Brenda Dalglish, 'Cheaters,' *Maclean's*, 9 August 1993, 18–21

40 'Undeclared Liquor Pours Over Ontario Border Crossings,' *The Ottawa Citizen*, 21 May 1988, A5

41 'Shopping Binge: The Cross-Border Spending Spree Has Become a Crisis,' *Maclean's*, 29 April 1991, 36–41

42 Amy Willard Cross, 'A Case of Borderline Crime,' *The Globe and Mail*, 25 July 1990

43 'Edmonton Tornado Victims May Face Fraud Charges for Outrageous Damage Claims,' *The Ottawa Citizen*, 16 October 1987, A3

44 Edith Skom, 'Plagiarism: Quite a Rather Bad Little Crime,' *AAHE Journal*

45 'Tempests in a Test Tube,' *Newsweek*, 2 February 1987, 64

46 'Medical Profession Reluctant to Open Hearings to Public,' *The Ottawa Citizen*, 9 January 1988, B5

47 P.R. Wilson, R. Lincoln, and D. Chappell, 'Physician Fraud and Abuse in Canada: A Preliminary Examination,' *Canadian Journal of Criminology* 28 (1986), 129–46

48 Larry J. Siegal, *Criminology*, 4th Ed. (St. Paul, MN: West Publishing Company 1992), 362

49 Quoted in Geoffrey York, *The High Price of Health: A Patient's Guide to the Hazards of Medical Politics* (Toronto: Lorimer 1987), 73–4

50 Ibid, 74

51 Ibid, 77

52 Jerome E. Carlin, *Lawyer's Ethics* (New York: Russell Sage 1966); Charles E. Reasons and Duncan Chappell, 'Crooked Lawyers: Towards a Political Economy of Deviance in the Profession,' *The New Criminologies in Canada*, 206–22 (Toronto: Oxford University Press 1985)

53 J. Nagler, 'Overbilling an Error, Kopyto Tells Tribunal,' *Globe and Mail*, 12 August 1989, A8

54 William Blackstone, Jr, *Don't Ask Your Lawyer: How to Judge, Deal, and Win In and Out of Court* (New York: Beaufort Books 1981), ch. 9

55 Ibid, 166–77

56 Ibid, 167

57 Abraham S. Blumberg, 'The Practice of Law as Confidence Game: Organizational Cooptation of a Profession,' In William J. Chambliss, ed., *Crime and the Legal Process*, 220–37 (New York:, McGraw-Hill 1969)

CHAPTER 5

1 'Oh! God! that bread should be so dear, / And flesh and blood so cheap!' – from Thomas Hood's *The Song of the Shirt* (1843)

2 Lorne Gibson, Rick Linden, and Stuart Johnson, 'A Situational Theory of Rape,' *Canadian Journal of Corrections* 22 (1980), 51–65

3 Michael J. Hindelang, Michael R. Gottfredson, and James Garofalo, *Victims of Personal Crime: An Empirical Foundation for a Theory of Personal Victimization* (Cambridge, MA: Ballinger 1978); Holly Johnson and Vincent F. Sacco, 'The Risk of Criminal Victimization.'

In Robert A. Silverman, James J. Teevan, Jr, and Vincent F. Sacco, eds., *Crime in Canadian Society*, 4th ed., 92–8 (Toronto: Butterworths 1991)

4 Marvin E. Wolfgang, *Patterns in Criminal Homicide* (Philadelphia: University of Pennsylvania Press 1958)

5 Marc Reidel, 'Stranger Violence: Perspectives, Issues, and Problems,' *Journal of Criminal Law and Criminology* 78 (1987), 223–58; Margaret Zahn and Philip Sagi, 'Stranger Homicides in Nine American Cities,' *Journal of Criminal Law and Criminology* 78 (1987), 377–97

6 Neil Boyd, *The Last Dance: Murder in Canada* (Scarborough, ON: Prentice-Hall 1988)

7 David Luckenbill, 'Criminal Homicide as a Situational Transaction,' *Social Problems* 25 (1977), 176–86

8 Boyd, *The Last Dance: Murder in Canada*, 88–91

9 In a seminal work, Ezzat Fattah, in his book entitled *Understanding Criminal Victimization* (Scarborough, ON: Prentice-Hall 1991), cogently argues for the need to unravel interpersonal dynamics in understanding many forms of crime.

10 Wendy Darroch, 'Woman Jailed Year for Killing Abuser,' *The Toronto Star*, 16 October 1991, A22

11 Wolfgang, *Patterns in Criminal Homicide*, 329

12 Canadian Advisory Council on the Status of Women, *Sexual Assault* (Ottawa, February 1985)

13 D. Kinnon, *Report on Sexual Assault in Canada* (Ottawa: Canadian Advisory Council on the Status of Women 1981)

14 Alex Thio, *Deviant Behavior* (New York: Harper & Row 1988), ch. 6

15 Menachem Amir, *Patterns in Forcible Rape* (Chicago: University of Chicago Press 1971)

16 Ibid, 141–2

17 Gibson, Linden, and Johnson, 'A Situational Theory of Rape'

18 Thio, *Deviant Behaviour*, 142

19 Metro Action Committee on Public Violence Against Women and Children, *Curriculum Development Research Needs Assessment Report* (Toronto, 1986)

20 'What Is "Abuse"? A Striking Survey Provokes a Heated Reaction,' *Maclean's*, 22 February 1993, 54

21 Diana Russell, *The Politics of Rape* (New York: Stein and Day 1975)
22 Lorenne Clark and Debra Lewis, *Rape: The Price of Coercive Sexuality* (Toronto: The Women's Press 1977), 121
23 Ian Gomme, *The Shadow Line: Deviance and Crime in Canada* (Toronto: Harcourt Brace Jovanovich Canada 1993), 11
24 Mary P. Koss and Mary R. Harvey, *The Rape Victim: Clinical and Community Interventions* (Newbury Park, CA: Sage 1991), 89–90
25 'Campuses "Foster Rape," Crown Says,' *The Ottawa Citizen*, 23 December 1991, A4
26 Jim Coyle, 'It Takes Courage to Reveal MD's Sexual Abuse,' *The Ottawa Citizen*, 1 June 1991, B2
27 Ibid
28 Linda MacLeod, *Wife Battering in Canada: The Vicious Circle* (Ottawa: Canadian Government Publishing Centre 1980)
29 M. A. Straus, 'Leveling, Civility, and Violence in the Family,' *Journal of Marriage and the Family* 36 (1974), 13–30
30 Del Martin, *Battered Wives* (San Francisco, CA: Volcano Press 1981)
31 'Seminar Addresses Family Violence,' *Liaison* 15 (1989), 7
32 Martin, *Battered Wives*, 18–19
33 Ibid, 19
34 Richard J. Gelles, 'Violence Toward Children in the United States,' *American Journal of Orthopsychiatry* 48 (1978), 580–92
35 Richard Gelles and Murray Straus, 'Violence in the American Family,' *Journal of Social Issues* 35 (1979), 15–39
36 Diana Russell, 'The Incidence and Prevalence of Intrafamilial and Extrafamilial Sexual Abuse of Female Children,' *Child Abuse and Neglect* 7 (1983), 133–46
37 K. Ledger and D. Williams, *Parents at Risk* (Victoria, BC: Queen Alexandra Hospital 1980)
38 Robin Badgley, *Sexual Offences Against Children* (Ottawa: Government of Canada 1984)
39 'The Abuse of Children,' *Maclean's*, 27 November 1989, 56
40 Chris Bagley, 'Child Abuse and Neglect.' In Grant Charles and Peter Gabor, eds., *Issues in Child and Youth Care Practice in Alberta*, 52–72 (Lethbridge, AL: Lethbridge Community College 1988)
41 Glen Allen, 'A Church in Crisis: Sex Scandals Shake Newfoundlanders' Faith,' *Maclean's*, 27 November 1989, 66

42 Mike Blanchfield, 'Police Charge 19 Former, Current Brothers,' *The Ottawa Citizen*, 15, February 1991, C1
43 'The Martensville Scandal,' *Maclean's*, 22 June (1992), 26–8
44 *The New York Times*, 7 February 1968
45 Thio, *Deviant Behavior*, ch. 8
46 R. Gemme, A. Murphy, M. Bourque, M.A. Nemeh, and N. Payment, *A Report on Prostitution in Quebec* (Ottawa: Department of Justice 1984)
47 Thio, *Deviant Behavior*, ch. 8
48 Franz G. Alexander and Sheldon T. Selesnick, *The History of Psychiatry* (New York: Mento 1966), 96–7
49 B. Evenson, '"I Have Sinned": A Righteous Preacher Sunk by His Dark Side,' *The Ottawa Citizen*, 27 February 1988, B1
40 Roberta Perkins, *Working Girls: Prostitutes, Their Lives and Social Control* (Canberra: Australian Institute of Criminology 1991)
51 Ibid, 1
52 Gomme, *The Shadow Line*, 291

CHAPTER 6

1 'True Greed,' *Newsweek*, 1 December 1986, 48
2 Robert Sherrill, 'Murder Inc. – What Happens to Corporate Criminals?' *Utne Reader*, March/April 1987, 48–56
3 'A Queen on Trial,' *Newsweek*, 21 August 1989, 46–51
4 Ibid, 47
5 Anthony Solomon, 'The Risks Were Too Good to Pass Up,' *New York Times Book Review*, 29 October 1989, 26–8
6 Larry J. Siegal, *Criminology*, 4th ed. (St Paul, MN: West Publishing Company 1992), 360
7 Colin H. Goff and Charles E. Reasons, *Corporate Crime in Canada* (Scarborough, ON: Prentice-Hall of Canada 1978)
8 Marshall Clinard and Peter C. Yeager, *Corporate Crime* (New York: Free Press 1980), 118
9 Charles E. Reasons, Lois L. Ross, and Craig Paterson, *Assault on the Worker: Occupational Health and Safety in Canada* (Toronto: Butterworths 1981)

10 Ibid
11 Laura Schrager and James Short, 'Toward a Sociology of Organizational Crime,' *Social Problems* 25 (1978), 415–25
12 Daniel Seligman, 'Keeping Up: The Case for Unskilled Mechanics,' *Fortune*, 22 October 1979, 43
13 Robert Sikorsky, 'Highway Robbery: Canada's Auto Repair Scandal,' *Reader's Digest*, February 1990, 55–63
14 Peter T. Maiken, *Ripoff: How to Spot It: How to Avoid It* (Kansas City: Andrews and McMeel 1979)
15 Ibid, 6
16 J.W. Suthers and Gary Shupp, *Fraud and Deceit: How to Stop Being Ripped Off* (New York: Arco 1982)
17 Maiken, *Ripoff*, 29
18 Ibid, 97–8
19 Interview with Kevin Doucette and Cathy Thompson of the Consumers Association of Canada
20 Charles A. Jaffe, 'The Lure of Travel Scams,' *St Petersburg Times*, 21 June 1987, 1-I, 3-I
21 Clinard and Yeager, *Corporate Crime*, 218
22 Ibid, 219
23 Interview with the executive director of Ottawa's Better Business Bureau, Jane Belyea
24 Clinard and Yeager, *Corporate Crime*, 224
25 Ian Gomme, *The Shadow Line: Deviance and Crime in Canada* (Toronto: Harcourt Brace Jovanovich 1993), 407
26 Brad Evenson, 'Byward Market Restaurants Fail 40 Percent of Health Inspections,' *The Ottawa Citizen*, 27 April 1991, 1–2
27 Ibid, 2
28 Clinard and Yeager, *Corporate Crime*, 226
29 John Braithwaite, 'White Collar Crime,' *Annual Review of Sociology* 11 (1985), 1–25
30 Jay Livingstone, *Crime and Criminology* (Englewood Cliffs, NJ: Prentice-Hall 1992), 311
31 John Braithwaite, *Corporate Crime in the Pharmaceutical Industry* (London: Routledge and Kegan Paul 1985), 308
32 Clinard and Yeager, *Corporate Crime*, 208
33 'Cleaning Up the Teamsters,' *Maclean's*, 23 March 1992, 36–42

CHAPTER 7

1 R. Howard, 'Stevens Inquiry to Spawn New Rules for Ministers: Mulroney Package Expected in Weeks,' *Globe and Mail*, 3 December 1987, A14

2 Claire Hoy, *Friends in High Places: Politics and Patronage in the Mulroney Government* (Toronto: Key Porter Books 1987)

3 Raymond R. Corrado, 'Political Crime in Canada.' In Rick Linden, ed., *Criminology: A Canadian Perspective* (Toronto: Harcourt Brace Jovanovich, 1992), 444

4 Martin Woollacott, 'Corruption as a Way of Life,' *The Toronto Star*, 17 March 1993, A19

5 '20% of Chicago Executives Would Bribe Official: Poll,' *The Ottawa Citizen*, 28 March 1987, D3

6 'A Shaken Nation Bares its Anger: Canadians Are Suffering a Massive Loss of Confidence in Politicians and in the Political System Itself,' *Maclean's*, 7 January 1991, 10–38

7 'Five Liberal Workers in Nova Scotia Convicted of Buying Votes,' *The Globe and Mail*, 7 April 1989, A5

8 J.R. Duffy, 'How to Speak Like a Real Politician,' *The Ottawa Citizen*, 16 June 1990, B7

9 'Abuses Spoil Rights Group's 30th Birthday,' *The Ottawa Citizen*, 29 May 1991, A7

10 'Fresh Out of Miracles: Evangelists Jim and Tammy Faye Bakker Lose Their TV Ministry Over the Sex-and-Money Scandal,' *Newsweek*, 11 May 1987, 70–2

11 Paul Nowell, 'Bakker Convicted of Fraud,' *Boston Globe*, 6 October 1989, 1

12 'RC Church to Review Training, Says Bishop,' *The Ottawa Citizen*, 29 June 1989, A18

13 'When a Pastor Turns Seducer: Church Confronts Sexual Predators,' *Newsweek*, 28 August 1989, 48

14 Ibid

15 *The Knapp Commission Report on Police Corruption* (New York: George Braziller 1973)

16 'Police Official Sentenced to 18 Years for Extortion,' *Wall Street Journal*, 25 September 1984, 6

17 Larry J. Siegal, *Criminology*, 4th ed. (St Paul, MN: West Publishing Company 1992), 366
18 'Police-Force Scandals,' *Maclean's*, 9 May 1988, 28
19 'Blackened Blue: Scandal Strikes the Edmonton Police Force,' *Maclean's*, 26 August 1991, 43
20 Scott Edmonds, 'Manitoba Judges, Magistrates Charged: 11 Accused of Conspiracy in Traffic-Ticket Fixing Scam,' *The Ottawa Citizen*, 16 January 1988, A1, A20
21 Brian Bergman and Don Campbell, 'Police under the Gun: A Justice Scandal Rocks Winnipeg,' *Maclean's*, 29 July 1991, 20
22 Ellwyn R. Stoddard, 'The Informal "Code" of Police Deviancy: A Group Approach to "Blue-Coat" Crime,' *Journal of Criminal Law, Criminology, and Police Science* 59 (1968), 201–13
23 Ibid, 208
24 Mark Baker, *Cops: Their Lives in Their Own Words* (New York: Pocket Books 1985) 253
25 Ibid, 253–4
26 Ibid, 33–5
27 Ibid, 286–7
28 Personal interview with a veteran police officer in a medium-size Canadian city
29 Randall Guynes and Osa Coffey, *Employee Drug-Testing Policies in Prison Systems* (Washington, DC: National Institute of Justice 1988)
30 Tamar Jacoby, 'A Web of Crime Behind Bars: An Undercover Team Charges Philadelphia Prison Guards With Smuggling Drugs and Aiding Escapes,' *Newsweek*, 24 October 1988, 76–81

CHAPTER 8

1 D.I. MacDonald, *Drugs, Drinking, and Adolescents* (Chicago: Year Book Medical Publishers 1984)
2 'Trying to Say "No": The Drug Crisis,' *Newsweek*, 11 August 1986, 14–21
3 'Losing the War? The Drug Crisis,' *Newsweek*, 14 March 1988, 16–18
4 'Drug Abuse: Testing,' *Newsweek*, 14 September 1987, 4
5 William Long, 'War on Coca Leaf Angers Andean Natives,' *The Ottawa Citizen*, 24 September 1988, H15

6 The Canadian Gallup Poll Limited, *Alcohol, Tobacco and Marijuana Use and Norms Among Young People in Canada – Year 2* (Ottawa: Health and Welfare Canada 1984)

7 Addiction Research Foundation, 'Alcohol and Other Drug Use in Canada,' *The Journal*, 1 September 1988

8 Addiction Research Foundation, 'Alcohol Problems Studied,' *Ontario Report*, December 1989/January 1990, 3

9 Neil Boyd, *High Society: Legal and Illegal Drugs in Canada* (Toronto: Key Porter Books 1991), 224

10 Addiction Research Foundation, 'Ontario Report,' *The Journal*, (1988), 2

11 'The Doped-Up Games,' *Newsweek*, 10 October 1988, 54–7

12 Michael D. Whittingham, 'Vandalism – The Urge to Damage and Destroy,' *Canadian Journal of Criminology* 23 (1981) 69–73

13 Paul Wilson, *Graffiti and Vandalism on Public Transport* (Canberra: Australian Institute of Criminology 1987)

14 Thomas Gabor, 'Prevention Into the Twenty-First Century: Some Final Remarks,' *Canadian Journal of Criminology* 32 (1990), 197–212

15 Tim Foran, Public Deviance in the Form of the Mutilation of Library Materials.' Unpublished document, University of Ottawa, 1989

16 M. David Ermann and Richard J. Lundman, *Corporate Deviance* (New York: Holt, Rinehart, and Winston 1982)

17 J. Quig, 'Setting Traps for People Who Hunt Dirty: Poachers Insult Laws of Nature and Sneer at Laws of Man,' *The Montreal Gazette*, 11 October (1986), A1 A4

18 Ibid

19 'Of Pain and Progress: A Growing Social Movement Raises a Thorny Ethical Question: Do The Practical Benefits of Animal Experimentation Outweigh the Moral Costs?' *Newsweek*, 26 December (1988), 50–6

20 Frederick A. King, 'Animals in Research: The Case for Experimentation,' *Psychology Today*, September 1984, 56–8

21 'Of Pain and Progress ...,' 53–4

22 P. Elmer-DeWitt, 'A Bold Raid on Computer Security,' *Time*, 2 May 1988, 56

23 'Invasion of the Data Snatchers,' *Time*, 26 September 1988, 50–5

24 K. Makin, 'Computer Systems Hit by "Logic Bombs,"' *The Globe and Mail*, 3 November 1987, A1
25 Ibid
26 David Silburt, 'The Disk Takers,' *Canadian Business*, March 1987, 66–78
27 P. Lewis, 'Amnesty New Tactic to Fight Software Piracy,' *The Globe and Mail*, 10 July 1989, B1-B2
28 Dan Antonowicz, 'The Prevalence of Computer Software Piracy.' Manuscript, Department of Criminology, University of Ottawa, 1989
29 Silburt, 'The Disk Takers,' 66
30 Mary Gooderham, 'CBC Destroys Illegal Computer Software Following Rumors of Police Raiding Offices,' *The Globe and Mail*, 3 April 1990, A3
31 'A Scourge of Video Pirates: Fake Tapes Cost Hollywood $1 Billion in Revenues,' *Newsweek*, 27 July 1987, 39–41
32 Jamie Portman, 'Canadian Video Pirates Meet Their Match,' *The Montreal Gazette*, 5 September 1991
33 Charles Silberman, *Criminal Violence, Criminal Justice* (New York: Vintage Books 1978), 51–2
34 Larry J. Siegel, *Criminology*, 4th ed. (St Paul, MN: West Publishing Company 1992), 381
35 Vincent F. Sacco, 'An Approach to the Study of Organized Crime.' In Robert A. Silverman and James J. Teevan, Jr, eds., *Crime in Canadian Society*, 3rd ed., 214–26 (Toronto: Butterworths 1986)
36 Don C. Gibbons, *Society, Crime, and Criminal Behavior*, 6th ed. (Englewood Cliffs, NJ: Prentice-Hall 1992), 319
37 Francis A.J. Ianni, *A Family Business* (New York: Russell Sage Foundation 1972)
38 Sacco, 'An Approach to the Study of Organized Crime'

CHAPTER 9

1 Gresham M. Sikes and David Matza, 'Techniques of Neutralization: A Theory of Delinquency,' *American Sociological Review* 22 (1957), 667–70
2 Alex Thio, *Deviant Behavior*, 3rd ed. (New York: Harper and Row 1988), 456–7

3 Robert R. Ross and Elizabeth A. Fabiano, *Time to Think: A Cognitive Model of Delinquency Prevention and Offender Rehabilitation* (Johnson City, TN: Institute of Social Sciences and Arts, Inc. 1985)

4 Albert Bandura, 'The Social Learning Perspective: Mechanisms of Aggression.' In Hans Toch, ed., *Psychology of Crime and Criminal Justice* (New York: Holt, Rinehart and Winston 1977), 230

5 Samuel Yochelson and Stanton E. Samenow, *The Criminal Personality* (New York: Jason Aronson 1976)

6 James E. Coleman, *Abnormal Psychology and Modern Life*, 5th ed. (Glenview, IL: Scott, Foresman and Co. 1976), 122–31

7 Lawrence C. Kolb, *Modern Clinical Psychiatry*, 8th ed. (Philadelphia: W.B. Saunders 1963), 68

8 Leon Festinger, *A Theory of Cognitive Dissonance* (Stanford, CA: Stanford University Press 1957)

9 C.R. Snyder, 'Excuses, Excuses: They Sometimes Actually Work – To Relieve the Burden of Blame,' *Psychology Today* 18 (September 1984), 50–5

10 Paul F. Secord and Carl W. Backman, *Social Psychology* (New York: McGraw-Hill 1964), 76

11 Stuart Henry, *The Hidden Economy: The Context and Control of Borderline Crime* (Oxford: Martin Robertson 1978), 49

12 Eldridge Cleaver, *Soul on Ice* (New York: McGraw-Hill 1968), 14

13 Imamu Amiri Baraka, 'Black People!' In Richard Barksdale and Kenneth Kinnamon, eds., *Black Writers of America* (New York: Macmillan 1972), 750–71

14 William Ryan, *Blaming the Victim* (New York: Vintage Books 1971)

15 Ibid, 27–9

16 Peter T. Maiken, *Ripoff: How to Spot It, How to Avoid It* (Kansas City: Andrews and McMeel 1979)

17 Thomas Gabor, Micheline Baril, Maurice Cusson, Daniel Elie, Marc Leblanc, and Andre Normandeau, *Armed Robbery: Cops, Robbers, and Victims* (Springfield, IL: Charles C. Thomas 1987), 58

18 Enrico L. Quarantelli and Russell R. Dynes, 'Organizations as Victims in American Mass Racial Disturbances: A Re-Examination.' In I. Drapkin and E. Viano, eds, *Victimology: A New Focus*, 67–77 (Lexington, MA: D.C. Heath 1975)

19 Henry, *The Hidden Economy*, 53

20 Ibid, 57
21 'Memorandum on a Mass Murder,' *Newsweek*, 9 April 1990, 25

CHAPTER 10

1 Harold J. Vetter and Ira J. Silverman, *The Nature of Crime* (Toronto: W.B. Saunders 1978), 361
2 A.M. Rosenthal, *Thirty-Eight Witnesses* (New York: McGraw-Hill 1964)
3 Ibid, 78–9
4 Donna M. Gelfand, Donald P. Hartmann, Patricia Walder, and Brent Page, 'Who Reports Shoplifters? A Field-Experimental Study,' *Journal of Personality and Social Psychology* 25 (1973), 276–85
5 'Reported and Unreported Crimes,' *Canadian Urban Victimization Survey* (Ottawa: Solicitor General of Canada 1984)
6 B. Latane and J. Darley, *The Unresponsive Bystander: Why Doesn't He Help?* (New York: Appleton-Century-Crofts 1970)
7 Max C. Dertke, Louis A. Penner, and Kathleen Ulrich, 'Observer's Reporting of Shoplifting as a Function of Thief's Race and Sex,' *Journal of Social Psychology* 94 (1974), 213–21; Darrell J. Steffensmeir and Robert M. Terry, 'Deviance and Respectability: An Observational Study of Reactions to Shoplifting,' *Social Forces* 51 (1973), 417–26
8 Leonard Bickman, 'Attitude Toward an Authority and the Reporting of a Crime,' *Sociometry* 39 (1976), 76–82
9 Vetter and Silverman, *The Nature of Crime*, 363
10 John E. Conklin, *The Impact of Crime* (New York: Macmillan 1975), 222–3
11 Gustave LeBon, *The Crowd: A Study of the Popular Mind* (New York: Viking Press, 1960); Sigmund Freud, *Group Psychology and the Analysis of the Ego* (New York: Hogarth Press 1922)
12 Quoted in Freud, *Group Psychology*, 12
13 Freud, *Group Psychology*, 15
14 Martin R. Haskell and Lewis Yablonsky, *Crime and Delinquency* (Chicago: Rand McNally 1970), 321–6
15 Joseph B. Perry, Jr, and M.D. Pugh, *Collective Behavior: Response to Social Stress.* (St Paul, MN: West Publishing Company 1978), 108

16 Enrico L. Quarantelli and Russell R. Dynes, 'Property Norms and
    Looting: Their Patterns in Community Crises,' *Phylon* 31 (1970),
    168–182
17 Perry and Pugh, *Collective Behavior*, 186
18 R. Curvin and B. Porter, *Blackout Looting* (New York: Gardner Press
    1979), 17
19 Ibid, 10
20 Ibid
21 Quarantelli and Dynes, 'Property Norms and Looking'
22 'The Siege of LA,' *Newsweek*, 11 May, 1992, 36–7
23 Roland Boisjoli, 'Vigilantism in Canada.' Master's thesis, University
    of Ottawa, 1987; J.M. Torrance, *Public Violence in Canada,
    1867–1982* (Toronto: University of Toronto Press 1986)
24 P. Curran, 'Third Shopkeeper Shoots Intruder,' *The Montreal
    Gazette*, 11 December 1986, A1, A7
25 Leonard Berkowitz, *Aggression: Its Causes, Consequences, and Con-
    trol* (New York: McGraw-Hill 1993), 202
26 'Montreal Bus Drivers Arming Themselves,' *The Ottawa Citizen*, 26
    August 1986, A5
27 'Cool It, Montreal Transit Bosses Tell Drivers,' *The Ottawa Citizen*,
    27 August 1986, A18
28 William Johnson, 'Subway Vigilante Struck a Nerve,' *The Globe and
    Mail*, 18 January 1985, 8
29 David Gelman and David L. Gonzalez, 'The Bundy Carnival: A
    Thirst for Revenge Provokes a Raucous Send-Off,' *Newsweek*, 6 Feb-
    ruary 1989, 66

CHAPTER 11

1 Thomas Gabor, *The Prediction of Criminal Behaviour: Statistical
   Approaches* (Toronto: University of Toronto Press 1986)
2 George Vold, *Theoretical Criminology*, 2d ed., prepared by Thomas
   Bernard (New York: Oxford University Press 1979), ch. 2
3 Emile Durkheim, *The Rules of the Sociological Method*, trans. by
   Sarah A. Solovay and John H. Mueller; ed. by George E.G. Catlin
   (New York: The Free Press 1965)
4 Ibid., 68–9

5 Jeremy Bentham, 'An Introduction to the Principles of Morals and Legislation.' In John Bowring, ed., *The Works of Jeremy Bentham*, 1–154 (New York: Russell & Russell 1962)
6 August Aichhorn, *Wayward Youth* (New York: Viking Press 1963)
7 Sigmund Freud, *Civilization and Its Discontents*, trans. by J. Strachey (New York: Norton 1961), 105
8 John M. Rich and Joseph L. DeVitis, *Theories of Moral Development* (Springfield, IL: Charles C. Thomas 1985), ch. 5
9 Quoted in Marguerite Q. Warren and Michael J. Hindelang, 'Current Explanations of Offender Behavior.' In Hans Toch, ed., *Psychology of Crime and Criminal Justice* (New York: Holt, Rinehart, and Winston 1977), 173
10 Rich and DeVitis, *Theories of Modern Development*, 89
11 Travis Hirschi, *Causes of Delinquency* (Berkeley: University of California Press 1969), 31
12 Menachem Amir, *Patterns in Forcible Rape* (Chicago: University of Chicago Press 1971), 141–2
13 Edwin Sutherland, *Criminology*, 4th ed. (Philadelphia: Lippincott 1947), 6–7
14 Albert Bandura, *Aggression: A Social Learning Analysis* (Englewood Cliffs, NJ: Prentice-Hall 1973)
15 A Bandura, D. Ross, and S. Ross, 'Imitation of Film-Mediated Aggressive Models,' *Journal of Abnormal and Social Psychology* 66 (1963), 3–11
16 Robert J. Mundt, 'Gun Control and Rates of Firearms Violence in Canada and the United States,' *Canadian Journal of Criminology* 32 (1990), 137–54
17 Barry Krisberg, *Crime and Privilege* (Englewood Cliffs, NJ: Prentice-Hall 1975)
18 Milton L. Barron, 'The Criminogenic Society: Social Value and Deviance.' In A.S. Blumberg and J. Douglas, eds., *Current Perspectives on Criminal Behavior: Essays on Criminology*, 136–52 (New York: Alfred A. Knopf 1981)
19 Robert K. Merton, *Social Theory and Social Structure* (Glencoe, IL: The Free Press 1968)
20 Claude Brown, *Manchild in the Promised Land* (New York: Signet 1965)

21 Ibid, 263–5
22 Claude Brown, 'Images of Fear,' *Harper's,* May 1985, 44
23 Thomas Gabor and Tonia G. Barker, 'Probing the Public's Honesty: A Field Experiment Using the "Lost Letter" Technique,' *Deviant Behavior* 10 (1989), 387–99
24 Gwynn Nettler, *Lying, Cheating, and Stealing* (Cincinnati: Anderson 1982)
25 Ibid
26 E.O. Smigel and H.L. Ross, *Crimes Against Bureaucracy* (New York: Van Nostrand Reinhold 1970)
27 Enrico L. Quarantelli and Russell R. Dynes, 'Organizations as Victims in American Mass Racial Disturbances: A Re-examination.' In I. Drapkin and E. Viano, eds., *Victimology: A New Focus,* 67–77 (Lexington, MA: Lexington Books 1975); Thomas Gabor, Jody Strean, Gurnam Singh, and David Varis, 'Public Deviance: An Experimental Study,' *Canadian Journal of Criminology* 28 (1986), 17–29; L. Bickman, 'The Effect of Social Status on the Honesty of Others,' *Journal of Social Psychology* 85 (1971), 87–92
28 Bickman, 'The Effect of Social Status on the Honesty of Others'
29 Ronald V. Clarke and Patricia Mayhew, *Designing Out Crime* (London: HMSO 1980)
30 Stanley Milgram, 'Behavioral Study of Obedience,' *Journal of Abnormal Psychology* 67 (1963), 371–8
31 Walter Mischel, *Introduction to Personality* (New York: Holt, Rinehart, and Winston 1971), 507
32 Craig Haney, Curtis Banks, and Philip Zimbardo, 'Interpersonal Dynamics in a Simulated Prison,' *International Journal of Criminology and Penology* 1 (1973), 69–97
33 Derek B. Cornish and Ronald V. Clarke, 'Understanding Crime Displacement: An Application of Rational Choice Theory,' *Criminology* 25 (1987), 933–47
34 Cesare Lombroso, *L'uomo delinquente* [The Criminal Man] (Torino: Bocca 1889), Ernest Hooton, *Crime and the Man* (Cambridge, MA: Harvard University Press 1931)
35 Vold, *Theoretical Criminology,* ch. 7
36 B.F. Skinner, *About Behaviorism* (New York: Alfred A. Knopf 1974)

37 Vold, *Theoretical Criminology*, 312–15
38 Ibid
39 Bentham, 'An Introduction to the Principles of Morals and Legislation'
40 Maurice Cusson, *Why Delinquency?* (Toronto: University of Toronto Press 1983), 18–21
41 Ibid, 25
42 Derek B. Cornish and Ronald V. Clarke, 'Situational Prevention, Displacement of Crime, and Rational Choice Theory.' In Kevin Heal and Gloria Laycock, eds., *Situational Crime Prevention*, 1–16 (London: HMSO 1986)
43 Thomas Gabor, Micheline Baril, Maurice Cusson, Daniel Elie, Marc LeBlanc, and Andre Normandeau, *Armed Robbery: Cops, Robbers, and Victims* (Springfield, IL: Charles C. Thomas 1987), ch. 3
44 Rick Linden, ed., *Criminology: A Canadian Perspective* (Toronto: Holt, Rinehart, and Winston 1987), ch. 12
45 David D. Burns, *Feeling Good: The New Mood Therapy* (New York: Signet 1980)
46 Menachem Amir, *Patterns in Forcible Rape* (Chicago: University of Chicago Press 1971), 141–2
47 Lorne Gibson, Rick Linden, and Stuart Johnson, 'A Situational Theory of Rape,' *Canadian Journal of Corrections* 22 (1980), 51–65
48 Amir, *Patterns in Forcible Rape*
49 Alex Thio, *Deviant Behavior*, 3d ed. (New York: Harper & Row 1988), 277
50 Ibid, 278
51 Ronald V. Clarke and Patricia Mayhew, 'The British Gas Suicide Story and Its Criminological Implications,' In Michael Tonry and Norval Morris, eds., *Crime and Justice*, vol. 10, 79–116 (Chicago: University of Chicago Press 1988)
52 There is additional evidence that people do not always substitute methods when their preferred method of self-destruction is unavailable. For example, there is evidence that controlling the availability of firearms can reduce the number of suicides. See Sharon Moyer and Peter J. Carrington, *Gun Availability and Firearm Suicide* (Ottawa: Department of Justice Canada 1992).

53 Some experiments have shown that the rates of repeated violence decline when the most punitive measure (i.e., arrest as opposed to mediation) is taken by the police against wife batterers. See, for example, Lawrence W. Sherman and Richard A. Berk, 'The Minneapolis Domestic Violence Experiment,' *Police Foundation Reports* (Washington: Police Foundation April 1984), 10

CHAPTER 12

1 George Vold, *Theoretical Criminology*, 2d ed., with Thomas Bernard (New York: Oxford University Press 1979), ch. 8
2 Allen H. Barton, *Communities in Disaster: A Sociological Analysis of Collective Stress Situations* (Garden City, NY: Anchor Books 1969), ch. 5
3 James C. Davies, 'Toward a Theory of Revolution,' *American Sociological Review* 27 (1962), 5–19
4 Marshall B. Clinard, *Cities with Little Crime: The Case of Switzerland* (Cambridge: Cambridge University Press 1978)
5 Robert K. Merton, *Social Theory and Social Structure* (New York: Macmillan 1968)
6 Irvin Waller and Norm Okihiro, *Burglary: The Victim and the Public* (Toronto: University of Toronto Press 1978), 28
7 Thomas Gabor, Micheline Baril, Maurice Cusson, Daniel Elie, Marc Leblanc, and Andre Normandeau, *Armed Robbery: Cops, Robbers, and Victims* (Springfield, IL: Charles C. Thomas 1987), ch 3
8 See, for example, Diana Russell's, *The Politics of Rape* (New York: Stein and Day 1975)
9 Maurice Cusson, *Why Delinquency?* (Toronto: University of Toronto Press 1983)
10 Gabor et al, *Armed Robbery*, 63
11 Gwynn Nettler, *Lying, Cheating, and Stealing* (Cincinnati: Anderson 1982)
12 Marvin E. Wolfgang, *Patterns in Criminal Homicide* (Philadelphia: University of Pennsylvania Press 1958)
13 Gabor et al, *Armed Robbery*, 67
14 Philip G. Zimbardo, 'A Field Experiment in Autoshaping.' In C. Ward, ed. *Vandalism*, 85–90 (London: Architectural Press 1973)

15 D. Samdahl and H. Christiansen, 'Environmental Cues and Vandal-ism,' *Environment and Behavior* 17 (1985), 446
16 James Q. Wilson and George Kelling, 'Broken Windows,' *The Atlantic Monthly*, 1983, 31
17 Samdahl and Christiansen, 'Environmental Cues and Vandalism'
18 Mike J. Hough, Ronald V. Clarke, and Patricia Mayhew, 'Introduction.' In R.V. Clarke and P. Mayhew, eds., *Designing Out Crime* (London: HMSO, 1980) For other successful experiences in relation to the manipulation of targets see Ronald V. Clarke's *Situational Crime Prevention: Successful Case Studies* (New York: Harrow and Heston 1992)
19 Gabor et al, *Armed Robbery*, ch. 6
20 Patricia L. Brantingham and Paul J. Brantingham, 'Situational Crime Prevention in Practice,' *Canadian Journal of Criminology* 32 (1990), 17–40
21 Ibid, 29–30
22 Merton, *Social Theory and Social Structure*
23 Richard Cloward and Lloyd Ohlin, *Delinquency and Opportunity* (New York: Free Press 1960)
24 Charles R. Tittle, 'Crime Rates and Legal Sanctions,' *Social Problems* 16 (1969), 409–23
25 Edward Diener, Arthur L. Beaman, Scott, C. Fraser, and Roger T. Kelem, 'Effects of Deindividuation Variables on Stealing Among Halloween Trick-or-Treaters,' *Journal of Personality and Social Psychology* 33 (1976), 178–83
26 Gabor et al, *Armed Robbery*, 58
27 Thomas Gabor and Andre Normandeau, 'Armed Robbery: Highlights of a Canadian Study,' *Canadian Police College Journal* 13 (1989), 273–82
28 John F. Decker, 'Curbside Deterrence: An Analysis of the Effect of a Slug Rejector Device, Coin View Window and Warning Labels on Slug Usage in New York City Parking Meters,' *Criminology* 10 (1972), 127–42
29 Patricia Mayhew, Ronald V. Clarke, and David Elliott, 'Motorcycle Theft, Helmet Legislation and Displacement,' *The Howard Journal* 28 (1989), 1–8
30 For additional examples of successful preventive measures focus-

ing on risk and criminal opportunity reduction, refer to the case studies provided in Ronald V. Clarke's, *Situational Crime Prevention: Successful Case Studies.*

31 Hervey Cleckley, *The Mask of Sanity* (St Louis, MO: Mosby 1976); American Psychiatric Association, *Diagnostic and Statistical Manual of Mental Disorders*, 2d ed. (Washington, DC, 1968)

32 James C. Coleman, *Abnormal Psychology and Modern Life*, 5th ed. (Glenview, IL.: Scott, Foresman and Company 1976), 370

33 Ibid

34 Thomas Gabor, *The Prediction of Criminal Behavior: Statistical Approaches* (Toronto: University of Toronto Press 1986)

35 American Psychiatric Association, *Diagnostic and Statistical Manual of Mental Disorders*

36 Marvin E. Wolfgang and Franco Ferracuti, *The Subculture of Violence* (Beverly Hills, CA: Sage 1981)

37 Maynard L. Erickson and Jack P. Gibbs, 'Community Tolerance and Measures of Delinquency,' *Journal of Research in Crime and Delinquency* 16 (1979), 55–79

38 Maurice Cusson, *The Social Control of Crime* (Montreal: International Centre for Comparative Criminology, University of Montreal 1986), 94

39 For a discussion of the experience of British railway workers, see Stuart Henry, 'Fiddling as a Media Issue,' *The Media Reporter*, Winter (1992), 41–3

40 Jack Henry, 'The Employee Theft Triangle,' *Canadian Security*, August/September (1988), 26–7

40 Murray A. Straus, 'Leveling, Civility, and Violence in the Family.' *Journal of Marriage and the Family* 36 (1974), 13–30

CHAPTER 13

1 From the title of a book by Jeffery Reiman (see note 4, below)

2 Canadian Sentencing Commission, *Sentencing Reform: A Canadian Approach* (Ottawa: Ministry of Supply and Services 1987), 119

3 Ibid

4 Jeffery Reiman, *The Rich Get Richer and the Poor Get Prison: Ideology, Class and Criminal Justice* (New York: Wiley 1979)

5 Ibid, 97
6 Ibid, 96
7 The U.S. President's Crime Commission found, in 1967, for example, that a Los Angeles patrol officer could expect to detect a burglary every three months and a robbery once every fourteen years. For a more detailed discussion of the limits of preventive patrol, see Charles Silberman, *Criminal Violence, Criminal Justice* (New York: Vintage Books 1978), ch. 7.
8 Solicitor General Canada, 'Reported and Unreported Crimes,' *Canadian Urban Victimization Survey* (Ottawa: Ministry of the Solicitor General, 1985)
9 Ezzat A. Fattah, *Understanding Criminal Victimization* (Scarborough, ON: Prentice-Hall 1991), 50–1
10 Ibid, 51
11 Thomas Gabor, Micheline Baril, Maurice Cusson, Daniel Elie, Marc Leblanc, and Andre Normandeau, *Armed Robbery: Cops, Robbers, and Victims* (Springfield, IL: Charles C. Thomas 1987), ch. 3
12 Paul Ingram, 'Burglary in Ottawa,' Master's thesis, University of Ottawa, 1989
13 Donald Black and Albert J. Reiss, Jr, 'Police Control of Juveniles,' *American Sociological Review* 35 (1970), 63–77
14 U.S. President's Commission on Law Enforcement and the Administration of Justice, *The Challenge of Crime in a Free Society* (Washington, DC: Government Printing Office 1967), 79
15 Terence P. Thornberry, 'Race, Socioeconomic Status and Sentencing in the Juvenile Justice System,' *The Journal of Criminal Law and Criminology* 64 (1973), 90–8
16 Reiman, *The Rich Get Richer ...*, 104
17 Mary Owen Cameron, *The Booster and the Snitch* (New York: Free Press of Glencoe 1964)
18 Reiman, *The Rich Get Richer ...*, 119
19 Donald J. Newman, *Conviction: The Determination of Guilt or Innocence Without Trial* (Boston: Little, Brown 1966); Bureau Of Justice Statistics, *The Prevalence of Guilty Pleas* (Washington, DC: U.S. Department of Justice 1984)
20 Gabor et al, ch. 5
21 Reiman, *The Rich Get Richer ...*, 119

22 Ibid, 116
23 Ibid
24 John H. Hylton, 'The Native Offender in Saskatchewan,' *Canadian Journal of Criminology* 24 (1982), 121–31
25 Marvin Bohnstedt, 'Variables Common to Pre-Trial, Sentencing/ Parole Release and Institutional Custody Classification Instruments.' Paper presented at the Annual Meeting of the American Society of Criminology, Philadelphia, PA, November 1979
26 Edward L. Greenspan and George Jonas, *Greenspan: The Case for the Defence* (Toronto: Macmillan 1987), 383–4

CHAPTER 14

 1 Ezzat A. Fattah, *Understanding Criminal Victimization* (Scarborough, ON: Prentice-Hall 1991), 147–9
 2 Jeffrey L. Edleson and Richard M. Tolman, *Intervention for Men Who Batter: An Ecological Approach* (Newbury Park, CA: Sage 1992), 35–6
 3 John C. Ball, Lawrence Rosen, John A. Flueck, and David Nurco, 'The Criminality of Heroin Addicts When Addicted and When Off Opiates.' In James A. Inciardi, ed., *The Drugs-Crime Connection*, 39–65 (Beverly Hills, CA: Sage 1981)
 4 Thomas Gabor, Micheline Baril, Maurice Cusson, Daniel Elie, Marc Leblanc, and Andre Normandeau, *Armed Robbery: Cops, Robbers, and Victims* (Springfield, IL: Charles C. Thomas 1987), ch. 6
 5 George Kelling, *The Newark Foot Patrol Experiment* (Washington, DC: The Police Foundation 1981)
 6 Quoted in Stuart Henry, *The Hidden Economy: The Context and Control of Borderline Crime* (Oxford: Martin Robertson 1978), 53
 7 Ibid, 151–6
 8 Robert Trojanowicz and Bonnie Bucqueroux, *Community Policing: A Contemporary Perspective* (Cincinnati: Anderson 1990)
 9 Thomas Gabor and Ellen Gottheil, 'Offender Spatial Mobility: An Empirical Study and Some Policy Implications,' *Canadian Journal of Criminology* 26 (1984), 267–81
10 Floyd J. Fowler and Thomas W. Mangione, *Neighbourhood Crime,*

Fear and Social Control: A Second Look at the Hartford Program (Washington, DC: U.S.: Department of Justice 1982)

11 John Braithwaite and Gilbert Geis, 'On Theory and Action for Corporate Crime Control,' *Crime and Delinquency* 28 (1982), 292–314

12 Jay Livingston, *Crime and Criminology* (Englewood Cliffs, NJ: Prentice-Hall 1992), 313

13 Adam Podgorecki, 'Attitudes to the Workers' Courts.' In V. Aubert, ed., *Sociology of Law* (Harmondsworth: Penguin 1969), 142–9

14 Elliott Currie, *Confronting Crime: An American Challenge* (New York: Pantheon 1985)

15 J.B. Franz, 'The Frontier Tradition: An Invitation to Violence.' In H.D. Graham and T.R. Gurr, eds., *Violence in America: Historical and Comparative Perspectives* (New York: Bantam Books 1970)

16 Citizen's Crime Commission, *Tokyo: One City Where Crime Doesn't Pay! A Study of the Reasons for Tokyo's Low Urban Crime Rate and What Can Be Learned to Help America's Crime Crisis* (Philadelphia, 1975); Marshall B. Clinard, *Cities with Little Crime: The Case of Switzerland* (Cambridge: Cambridge University Press 1978)

17 Clifford R. Shaw and Henry D. McKay, *Juvenile Delinquency and Urban Areas*, rev. ed. (Chicago: University of Chicago Press 1969)

18 Claude S. Fischer, 'The Effect of Urban Life on Traditional Values,' *Social Forces* 53 (1975) 420–32; Thomas C. Wilson, 'Urbanism and Tolerance: A Test of Some Hypotheses Drawn from Wirth and Stouffer,' *American Sociological Review* 50 (1985), 117–23

19 Marshall B. Clinard and Robert F. Meier, *Sociology of Deviant Behavior*, 8th ed. (Fort Worth: Harcourt Brace Jovanovich 1992), 72

20 M. Roy, *Battered Women: A Psychosociological Study of Domestic Violence* (New York: Van Nostrand Reinhold 1977)

21 Maurice Cusson, *The Social Control of Crime* (Montreal: International Centre for Comparative Criminology, University of Montreal, 1986), 97–8

22 Currie, *Confronting Crime*, ch. 6

23 Ibid, 191–2

24 James Q. Wilson, *Thinking about Crime* (New York: Random House 1975), 236

25 In the United States, the Uniform Crime Reports have been collected since 1931; however, it took many years before full reporting

of crime statistics by police departments to the FBI took place. In Canada, the uniform crime-reporting system was not introduced until 1962.

26 Ted Robert Gurr, *Violence in America* (Newbury Park, CA: Sage 1989)
27 Henry, *The Hidden Economy*, 50
28 Ibid
29 Gary S. Green, *Occupational Crime* (Chicago: Nelson-Hall 1990), 231

Photo Credits

Photo on page 63 (on car vandalism) reproduced by permission of Professor Philip Zimbardo, School of Psychology, Stanford University

Photo on page 204 (blackout looting in New York) reproduced by permission of the Associated Press. Permission was obtained through Canapress Photo Service in Ottawa.

Cartoon on page 210 (Bundy execution) reproduced by permission of Michael Schultz, Marketing Department of the *Baltimore Evening Sun*.

Photos on page 221 (children imitating model) reproduced by permission of Professor Albert Bandura, School of Psychology, Stanford University.

CREDITS FOR USE OF TEXT

Material on hotel linen lifting appearing on pages 84–6 reproduced by permission of Rick Laiken of the *Ottawa Citizen*.

Material on the 'Victor Morrison' case appearing on pages 101–3 reproduced by permission of Neil Boyd.

Index